RUMI ESSAYS

On the Life, Poetry, and Vision of the Greatest Persian Sufi Poet

Rasoul Shams

RUMI PUBLICATIONS
an imprint of
RUMI POETRY CLUB
2016

Rumi Essays: On the Life, Poetry, and Vision of the Greatest Persian Sufi Poet
Rasoul Shams

Copyright © 2016 Rumi Poetry Club
All rights reserved.
No part of this book may be published, reproduced, translated or transmitted in any form or by any means without written permission of the publisher, except in the case of brief quotations (with citation) embodied in critical articles and reviews.

ISBN-13: 978-0-9850568-1-0
ISBN-10: 0-9850568-1-9

Library of Congress Control Number: 2016913327

First Published in 2016
RUMI PUBLICATIONS
Rumi Poetry Club
P.O. Box 521376
Salt Lake City, UT 84152-1376
Email: info@rumipoetryclub.com
Website: www.rumipoetryclub.com
Facebook: www.facebook.com/rumipoetryclub

Cover painting of Rumi by Setsuko Yoshida based on the oldest miniature portrait of Rumi

Printed in the United States of America

CONTENTS

	Preface	8
[1]	Introduction: Why Rumi Matters	9
[2]	Inspiration: Be Like Melting Snow	17
[3]	Poet of Love and Peace	23
[4]	Master Rumi: The Path to Poetry, Love and Enlightenment	28
[5]	Rumi's Life and Spiritual Journey	38
[6]	Rumi's Roots: The Historical Rumi	49
[7]	Rumi and the Buddha: Correlative Ideas on Spiritual Awakening	57
[8]	Sufi and Buddhist Teachings: Views from Rumi's Poetry and Life	72
[9]	Jesus Christ in Rumi's Poetry and Parables	80
[10]	Rumi's Poems on Jesus' Breath	86
[11]	In the Ocean of Rumi	90
[12]	Love and Life in Rumi's Poetry	96

[13]	A Map of the Heart in Rumi's Poetry	*102*
[14]	Rumi's Poetry as a Guiding Light	*109*
[15]	Rumi's Poems for Meditation and Life	*115*
[16]	Rumi Comes to America	*122*
[17]	Why is Rumi a Best-Selling Poet in America?	*130*
[18]	Book Reviews	*143*

[Appendix I] A Chronology of Rumi's Life & Family   *159*

[Appendix II] Glossary and Transliteration   *165*

[Appendix II] Rumiyât: A Guide to Rumi Studies   *176*

    Notes and References   *189*

    Index of Names   *205*

    Acknowledgments   *213*

"Speech is like the Sun. All humans gain warmth and life from it. However, because the Sun is not always visible, people forget that their warmth and life come from it. Although the celestial Sun continuously shines, it does not come to our sight until its rays strike and illuminate a wall. In the same way, the sunlight of speech cannot be seen without the medium of words and sounds."

From the *Discourses of Rumi*, No. 53

Preface

We all wait for the letter. I do not mean any letter. We wait for the letter – from whom we do not know, but one which brings us the richest fragrance of love and life, one which liberates us totally. The Rumi essays in this volume are essentially the letters I wrote to myself over a period of several years. Inspired by Rumi's enlightened life and poetry, I thought these writings may also be of some use to others. Rumi himself says: *"I am a mirror; I am not a man of speeches and essays. Nevertheless, you will see my mind if your ears become eyes."*[1]

Rasoul Shams
Salt Lake City
September 2016

---

1. *Divân*, 492

[1]
Introduction: Why Rumi Matters

"In looking for poems and poets, don't dwell on the boundaries of style, or time, or even of countries and cultures. Think of yourself rather as one member of a single, recognizable tribe."

Mary Oliver[1]

This book has its origin in 2007. That year marked the 800th anniversary of Rumi's birth. The full name of this thirteenth-century Persian Sufi poet is Mawlânâ Jalâluddin Mohammad Balkhi Rumi. He was born on September 30, 1207 in the city of Balkh in present-day Afghanistan, and died on December 17, 1273 in the city of Konya in present-day Turkey. People in the East have traditionally called him "Mawlânâ," an Arabic word meaning "Our Master" (pronounced Mowlânâ in Iran and Mevlânâ in Turkey). In the West, he is simply known as Rumi, a reference to the fact that he lived most of his life in "Rūm," an Arabic-Persian noun for the "Eastern Roman or Byzantine" Empire, which ruled Anatolia (Asia Minor) for centuries before the region fell to the Moslem Saljug (Seljuq) Kingdom in the eleventh century.

Since the 1990s, Rumi has been one of the most widely-read and bestselling poets in North America – thanks to popular translations and renditions of his poetry into contemporary English. Given Rumi's universal message of peace and compassion expressed through his elegant poetry, the United Nations Educational, Scientific and Cultural Organization (UNESCO) included Rumi among sixty-three world figures to be celebrated during the "Anniversaries 2006-2007." The initiative for this came from the representatives of Afghanistan, Egypt and Turkey, which were members of the Executive Board of UNESCO in Paris in 2005, the year the decisions for the anniversaries were made. In its 175th session (October 3, 2006), UNESCO approved to issue a Commemorative Medal in honor of Rumi in 2007, and praised Rumi as "one of the great humanists, philosophers and poets who belong to humanity in its entirety."[2] In this way, mass media around the world celebrated 2007 as the International Year of Rumi designated by the United Nations. A large number of lectures, poetry recitations, and music concerts were organized; newspapers and magazines published articles about Rumi; several websites were launched to commemorate Rumi's life and poetry; and postal stamps depicting like-images of Rumi were issued in Afghanistan, Iran, Turkey, and Syria.

It was also in 2007 that I founded the Rumi Poetry Club in Salt Lake City, Utah. Our efforts have been modest but steady and, hopefully, beneficial. We have held monthly meetings on the first Tuesday of every month at the public library to read and discuss Rumi's poems, and an annual Rumi Festival usually in September in honor of Rumi's birth month. Both gatherings have always been free and open to the public. We have also maintained a Website and a Facebook page. Since 2007, I have published dozens of articles related to Rumi's life, thought and poetry in various magazines in the USA, Europe, and Asia. This book is, indeed, a collection of those articles, with revisions and new material, now offered in a single volume for the convenience of interested readers.

We Eat Love

For the past thirty five years, I have been fascinated by the poetry of Mawlânâ Rumi. The poems and parables of this great Persian Sufi poet have given me consolation, insight, and joy wherever I have been. In recent years, Rumi has become one of the most-widely read poets in North America. And I am delighted to see this phenomenon, not merely because he was a Persian poet and thus a part of my cultural roots, but because his poetry epitomizes love, or as Rumi himself says, "We eat love."

Love is like food to be eaten and also to be shared. When you enjoy a particular dish, you like to offer it to others so that they also enjoy the fragrance, texture, saltiness, sweetness, and warmth of your favorite dish. When people from various walks of life read Rumi's poems, they eat the food of love. Good poetry enriches our lives, and Rumi's poetry is a treasury of gems: It offers us mental peace, compassion, timeless wisdom, healing words, inspiration, and intimacy. And all of this at no cost other than a willingness to listen and a calmness to enjoy. It is for these reasons that I believe Rumi and sages of his caliber are the answer to all of our problems – personal, interpersonal, social, and global.

Before you judge me as a naïve person, let me tell you a story. Soh'râb Sepehri was a renowned twentieth century Persian poet. In one of his famous poems, "Water" (*Âb*), Sepehri imagines a beautiful rural landscape and says that we should not pollute the stream flowing through the village because pigeons drink water from the stream. When this poem was published in the mid-1960s, some critics blamed Sepehri for his shallow concern about pigeons' drinking water while the world was facing so much bloodshed and nuclear war threat (those were indeed days of war including the Cold War and Vietnam War). Sepehri, who rarely replied to his critics, is recorded to have said that his poetry actually points to the root of our problems: If politicians are compassionate enough to care about the birds' drinking water, they will be even more concerned about the death of thousands of humans caused by bloody wars.

Rumi views love as rays of the Divine light shining upon our hearts and guiding our life on a beautiful path. The more we read and enjoy Rumi's poems, the more compassionate and less selfish we become. The more Rumi's poetry spreads around communities and enlightens people's minds, there will be more peace and happiness. If our political leaders also read and understand spiritual poetry and live up to that understanding, the less violent and more friendly our world will be. If there are violent religious fanatics destroying life, civilization and peace in various parts of the world, Rumi is the answer to that also because his poetry calls for compassion, tolerance, joy, and beauty. Rumi is the answer not because he has a monopoly on truth, but because his message (as the messages of other sages) is an essential part of the spiritual solution to many of our life and social problems.

The fact that Rumi's poems are sweet on our lips even seven centuries after his death testifies to the truth of his vision. Rumi's constituency is not a particular creed or community but the human heart, and the wisdom of the heart is urgently needed in our increasingly interdependent world. Once I was talking with Nevit Ergin, a well-known English translator of Rumi, and he said, "If you think deeply, the alternative to Rumi is misery, suffering and destruction because what Rumi teaches is nothing but awareness, compassion, joy, peace." Those who read, enjoy, and understand Rumi will see much truth in Ergin's statement. Rumi's significance for the Islamic world today must also be highlighted. Not only is Rumi, as a planetary poet and spiritual teacher, a pride of the Islamic world; but also, as an eminent Muslim scholar, his understanding of Islam as an inclusive, compassionate, and progressive religion can be inspirational and educational to the Muslim nations.

Why Poetry Matters

In his 2008 book, *Why Poetry Matters*, Jay Parini writes that most people do not care about poetry and may even wonder why some people do not have more important things to do than to read or write poems. Poetry, indeed, has become less present in our lives (poetry books sell the least, for example), partly because people do not have (or do not try to have) quiet, quality time. TV with its numerous channels, cell phones, emails, internet, traffic, gossip, and so forth have occupied our space and mind. Daily life has thus become clamorous. Most people feel that they do not have the time or patience to add poetry to their already busy, noisy schedule. And yet, I think, poetry can actually save us from the noise and stress of modern life because the reading or writing of poetry helps people to sit alone or with others in a friendly atmosphere, listen to their inner voice or that of others, and relax, meditate, explore, and enjoy. So poetry is not simply a theoretical occupation with words but very much utilitarian; it has practical applications in our lives and society. We do need poets and their creative works.

What is a poem? What is poetry? William Henry Hudson in *An Introduction to the Study of Literature* (published in 1917, an out-of-print book which I discovered during my university education in India years ago), lists various definitions of poetry by some of the eminent minds in literature. Here are some of these definitions: "A metrical composition" (Samuel Johnson); "thought and words in which emotion spontaneously embodies itself" (John Stuart Mill); "the breath and finer spirit of all knowledge" (William Wordsworth); "simply the most delightful and perfect form of utterance that human words can reach" (Matthew Arnold); "the rhythmic creation of beauty" (Edgar Allan Poe); and "the suggestion, by the imagination, of noble grounds for the noble emotions" (John Ruskin). Although one can find some common elements in these definitions of poetry, the variety of definitions also indicates that poetry has many facets and forms, and that there can probably be no consensus on a single, comprehensive definition. Indeed, some of the statements about poetry are poetic themselves. Therefore, Hudson, suggests that what makes a writing "poetical" is that it is "emotional and imaginative." Of course, this requires that a poem uses some literary form that contains rhythm (if not rhyme), music, beauty, elegance, symbolism, and figures of speech such as metaphor, simile, etc.

Rumi is renowned as a spiritual or mystical poet. What exactly is spiritual poetry? This is even more difficult to answer. Is it possible to divide poets and poetry into spiritual versus non-spiritual, or into sacred versus profane? Good poetry, I believe, is essentially spiritual. When we read or hear a poem that touches our heart, uplifts our spirit, illuminates our mind with a glimpse of hidden reality, inspires in us something positive, sacred, peaceful, beautiful and compassionate, or connects us to nature, life and God, that is a good poem and a spiritual one too. When life, whether individual or social, is too materialistic, greedy, possessive and selfish, our whole movement and energy becomes destructive (sooner or later, for ourselves, others or future generations) because that kind of life and society lacks a true understanding of life, and deprives our soul of its food – love and joy. Poetry is closely related with music, meditation, and nature; and all of these are vital tools that take us beyond our small self, connects us to the vast reality, and gives a balanced perspective on life, society, and the world.

Back to Parini's book. He writes that one reason poetry matters is that it provides a voice for the poet as a member of the human community. Rumi, indeed, represents a rare enlightening voice. He integrated in his own person three significant qualities seldom combined in a single life: (1) Perennial wisdom and philosophical insight; (2) marvelous poetic imagination and literary skills; and (3) spiritual living – all of them to a very fine degree. Rumi's words were not shallow intellectualism or hot-air preaching; his teaching of love was deeply rooted in the millennia-old cultural traditions of the Middle East, notably the Abrahamic religions, Sufi heritage, and Persian poetry.

I regard Rumi as an icon of spiritual poetry; he was a master poet who mapped the world of the heart. Yet, we should not lionize, idealize,

Westernize, Easternize or misinterpret him. Yes, he was a passionate poet of love and ecstasy; he was also a man of faith, prayer, meditation, and ethical living. He was a simple human with no claims for titles (not even for being a poet). Rumi himself enjoyed reading other literary, spiritual works. It is in this light that we should read and understand Rumi. The fact that poetry, like music, is found in all cultures and languages is a testimony to its value. But mystical poets of Rumi's caliber are hard to come by, and yet very much needed in our world in which there is so much suffering, misunderstanding, and violence. Rumi does not speak for a particular creed or community but for the human heart which, as he elegantly articulates, is the garden of secrets, joy, love, and intuitive knowledge.

* * *

I was introduced to Rumi's poetry in my Persian textbooks as a young boy growing up in Iran during the 1970s. Iran, or what is historically called Persia, is a land of eminent poets, and Rumi is a giant among them. When I left Iran about thirty five years ago, I took with me a few Persian poetry books, including of course Rumi's. All through those years in India, Japan and the USA, where I have spent most of my life, these poetry books have given me consolation, insight, and joy.

This book, as mentioned before, is a collection of my Rumi essays published in various magazines. To better fit in this volume, I have revised and edited the essays in order to reduce some repetitions and overlaps; I have also added new information and a few previously unpublished chapters. Nevertheless, there are certain facts and ideas repeated here and there in the book (especially in the biographical part) because the information was essential to the structure of the chapter (originally published as a magazine article) and I also wanted to reinforce those historical points. I have retained repetition of certain poems in a few chapters mainly because they convey elegant phrases and insightful teachings, and, as a Persian proverb says, "Recurring sweetness (*gand-e mokarrar*) is desirable." The Rumi poems in this book are my own translations for which I have used authentic editions of Rumi's works.[3]

After this introductory chapter, I present a personal contemplative essay, "Be Like Melting Snow," inspired by a poem from Rumi. These two chapters constitute a setting for the remaining sixteen chapters of the book, which may be divided into several themes. Chapters 3-6 are biographical — describing Rumi's life and how he became the personality we know as Rumi, the poet and the mystic. Chapters 7-8 juxtapose Rumi's words and vision with Buddhist teachings, and draw some important parallels between the Sufi and Buddhist traditions. Chapters 9-10 review the sacred position of Jesus Christ in Rumi's poetry and faith. These chapters related to the Buddha and Jesus have significant implications for interfaith dialogue, interreligious insight, and East-West understanding, as Islam (Rumi's religion), Christianity (the predominant Western religion), and Buddhism (a major Eastern religion) together account for more than sixty percent of world population. Chapters 11-15 present some of the essential teachings of Rumi through his poetry, and how we can use these insightful words for meditation and life transformation. Chapters 16-17 are an analysis of why Rumi's poetry has become so popular in the West, particularly in North America. Chapter 18 is a collection of my reviews of several Rumi-related books. There are also three appendices at the end of the book. Appendix I provides a chronology of Rumi's life and family; appendix II gives a glossary and transliteration of Persian terms related to Rumi. Finally, appendix III suggests some print and online sources about Rumi and his works; I categorize these information resources as "Rumiyât" — all that is related to Rumi.

Although I have adopted a scholarly approach to researching this book and documenting the sources used, *Rumi Essays* is primarily for the average reader interested in Rumi's poetry who would like to learn more about his life, poetry, and thinking. I hope that academic students of Rumi will also find it informative in some respects. There is no general consensus on a transliteration system for Arabic and Persian names and words in English. I have adopted an easy-to-read English system that closely reflects the Persian pronunciation, as Rumi wrote all of his works in the Persian language. Where necessary, I have also given the Arabic or Turkish variants of the words for the information of interested readers. For example, *Masnavi* (or *Masnawi*) is Persian; *Mathnawi* is Arabic, and *Mesnevi* is Turkish.

The year 2017 will mark the tenth anniversary of the Rumi Poetry Club. These ten years have been an immense journey for me; I have met many friends with beautiful souls and warm hearts. It is also apt here to recall the following passage from Rainer Maria Rilke's *Letters to A Young Poet*: "There is here no measuring with time, no year matters, and ten years are nothing."

Rilke continues to say that an artist should not measure time but grow and ripen like a tree "which does not force its sap" but rather stands still and confident in the stormy spring with no concern whether the summer will come or not. "It does come. But it comes only to the patient, who are there as though eternity lay before them ... Patience is everything!" In that spirit of patience and attention, I invite you to read and explore this book; this is a journey that, I hope, will bring a better understanding of Rumi as well as joy, peace, and expansion to the reader's soul.[4]

Parts of this introductory chapter were published in the following essays:
"Celebrations of the 800th Birth Anniversary of Moulana Rumi," *Persian Heritage Monthly*, English section, p. 1, April 2007; also posted on the website of *Sufi News and Sufi World Report* (htpp://sufinews.blogspot.com), April 9, 2007.
"Rumi is the Answer to All of Our Problems," *The Payvand Online* (www.payvand.com), March 2, 2007; also posted under the title "Ma Eshg Khoreem: We Eat Love" on the website of *Sufi News and Sufi World Report* (htpp://sufinews.blogspot.com), March 4, 2007.
"Why Rumi Matters," a blog posted on the website of the Rumi Poetry Club (www.rumipoetryclub.com) in June 2010.

[2]
Inspiration: Be Like Melting Snow

"If there is magic on this planet, it is contained in water."

Loren Eiseley[1]

Salt Lake City is actually a city of snow. Some years, it snows even in the summer. Cold storms lift off the warm water of the Great Salt Lake, located on the west side of the city, and precipitate the moisture as rain or snow on the Wasatch Front. This process is part of what is called the "lake effect." The lofty Wasatch Range on the east side of Salt Lake City, which acts as a barrier to winds and clouds, is snow covered for the better part of the year. In the spring as the climate begins to warm, the mountain range provides snow-melt water rushing through canyons and creeks toward the city, which sits on the sediments of an ancient lake. Apart from the uplands and canyons, one particular place I go to enjoy the spring and the revival of greenery is Sugar House Park. The Park's lake, which is a gathering place for ducks and seagulls, has a spectacular background of the Wasatch Mountains on the east side. Streams bring water from the mountains down to the valley, and one of these streams feeds water to the Park's lake. It was in this setting, on a spring day of 2010, that I contemplated on the following poem from Rumi (*Divân*: 23022):

Be like melting snow.
Wash yourself of yourself.[2]

As the mountain snow melts, it flows; it washes itself of itself on solid ground; it becomes a stream; it creates greenery and life; and it eventually joins the sea – its source. This journey also articulates the path of spiritual awakening in human life. Let's reflect on this short poem in some depth and detail.

"Melting snow" refers to a state of consciousness which Buddhists call *nirvâna* and Sufis call *fanâ*. Both of these words (the first Sanskrit and the second Arabic) mean the "extinction" of the ego and its illusions, attachments, and miseries. How does this happen? Snow melts by the warmth of sunshine; similarly, the warmth of love in the heart melts the ego. The heart is very much treasured in Rumi's poetry because it is the source of joy, love, and awareness. "Wash yourself of yourself" is the principal teaching of all spiritual traditions. It means that the brilliant mirror of the heart is covered and concealed by the rust and dust of the small, selfish, ever-desiring ego. Selfishness veils the true human nature and brings suffering to the individual as well as to society. Enlightenment is nothing other than the removal of this veil and obstacle; it is to let the heart shine and illuminate life.

Nonetheless, there is a subtle point in this process of enlightenment. For the snow to melt it should not reject or blame its being as a snow flake in the first place. A snow flake in its own place has a value and function. This is valid for the journey of the soul too. Enlightenment does not mean rejecting the ego in a negative, hostile, dualistic manner, but transcending it and transforming its power in a positive joyful way. This means bringing the totality of one's being onto the right path – the path of love and light. The Japanese Zen teacher Daisetz Suzuki once remarked: "Our consciousness is nothing but an insignificant floating piece of island in the Oceanus encircling the earth. But it is through this little fragment of land that we can look out to the immense expanse of the unconscious itself."[3]

The snow, which melts to become a stream, does so on the bedrock of a majestic mountain. Our life too is situated on solid high ground. For a flower or a human to appear on Earth it takes the participation of the entire universe and billions of years of evolution. Science, despite how it may appear under the materialistic lens, has actually found great significance to humankind's existence. Nature, much like the solid mountain beneath the snow cover, is in flux – a state of ceaseless changes sometimes sudden but usually at a slow rate (according to our scale of time). Nevertheless it is only because of this dynamism in nature that every being is rooted in a supportive net. If molecules of hydrogen and oxygen, for instance, do not want to interact and participate in the great flux of nature, no water can form, and no life can emerge. According to mystics from various religions, the ever-flowing universe with its laws and evolutionary journey is ultimately dependent upon God. Rumi calls God the Beloved because he sees love as the foundation and fabric of existence. Mesiter Eckhart views God as the *Urgrund* (the Primordial Ground); akin to the theologian Paul Tillich's notion of the Ground of Being. So whether one has a secular or a particular religious view, one can appreciate the fact that human life is rooted in a majestic, mysterious, beautiful, and shared ground of existence. This is indeed a basis of spiritual worldview.

Melting snow is free to flow. Spiritual enlightenment and transcendence also liberate the human soul from the illusions and attachments of the small self. Indian religions call this *muksha* (freedom from *samsara*, the wheel of birth, death and rebirth); Middle Eastern religions call it "salvation" of the soul from hell and its entry into heaven. So while folk religions postpone liberation or salvation until death, mystics from these same religions emphasize spiritual liberation and salvation in this very life; namely, the liberation of the soul from the man-made prison constructed with the walls of ignorance, greed, envy, hatred, violence, and suffering. Spiritual liberation brings joy, love, insight, and freedom to our daily life. "Melting snow" in Rumi's poem does not refer to physical death but rather to washing one's life of the false selves, and thus becoming transparent to the reality of existence, and being available to do the real work – the work we love and to work with love – in this very life.

Spiritual liberation is not a loss of our power or our life; it is rather the release of our inner forces that are otherwise dormant; it is the transformation of the potential into the actual; it is growth and blooming. Liberation has immense power. When snow that was once sitting idly on strong granite becomes stream water, it can erode and wash away even rocks, or as the *Tao Te Ching* says, "The softest thing on earth overtakes the hardest thing on earth."[4]

One wonders if Rumi used the symbolism of "melting snow" to describe his own transformation as well. Before meeting Shams, Rumi led the life of a reputed preacher and religious teacher. He was a snow flake, but Shams melted him, and from this melting flowed all that energy and poetry. By melting, Rumi became more, not less. Spiritual liberation does not diminish our personality and value in life; it actually makes us more aware, more alive, and more dignified. This holds true for water too. An interesting property of water is that, unlike other liquids in nature, its liquid form is denser than its solid form. Ice floats on water and that is why marine animals in the icy polar regions can survive. Snow melt is denser and flows downward, and gives life to plants and greenery to the dry land.

Another subtle point is that an enlightened, liberated human is not one who negates the world and society merely for the sake of his or her own salvation. This would be a contradiction with spirituality itself; it is another form of selfishness. In Rumi's view, this world and life provide a window of opportunity for the human to know the reality of Self and experience true joy and insight. Furthermore, each human being is a passenger in this life and is born to perform and participate in the world of creation using his or her talents. Spiritual enlightenment and liberation is inherently full of service, generosity, compassion, and work. The Indian Bengali poet Tagore writes a beautiful line that touches on this point: "I slept and dreamt that life was joy. I awoke and saw that life was service. I acted and behold, service was joy."[5] In other words, the joy of the human soul does not lie in greed and selfishness but in serving and loving. In fact, participation and contribution are embedded in the very fabric of the world.

Of course, "self-love" and "self-interest" exist in all creatures in the sense that they take care of themselves and their offspring in order to survive and grow, but that is different from greed, selfishness, and hatred. In 1976, the British biologist and atheist Richard Dawkins published a best-selling book titled *The Selfish Gene*; thirty years later, he wrote a new introduction to the revised edition of the book and suggested that perhaps *The Cooperative Gene* would equally express his ideas on natural selection and evolution of life even at the tiny scale of genes. (Biologist Lynn Margulis has better described symbiosis and mutualism as important processes in the evolution of life.) On a deeper level of understanding, according to Buddhist and Sufi teachings, no being really has a fixed, permanent and independent self; Buddhist call it a world of "no-self"; Sufis say that the existence of this world is simply a shadow of God's being.

All of these insights and many more are contained in this simple line: *Be like melting snow. Wash yourself of yourself.* Two questions. How does a poet observing nature come to deep spiritual insights? John Muir has answered this question from his own experience: "I only went out for a walk and finally concluded to stay out till sundown, for going out, I found, I was really going in."[6] Second question: When a poet composes a beautiful insightful poem inspired by nature, is it really the poet saying the poem or is it nature expressing itself through the poem? Consider this famous Japanese poem by the thirteenth century Zen master Dōgen:

Haru wa hana	In spring, cherry blossoms.
Natsu hotogisu	In summer, the cuckoo's song.
Aki wa tsuki	In autumn, moonlight.
Fuyu yuki kiede	In winter, frozen snow.
Suzushi kari keri	How fresh are the seasons!

Is this Dōgen's own poem or that of Nature which has four seasons? Perhaps, the poem belongs to both Dōgen and Nature. Why should we view the poet and Nature as separate? The poet may only be a verbal aspect of Nature. The articulation of such deep poetry and insight is possible when human beings like Rumi and Dōgen have become like melting snow – washing and transcending themselves.

Mountain snow melts, clouds pour down rain water, and rivers eventually join the sea – their origin. But even as snow, rain or stream water, they already contain something of the sea. In fact, the snow, the cloud, and the sea are all water molecules in various physical forms. Enlightenment is awakening to this oneness of existence and realizing that we as individuals are part of a great Whole, woven into the fabric of an immense mystery and traveling along with every other being on an adventurous path. The return of tiny water molecules to the majestic sea symbolizes the great cycle of creation that the Sufis express in this famous phrase: We (and the entire creation) come from God and unto God we shall eventually return (*Quran*, II, 156: *innâ lil'lâh-i wa innâ ilayhi râje'un*). In fact, lines preceding the phrase "Be like melting snow" in Rumi's poem shed much light on the poem:

"*And He is always with you.*" (*Quran*, LVII: 4)
This means that He is with you in your search.
When you are seeking,
      seek Him too in that search.
"*He is closer to you than yourself.*" (*Quran*: L: 16)
Why wander outside?
Be like melting snow.
Wash yourself of yourself. *Divân*: 23021

What more can be said about melting snow? Rumi concludes:

Through love, a tongue as fragrant as the lily grows in your soul.
Keep your tongue silent; be like the lily.

Divân: 23023

Melting snow is our emptiness, love, joy, journey, and homecoming. Melting snow is the state of flowing in love and being regenerated afresh in life. In another poem, also using the snow flake as a symbol of spiritual journey, Rumi says:

I was snow; I melted and
    the Earth drank me.
Then, I became a vapor in the heart of Earth,
    rising high to the sky.

Divân: 14922

This chapter has not been published previously.

[3]
Poet of Love and Peace

I am the wind; you are the leaf. How can you not dance?
Rumi, *Divân*: Quatrain 1900

Rumi lived in the thirteenth century (some three hundred years before Shakespeare) and in a part of the world today known as the Middle East, which has been a largely Muslim population for nearly 1400 years. The language Rumi spoke and wrote in – Persian – is also something exotic to the Western world. Therefore, Rumi's remarkable popularity in twenty-first century America may appear to be an odd phenomenon. But perhaps not. The views of a deep thinker and the words of an insightful poet transcend spatial and temporal boundaries. Rumi's poetry conveys teachings and vision which are essential to a human's spiritual life; moreover, he portrays his feelings and ideas in beautiful words and images that heal the soul and resonate with the reader. Rumi's teachings are sorely needed in our world and age. Rumi is perhaps even more of today's and tomorrow's poet than that of the past. In this chapter, I am delighted to share with readers some of Rumi's poems and ideas; but first, a brief review of his life.

A Poet is Born

Rumi was born on September 30, 1207 in the city of Balkh (in present-day Afghanistan) which was then was a major intellectual, commercial and political center in the Persian Kingdom. His name was Jalâluddin Mohammad. His father, Bahâ'uddin Valad, was a great Muslim scholar, mystic, and indeed Rumi's first teacher. When Rumi was still a young boy, his family left Balkh, both because his father's teachings were in conflict with the views of Muslim scholars and the king in Balkh, and because of the imminent threat from Genghis Khan's brutal army. After traveling widely in the Middle East, Rumi's family finally settled in the town of Konya in Anatolia (present-day Turkey), which was then ruled by the Seljuq (Saljug) Dynasty. "Rūm" is an Arabic-Persian word for Rome (Byzantium) that once included Anatolia, and where Rumi lived most of his life – hence the name "Rumi." The Middle Eastern people usually call him Mawlânâ (Arabic), Mowlânâ (Persian pronunciation) or Mevlânâ (Turkish pronunciation), all of which mean "Our Master." It is interesting that a common title for a spiritual teacher has become a proper noun for Rumi; this shows the reputation and eminence that this poet and mystic has enjoyed through the centuries in his cultural lands.

Rumi's father, Bahâ Valad, continued to teach and preach in seminaries in Anatolia. He died in 1231, when Rumi was twenty four. Rumi studied Islamic subjects and literature with several prominent teachers, and eventually succeeded his father a decade later. Rumi served as a reputed religious scholar and teacher in Konya. One day in late 1244, he met a wandering dervish, Shams of Tabriz, and this opened a new chapter in his life. Long sessions of *soh'bat* (dialogue) and retreats with Shams transformed Rumi into a mystical poet intoxicated with Divine love. He began to conduct whirling dances (*samâ*), and in the ecstasy of his dances, in the tranquility of his contemplation and in the climax of his speeches, amazing poems poured out from his lips. Shams' disappearance in 1248 (which still remains a historical mystery) was an emotional blow to Rumi, but he continued with his spiritual practices, teachings, and poetry. His poems have been collected in two masterpieces: (1) the *Divân-e Shams-e Tabrizi*, comprising about 44,000 verses of lyrical odes (*ghazaliyât*) and quatrains (*rubâiyât*); and (2) the *Masnavi* (*Mathnawi* in Arabic pronunciation, *Mesnevi* in Turkish) comprising about 26,000 "rhyming couplets" (*masnavi*) which amount to six volumes of stories and parables in verse.

A Poet in Love

Rumi's poems are filled with words like Love, Beloved, Friend, Compassion, Mercy, Bliss, Joy, Grief, Heart, Wine, Drunkard, Selflessness, God, Separation, Union, Oneness of God, Unity of the World, and so forth. Rumi was a poet in love with the Divine and the whole world, and was finely tuned to his heart and spiritual core. Of course, he could not define or prove what love is; love can be only experienced:

Someone asked: What is love?
I said: Don't ask about its meaning.
You will see love when you become like me.   Divân: 29050-51

Rumi's notion of love is not a transient, shallow feeling that would soon turn into hatred when someone "left him." Rumi considers genuine human love as a reflection of Divine love. Love is not unreachable metaphysics; it is embedded in life, both its joys and sorrows:

One night I asked Love: Tell me truly, what are you?
It said: I am life eternal, I multiply the joyful life.
I asked: Oh you, who are outside of space and time,
    where is your real home?
Love said: I am a companion to the heart's fire;
    I sit beside wet eyes.   Divân: 14851-52

Abstract love has no place in Rumi's vision: "God is Love" and "Love Thy Neighbor" either go together or go nowhere. From his biographical records, we read many stories of Rumi's compassion and humility toward all people. In one instance, a Christian monk who had heard about Rumi's scholarly and spiritual reputation went to meet him in Konya. Out of respect, the monk prostrated before Rumi, and when he raised his head, he saw that Rumi had been prostrating before the monk too. Recall that those were the days of the Crusades and the bloody wars between the Christians and the Muslims.

A Poet of Peace

Rumi expands love from interpersonal to international and interfaith relations. In one poem, he says that the objective of love is inherent in all religions, and yet separate from all forms of religion:

The religion of love is separate from all religions:
The nation and religion of lovers is God.   Masnavi, II: 1770

In one story in the *Masnavi* (II: 3681-3691), a story that suggests how Rumi would have reacted to today's superficial, superstitious, sectarian, and literalist notions of religion, he tells us about four men who were given only one *dirham* (silver) coin to buy whatever they desired. These men spoke in different tongues:

The Persian said: I want anghoor.
The Arab said: I want enab.
The Turk said: I want uzum.
And the Greek said: I want stafil.

These men were quarrelling because they were not aware of the fact that all of those words meant the same thing: "Grapes." Rumi does not hide his disdain that human history is full of such childish, unnecessary conflicts over symbols, appearances, and names. An effective conflict resolution is a realization of truth and meaning in our hearts. Truth-consciousness, self-realization, and mutual understanding are the keys to peace. A Persian proverb says, "Two worldly kings cannot be contained in one country, but ten dervishes can sleep on a single carpet."

Hatred in response to hatred (whether religious, political or racial) does not bring about peace; it breeds more hatred and perpetuates violence in history. Rumi is right: Love is the ultimate answer to all of our problems. Love does not solve but dissolves conflicts. And that is why Rumi emphasizes love in his poetry he invites us to join the caravan of love. First, however, the would-be lover should be free from dishonesty:

Put aside tricks and deceit;
    be honest and love-mad.
Then like a moth
    enter the heart of this fire.
Go and wash off all the hatred from your chest,
    seven times with water.
Then you can become our companion,
    drinking from the wine of love.   Divân: 22547-49

Peace comes from baptism by the Fire of Love. When love and its various behavioral manifestations like empathy, kindness, understanding, friendship, and forgiveness give way to ignorance, egoism, greed, and hatred, the result is what Rumi calls "the wars of seventy two nations or religions."

Rumi is Born Everyday

Rumi died at sunset on Sunday December 17, 1273 in Konya. People from various religions and walks of life – Muslims, Jews and Christians, poor, rich, educated, illiterate – all came to his funeral to pay their respects and mourn the loss of their beloved teacher and poet. His tomb in Konya is a shrine for lovers of peace and seekers of truth. And seven centuries later, Rumi's sweet poems are alive on our lips. Rumi is reborn every day. He says:

Although words circle around the mouth,
wonderful images circle around each poem.

Divân: Quatrain 482

An earlier version of this chapter was published in *New Perspectives: Journal of Conscious Living*, Summer 2007, pp. 14-15. Its Italian translation, "Rumi: Poeta di amore e pace," appeared in *Aam Terra Nuova* (Italy), October 2007, pp. 57-60.

[4]
Master Rumi:
The Path to Poetry, Love and Enlightenment

Eight hundred years ago, in a northeastern town of the Persian Kingdom, a boy was born. When he was twelve years old, he chanced to meet the great Persian poet and Sufi master Attâr who told the boy's father: "The fiery words of this boy will kindle the souls of lovers all over the world." That boy was later to be known as Rumi. In 2007, many literary, cultural and spiritual organizations celebrated his 800th birth anniversary. UNESCO issued a medal in Rumi's honor. According to various sources, such as *The Christian Science Monitor*,[1] *TIME Asia magazine*,[2] and the US Department of State's *Washington File*,[3] Rumi has become one of the most widely-read poets in North America, and translations of this poet are increasingly popular in the other Western countries. For three decades, I have read Rumi everywhere I have been – India, Japan, and the USA. It is thus a delight for me to see more people enjoying Rumi's poetry.

Who was Rumi really? How did a Muslim preacher become a poet of love? Who were Rumi's masters? What does Rumi mean by love? What was the visionary ground underlying his poetry? These are the questions I will explore here: Rumi's path to poetry, the source of his poetry – spiritual enlightenment – and the content of his poetry – love. In this analysis, I draw on the original documents[4] and scholarly biographies of Rumi,[5] and also offer some new translations of Rumi's poems. Good poetry enriches our life, and Rumi's poems are full of pearls of wisdom and inspiration. Technological developments over the past two centuries have created a world in which we utilize amazing instruments and enjoy convenient services, but our fast-paced industrial and digital civilization has also brought humanity to a point where we need more spiritual art, reflection, and practice to balance our lives, both personally and collectively.

In Search of Rumi

Today in the West, Rumi is famous for his poetry. While he was a prolific poet, Rumi was not a poet by profession; he was a religious teacher and leader. Above all, Rumi was a "gnostic" (*Âref:* one possessing esoteric knowledge of spiritual matters). For centuries, Rumi has been known as Mawlânâ ("Our Master") to the people of Turkey, Iran, Afghanistan, Tajikistan, and parts of India and Pakistan. The name Rumi, meaning "belonging to Rūm," refers to the Roman-Byzantine Empire which once included Anatolia, a vast plateau in Asia Minor, lying between the Black and Mediterranean seas – the vibrant setting in which Rumi lived most of his life.

Rumi's major works of literature include (1) the *Masnavi-ye Ma'navi* ("Spiritual Couplets"),[6] a six-volume book of stories and parables narrated in about 26,000 verses of didactic poetry; (2) the *Divân-e Shams-e Tabrizi*,[7] a poetry book consisting of about 44,000 lines of lyrical odes (*ghazaliyât*) and quatrains (*rubâiyât*); (3) a collection of seventy one discourses called the *Fihi Mâ Fih* ("In It What is in It");[8] and (4) the *Majâlis-e Sab'a* ("Seven Sermons"), his formal lectures; this last book is yet to be translated into English.

There is a line attributed to Rumi which summarizes his life work:

The outcome of my life is no more than these three lines:
    I was a raw material;
    I was cooked and became mature;
    I was baked and burned. [9]

Rumi's Life: Act I

Rumi's given name was Jalâluddin ("Splendor of Religion") Mohammad. He was born on September 30, 1207, most likely in the city of Balkh in present-day Afghanistan. The Swiss scholar Fritz Meier, who has researched the life of Rumi's father Bahâ Valad[10], argues persuasively for the small town of Vakh'sh (about 150 miles northeast of Balkh) in present-day Tajikistan. In any case, we know that Rumi grew up in Balkh, in that era a political, commercial and intellectual center of the Persian Kingdom, a city where his father was honored as the *Sultân-e Ulamâ* ("King of Scholars"). It is recorded that even the king, Mohammad Khârazm-Shah, attended Bahâ Valad's lectures.

To understand Rumi it is useful to understand his father – fifty six years his senior, and indeed, Rumi's first teacher. Bahâ Valad was not merely a preacher but also a Muslim gnostic, a Sufi. In the Islamic tradition, the Sufis have often been contrasted with the *Falâsafeh* (Philosophers). While the Sufis called for direct spiritual experience, meditation, and love, the *Falâsafeh* focused on rational thinking, intellectual knowledge, and logical arguments. These two fields are not necessarily contradictory, but philosophy, the Sufis contend, can never replace practice and experience. On the path of love, Rumi himself once said, *"The legs of argumentative logicians are made of wood!"* (*Masnavi*, I: 2128) In other words, they can talk but cannot walk. The Sufis have also had their differences with the *Fuqahâ*, or Islamic law-experts, who deal with rigid formalities and rituals.

In his public talks, Bahâ Valad would criticize the philosophers. His words and public influence obviously hurt the feelings of Imâm Fakhruddin Râzi, an eminent Muslim theologian and the King's teacher in Balkh. All of this came to make life difficult for Bahâ Valad. Moreover, there was a prevalent fear of the invasion of Persia by Genghis Khan's brutal army (this invasion and its attendant bloodshed eventually came to pass). Bahâ Valad decided to emigrate from Balkh and take his family westward. En route to Baghdad, Bahâ Valad's caravan stopped at the city of Nishâbur. This is where Attâr met the twelve-year-old Rumi and presented him with a copy of his book on mysticism, *Asrâr Nâmeh* ("The Book of Mysteries").

Bahâ Valad and his family made a pilgrimage to Mecca, stayed for a while in Baghdad and Damascus, and finally went to Anatolia, which was then under the rule of the Seljuq (Saljug) Dynasty, far from the Mongolian influence. For a while, they lived in the town of Lâranda (today called Karaman), where Rumi, at age eighteen, married his childhood friend Gowhar, whose family had accompanied Bahâ Valad from Balkh. Rumi's two sons, Alâ-eddin and Sultân Valad, were born in Lâranda. Rumi's mother, Mo'meneh Khâtun, also died in that town (her tomb is still there). Sometime later, at the request of the Seljuq king Alâ'eddin Kaygubâd, Bahâ Valad and his family moved to the town of Konya, where a seminary was provided for him. Two years later, in 1231, Bahâ Valad, aged eighty, passed away. And Rumi, then twenty four, took over his father's position.

Burhânuddin Termezi – Bahâ Valad's disciple and Rumi's tutor back in Balkh – soon rejoined Rumi in Konya. There he undertook a systematic training of the young man, and suggested that Rumi study Bahâ Valad's book of teachings, the *Ma'âref*.[10] Rumi also spent several years learning from great Sufi masters and Muslim scholars in Aleppo and Damascus (both in present-day Syria).

What was the content of Rumi's education? A Muslim scholar would have studied Arabic literature, the *Quran*, the sayings and acts of Prophet Muhammad, Islamic rituals and law, and theology. Rumi's books indeed show us that he possessed a vast knowledge of literature, both Arabic and Persian, and both prose and poetry. He was fond of at least one classic Arabic poet, Al-Mutanabbi, and two Persian Sufi poets, Attâr and Sanâ'ie.

Rumi returned to Konya some time before 1240, and Burhânuddin told him that although he had become a master of "the science of apparent subjects" (*ulum-e zâher*) he had yet to master "the science of hidden affairs" (*ulum-e bâten*). Rumi is said to have taken three successive *chelleh* (a forty-day period of retreat, fasting, and meditation) to the satisfaction of Burhânuddin. Rumi then began to serve as a reputed religious scholar in Konya. Burhânuddin would die in 1241.

Act II: When Two Oceans Meet

Now we are in a better position to consider the climax of Rumi's life – his meeting with a wandering dervish, Shams Tabrizi. This was a rebirth and Act II in Rumi's life. There are several versions of how this meeting took place. A fifteenth-century Persian poet, Jâmi, writes that one day in the late autumn of 1244, Rumi was sitting by a pool along with his disciples and books. Shams, who was unknown to Rumi, came along, greeted, and sat down. Interrupting Rumi's lecture, he pointed to the books and asked, "What are these?" Rumi replied, "This is some knowledge you wouldn't understand." Shams threw all those books into the water. Rumi protested; Shams then pulled the books out of the pool and they were dry! Rumi was marveled by it, and inquired about it. Shams said, "And this is some knowledge *you* wouldn't understand."[11]

I narrate this story not because I myself believe it, but because this story best illustrates how people have dramatized Shams' influence in Rumi's life:

A dry, bookish theologian suddenly turns to mysticism after meeting an old mystic who disliked bookish knowledge. The fact is that the meeting of Shams and Rumi was like the convergence of two oceans. Rumi's upbringing and education had nurtured him for a mystic's life. (A good analogy is this: Millions of people have observed apples falling down, but only Newton could discover the laws of universal gravitation from such an observation.) On the other hand, Shams was not an illiterate person. Born in Tabriz, a city in northwest Iran, some six decades before coming to Konya, Shams had studied with many masters, and his book of discourses, the *Magâlât-e Shams-e Tabrizi*,[12] indeed shows him to be a very knowledgeable person. Nevertheless, it is true that Shams galvanized Rumi's mystical and artistic senses. After that, Rumi turned to music, dance and poetry, and was detached from books. Shams would not even allow Rumi read his father's book.

The most likely story of the first encounter between Rumi and Shams in Konya in 1244, as narrated in authentic sources, is this: Rumi and his students and disciples were walking in the market when an old man (Shams) approached them and asked Rumi directly, "Who was spiritually superior: Prophet Muhammad or the Sufi Master Bâyazid Bastâmi?" Rumi replied, "Of course, Prophet Muhammad." Shams continued, "How is it that the Prophet regarded himself as God's servant and used to ask for God's forgiveness, while Bastâmi famously declared, 'Glory be to me, how great is my position. There is none in my cloak but God!'" Rumi was very moved by Shams, and noticed that his loaded question contained sublime mystical teachings. Rumi is quoted to have answered that it was a matter of the capacity of these individuals. Bâyazid Bastâmi became completely intoxicated and selfless after having only a glass of Divine wine, but the Prophet was more aware and more humble, and his inner space was more spacious. This was the beginning of the Rumi-Shams retreats and conversations, which often lasted for days and weeks.[13]

In the *Divân-e Shams*, Rumi has many expressions of love, respect, admiration, and longing for Shams. How can one explain Rumi's relationship with Shams? In Sufism, there is a tradition called *soh'bat* ("dialogue" in retreat), which takes place between two seekers as they share their knowledge, stories, and experiences. The *soh'bat* is believed to strengthen the mind and soul of the seekers. In those days (before automobiles and airplanes), a seeker may have journeyed for weeks or months to visit his favorite master for spiritual conversation and counseling. Rumi himself has a poem about this tradition:

Oh my heart, sit with a person
    who understands the heart.
Sit under a tree
    which has fresh flowers.
In the market of drug sellers
    do not wander hither and thither aimlessly.
Go to the shop of someone
    who has the sweet healing medicine.
Not every eye has eyesight.
Not every sea contains jewels.   *Divân*: 5960-61

    My interpretation of the Rumi-Shams relationship is based on a parable which both Shams and Rumi used in their speeches – the parable of the "mirror" (*âyeeneh*). A mirror reflects what is cast on it without judging, and thus we see ourselves in the mirror as we are, in a good or bad state of mind. A spiritual friend is like the mirror; it reflects and encourages our goodness and inner beauty; it also shows our weaknesses and dark sides in a friendly manner so that we can see them for ourselves and strive to resolve them.

    In 1248, Shams disappeared from Konya and, for that matter, from history. Some scholars believe that he was murdered by jealous disciples of Rumi who had lost their master to this strange old man. Other scholars believe that Shams left Konya on his own (as he had done once before, by going to Damascus, for a brief period) because Rumi's disciples had made life too difficult for him. We do not know for sure what happened.

    In any case, Shams had accomplished his task of Rumi-making in Konya. Nevertheless, Shams' disappearance was an emotional blow to Rumi. He traveled twice to Damascus in search of him. As time passed, Rumi found two other spiritual friends, the goldsmith Salâhuddin Zarkub and a young chivalric disciple (*Akhi*) Husâmuddin Chalabi. If Shams is the hero of Rumi's *Divân*, Husâmuddin is the hero of the *Masnavi*. It was Husâm who suggested Rumi compose this book and it was Husâm to whom Rumi recited the entire *Masnavi* during the last decade of his life, and he faithfully wrote it down.

Love in Rumi's Poetry

Love (*eshg*) is a common thread that runs through all of Rumi's poems, directly or implicitly. The intensity of the language and imagery that Rumi uses to express love is rarely seen in other mystical poets. As Coleman Barks aptly remarks, Rumi's love is not of the kind, "she left me, he left me; she came back; she left me."[14]

Love in Rumi's poems stems from his realization of Divine love and its extension to the world and human life. Rumi says:

In the Realm of the Unseen,
    there is a sandal wood, burning.
This love
    is the smoke of that incense.   Divân: 31322

Rumi views genuine human love as an integrated part of this cosmic love matrix. I use the term "love matrix" in a modern scientific sense. The best explanation physicists have for the gravitational force is that it is not a simple attraction between two isolated bodies but a force embedded in the very fabric of the universe. Here again, Rumi has a say:

If the Sky were not in love,
    its chest would not be pleasant.
If the Sun were not in love,
    its face would not be bright.
If the Earth and mountains were not in love,
    no plant could sprout from their heart.
If the Sea were not aware of love,
    it would have remained motionless somewhere.   Divân: 28369-72

How does this Divine cosmic love manifest and function in our life? Where does it take us? To answer this, I propose two love-based processes in Rumi's poetry: Transformation and transcendence.

Rumi assigns a transforming power to love like nothing else. Through love, he says, everything changes in a positive way, and far more rewardingly than through other means. In the *Masnavi*, Rumi tells us the story of Lugmân, a famous sage in the ancient Middle East, who one day was eating watermelon at his master's residence. When the master also ate the watermelon, he found it to be very bitter. The master scolded Lugmân over why he had not informed him that the watermelon was bitter. Lugmân replied that it was not bitter for him at all, as he was eating the watermelon with love in the home of his master:

Through love
> *bitter things become sweet.*

Through love
> *bits of copper turn into gold.*

Through love
> *dregs taste like pure wine.*

Through love
> *pains are healed.*   *Masnavi* (II: 1529-31)

Sometimes we are stuck in a problem or in a conflict, and our ever-calculating mind is unable to find a "rational" solution that satisfies our ego. In the alchemy of love, problems are not solved; they are dissolved. The school of love teaches us that the "six directions" (north, south, east, west, up, and down) surrounding us are not the limits of our being and life:

Reason says:
> *These six directions are the limit.*
> *There is no way out!*

Love says:
> *There is a way.*
> *I have traveled it many times.*

Reason sees a market and begins to trade.
Love sets its eye on superior bazaars beyond this market.   *Divân*: 1522-23

Similar to the Buddhist concept of *nirvâna*, Sufis say that *fanâ* is annihilation of the ego and dissolution in Divine love. In that state of consciousness, you are one with everything and you see everything as one. In other words, the seeker goes beyond dualities (a quality of the mind that Buddhism also fosters) and becomes one with the Beloved. Let's listen to a famous poem attributed to Rumi on what this transcendence means:

What is to be done, O Muslims, for I can't identify myself?
I'm neither Christian nor Jewish;
  neither Zoroastrian nor Muslim.
I'm neither Eastern nor Western;
  neither of the land nor of the sea.
I'm not from Nature's mine, or from the circling Heavens.
I'm not from this world, or from the next;
  neither from Paradise nor from Hell.
I'm neither from Adam nor from Eve.
My place is placeless; my trace is traceless.
This is neither body nor soul;
  for I belong to the soul of the Beloved.[15]

A Global Soul

Why is Rumi such a popular poet seven centuries after his life, and in different lands? To answer this question, perhaps I can offer one of Rumi's own poems:

I had a sea, but it was drowned in itself,
  for I am in an ocean without shore.
Don't seek me in this or that world.
They both have vanished in the world where I am.   Divân: 18440-41

    Rumi was a planetary poet and a world citizen because he was an "out of the world" soul. Although his life was rooted in the Islamic and Persian culture, his constituency was the human heart. That is why his poems lift us from mundane situations and offer us the purity, clarity and beauty of an extraordinary vision – and when our feet touch the earth again, we feel not simply relaxed, but relieved and liberated.
    Rumi does not view Divine love as an abstract, verbal subject for poets or philosophers; it is the source of our being and a foundation on which we should build our lives. He views God not as a remote father in Heaven but a friend (*doost*) on Earth. Rumi spoke his poems spontaneously – oftentimes during the whirling dances, listening to music, or contemplation. He appears to have practiced what he preached in his poetry. Rumi's message of love

was also his ethical practice. Rumi's biographers have recorded many stories of his humbleness and kindness towards people, whoever they were. For instance, Aflâki[4] recounts that a Christian monk, who had heard of Rumi's scholarly and spiritual reputation, went to meet him in Konya. Out of respect, the monk prostrated himself before Rumi three times, and each time he raised his head, he saw that Rumi had been prostrating himself as well, before the monk.

When Rumi died on December 17, 1273 (at sunset on Sunday) in Konya, people of the town – Muslims, Jews and Christians – all came to his funeral and mourned. Aflâki writes that some fanatic Muslims objected because non-Muslims were attending the services. But the Jews and the Christians told them just as their Muslim friends had understood Prophet Muhammad through Rumi, they had also understood Moses and Jesus through him. Perhaps, then, Rumi's poetry can serve as an enlightening vision and unifying voice for our divided world and violent era.

I am a Moon that shines in a placeless universe.
Do not seek me outside; I abide in your very soul and life.
Everybody calls you toward himself;
I invite you nowhere except to yourself.
Poetry is like the boat; its meaning like the sea:
Come onboard at once!
Let me sail this boat! *Divân*: 15976-85

An earlier version of this chapter appeared in *Kyoto Journal*, No. 66, pp. 16-21 as well as on the magazine's website (www.kyotojournal.org). It was also posted under the title "In the Alchemy of Love, Problems are Dissolved" on the website of *Sufi News and Sufi World Report* (htpp://sufinews.blogspot.com), June 20, 2007.

[5]
Rumi's Life and Spiritual Journey

Our wilderness has no bounds.
Our hearts and souls, no rest.
World within world, there are images and forms.
But which one of them is ours? Divân: 2689-90

Poetry has become less and less present in our modern life. Poetry books do not generally sell well. Even the word "poetry" is sometimes (mis)used to imply non-serious thoughts or irrelevant talk. This is in sharp contrast to the reputed position that poetry enjoyed in earlier times. Poetry played a practical role in society: Parents used to read poems to their children; students memorized poems in school; people recited poems as proverbs; and eminent poets were icons of wisdom and a refined soul. Against this backdrop of the marginalization of poetry in our life, it is heartening to see Rumi shelves in major bookstores with Coleman Barks' *The Essential Rumi* as a best-selling book – a rare achievement for a poetry book and a glimmer of encourgament for our times.

Despite the popularity of his poetry books, we will not see Rumi in book-signing events, lecture halls or television interviews. He lived in the thirteenth century. In 2007, many literary, cultural and spiritual organizations around the world organized events to celebrate the 800th anniversary of Rumi's birth. UNESCO hosted an international seminar, performance and exhibition from September 6-14 in Paris, and issued a Commemorative Medal in honor of Mowlânâ Rumi. On June 26, the United Nations Organization hosted a gathering in New York (with the participation of representatives from Afghanistan, Iran, and Turkey), and the UN Secretary-General Mr. Ban Ki-moon commented: "Rumi's poetry is timeless. But its celebration at the United Nations is extremely timely. Events of recent years have created a growing gulf between communities and nations. They have led to a worrying rise in intolerance and cross-cultural tensions ... As Moulana teaches, we must be mindful of the people around us, and love them as human beings and God's creatures."[1]

A Celestial Bird

I am a bird from the celestial garden;
I am not from this world of mud.[2]

Who was Rumi? How did he become an ecstatic poet of love and a teacher of wisdom and spiritual philosophy? What does he say in his poems? What is his vision of life and of the world? Why is he so popular? Why is this thirteenth-century poet even relevant to our generation? This article explores these questions, and briefly reviews Rumi's biography intertwined with his poems and ideas.

In his works Rumi very rarely talks about himself, his family or his past. This should not come as a surprise. He was first and foremost a deeply spiritual person living his life "here and now." Rumi did not even write down his own poems; he simply recited to his disciples who recorded them. What we know of Rumi's life comes from three historical documents (hagiographies): (1) *Valad Nâmeh* ("The Book of Valad"), a book of narrative poetry by Rumi's eldest son, Sultân Valad (1226-1312); (2) *Risâle-ye Sepah-sâlâr* ("The Treatise of Sepah-sâlâr"), written by his disciple Feridoon Sepah-sâlâr (?-1319); and (3) *Manâqeb ul-Ârefin* ("The Virtuous Acts of the Mystics") compiled by another disciple Ahmad Aflâki (?-1356). These are all in the Persian language, and only the third book[3] has been recently translated into English.

Modern authors, who have researched Rumi's life in detail, include the Iranian scholars Badi uz-Zamân Foruzânfar (1900-1970)[4] and Abdul Hossein Zarrinkub (1922-1999),[5] the Turkish scholar Abdulbâki Gölpinârli (1900-1982),[6] the Pakistani scholar Afzal Iqbâl (1919-1994),[7] the German scholar Annemarie Schimmel (1922-2003),[8] and more recently the American scholar Franklin Lewis.[9]

From Balkh to Konya

Since not a single straw can move save by a wind,
how can this universe move without the wind of passion and longing?
All parts and particles of the universe are lovers;
and each one is intoxicated by the sight of beauty.   Divân: 28365-65

Historical records place the birth of Jalâluddin Mohammad on September 30, 1207 in the city of Balkh (in present-day Afghanistan) which was then a political, economic and cultural center in the eastern part of the Persian Kingdom. Through the centuries, Balkh was a hub for various spiritual traditions, including Zoroastrian, Buddhist, and Islamic faiths. Rumi's father, Bahâ Valad, was a Muslim mystic and preacher, and indeed his first teacher.

When Rumi was a young boy, his family decided to leave Balkh and migrate westward. Two reasons are cited for this emigration from Balkh. First, Bahâ Valad in his speeches often criticized the philosophers who based their understanding of truth merely on logical, verbal arguments. Such criticisms surely angered powerful philosophers who were friends with Sultan Mohammad Khârazm-Shah, who ruled over the Persian Kingdom including one of its largest cities, Balkh. The king, who sometimes attended Bahâ Valad's sermons, apparently did not like the growing gathering around a pious, mystic preacher who kept distance from the court. The king's followers may thus have intimidated Bahâ Valad. The second reason for his departure from Balkh was that Bahâ Valad who, being a preacher, sometimes traveled to towns and villages close to Mongolia, must have sensed the growing power of Genghis Khan and his imminent threat to the unpopular and tyrant Khârazm-Shah.

Around 1219, Rumi's family left Balkh. About 300 people were in Bahâ Valad's caravan. They travelled along the historical Silk Road, and on their way, stopped for a while at the city of Nishâbur (in northeast Iran) where the great Persian poet Attâr lived. There is a famous story that Attâr was so impressed by the young Jalâluddin that gave him a copy of *Asrâr Nâmeh* ("The Book of Secrets") – a book Attâr had composed during his own youth. He also told the boy's father: "The time will come when the fiery words of this boy will kindle the hearts of lovers all over the world." If this conversation did take place, Attâr's prophecy has indeed come true. This story, however, is not recorded in Rumi's earliest biographies and appears in literature centuries later. In any case, we know that Rumi was fond of reading Persian poetry, especially that of Attâr (who was killed in 1221 by the Mongols) and Sanâ'ie (?-1131). Rumi regarded himself as a poet continuing the spiritual and literary tradition of these poets. There is a famous line attributed to Rumi: *"Attâr was the soul, and Sanâ'ie its two eyes. After them, I came."*

Bahâ Valad and his family were in Baghdad in 1221 when the Mongols sacked Balkh and Nishâbur, and massacred their inhabitants, including cats! (A famous Persian saying about the Mongol invasion is, "They came, they killed, they burned, and they departed.") After making a pilgrimage to Mecca, Bahâ Valad and his family moved to Anatolia (Asia Minor or Byzantine) which was then called Rūm in Arabic and Persian – hence the name Rumi as he is known in the West. The Eastern people respectfully call him Mawlânâ, "our master." Interestingly, this general title (Mawlânâ) for an eminent sage, scholar or poet, has become a specific name for Rumi.

In the thirteenth century, Anatolia was ruled by the Seljuq (Saljug) Dynasty who had conquered the Byzantine Empire two centuries earlier. The Seljuq kings were of Turkish origin, but over time, they had blended with the Persians, adopted their culture, and converted to Islam; the Seljuq courts were supporters of Persian poets and Sufi scholars. In the town of Lâranda (now called Karaman), Rumi's mother died; her tomb still exists there. In 1224, the eighteen-year-old Rumi married Gowhar Khâtun ("Lady"), a girl whose family had accompanied Bahâ Valad's westward sojourn. The couple soon had two sons – Sultân Valad (who became Rumi's successor) and Alâ'eddin (who died in about 1262, a decade before Rumi).

In 1229, Bahâ Valad and his family moved to the city of Konya (now in southern Turkey) at the request of the Seljuq king Sultan Alâ'eddin Kaygubâd. Konya (an ancient Greek city called Ikónion) was the Seljuq capital where peoples of various religions, languages, and ethnicities peacefully lived together. A school was given to Bahâ Valad to hold his classes and sermons. In 1231, Bahâ Valad died at the age of eighty. Rumi took over his father's position as the head of the family and the school, but he still needed to complete his own education. A year later, Burhânuddin Termezi, who was a disciple of Bahâ Valad and a tutor of Rumi back in Balkh, came to Konya and undertook a systematic training of the young scholar in various subjects of learning. In 1233, Rumi was sent to Aleppo and Damascus (both cities now in Syria) to study with the great teachers of the day. A few years later, Rumi returned to Konya. A scholar *par excellence* Rumi became a popular preacher and teacher in Konya with hundreds of students and followers. This was also a time of great loss for Rumi: His teacher and mentor Burhânuddin passed away in 1241, and also his beloved wife Gowhar probably died of illness at about this time.

Rumi married Kerâ Khâtun, a widow and mother of a son (and probably also a daughter named Kimiyâ) from her first marriage. The second marriage brought two more children (a son and a daughter) to Rumi's family. Kerâ was praised for her beauty, elegance, and devotion to her family. Rumi and Kerâ loved each other until the end of their lives; together they raised six children. Kerâ outlived Rumi by two decades and died in 1292, without marrying again. Rumi's descendants from the line of Sultân Valad (who died in 1312) still live in Turkey, and are called Chalabi (Chelebi, a Turkish title meaning "respected or distinguished").

I Became Alive

I was dead; I became alive.
I was all cries; I became laughter.
The glory of love came upon me, and
I became everlasting glory.   *Divân*: 14742

November 29, 1244 is a second birthday for Rumi. On that day, he met Shams Tabrizi in Konya's marketplace. Shams (literally "Sun") was a wandering dervish born in Tabriz, a city in northwest Iran, and had led a long life of travel, studies, and practice with the Sufis. Because of his constant moving and extensive travels, he was called *Shams-e Parandeh* ("Flying Shams" or "Shams the Bird").

In their very first meeting, Rumi (then thirty seven) and Shams (probably about sixty) were impressed by each other's spiritual insight. Subsequent conversations and retreats with Shams (a Sufi tradition called *soh'bat* or "conversation") drastically changed Rumi's life and worldview. He was transformed from a scholar (*âlem*) to a mystic (*âref*), from a preacher (*wâ'ez*) to a poet (*shâ'er*). Of course, Rumi himself was ripe for this spiritual transformation. After meeting Shams, Rumi did not read books much, and reduced his teaching schedule. Instead, he spent days and nights in poetry, meditation *(morâgibah)*, music and dance *(samâ,* later developed by his son Sultân Valad into the tradition of the Whirling Dervishes).

Shams was an enigmatic figure. He was a blunt and an extremely difficult person to deal with, mainly because he was honest and insightful, and resented pretense and hypocrisy from anyone. Shams' speeches collected in *Magâlât-e Shams-e Tabrizi* ("Discourses of Shams") portray him as a learned and wise man. Nevertheless, Rumi's students and disciples disliked Shams who, in their opinion, had kidnapped their teacher from them. At one point, Shams left Konya for Damascus in protest of the disciples' rudeness toward him; Rumi dispatched his son to bring him back. Shams returned, but after a while the same problems surfaced. In 1248, Shams disappeared for good. Nobody knows where he went or what happened to him. Some scholars believe that he was killed by Rumi's angry disciples; others, however, doubt this story as well as the authenticity of the tomb in Konya attributed to Shams. Nevertheless, Shams' disappearance devastated Rumi. He went to Damascus twice to look for him, but finally realized that Shams was within him. In the following years, Rumi found two other soul brothers: Salâhuddin Zarkub, a goldsmith and a former disciple of Burhânuddin Termezi who died in 1258, and Husâmuddin Chelebi, a young disciple from the chivalry class of Konya who died in 1284, a decade after Rumi.

It can be said that the first three-and-half decades of Rumi's life and education were a period of preparation for his poetic period. Rumi's meeting with Shams ignited his soul, triggered his poetic genius, and thus started a new chapter in his life. However, Rumi was not trained as a poet, nor did he anticipate becoming one. In fact, he was not a poet by profession; he earned his living by teaching Islamic subjects and guiding the public, for which he was given a modest salary from the government in Konya. Rumi's "poetic period" was limited to the last three decades of his life; nevertheless, he is one of the most prolific poets in the history of Persian poetry. Rumi's poems (ninety eight percent in Persian and about two percent in Arabic) are collected in two great works: (1) *Divân-e Shams-e Tabrizi*[10] ("The Poetry Book of Shams") or the *Divân-e Kabir* ("The Great Book of Poetry") contains some 3,300 lyrical odes *(ghazaliyât)* and about 1900 quatrains *(rubâiyât),* and is dedicated to Shams Tabrizi. This book is full of ecstatic love poems, many of which Rumi ends with his pen name of *Khamoosh* ("Silent") or *Shams* ("Sun") (out of respect and affection for his beloved friend). (2) *Masnavi-ye Ma'navi*[11] ("Rhyming Couplets on Spiritual Matters") is a six-volume book of didactic poetry (stories and parables) which Rumi recited to Husâm Chelebi during the last decade of his life. The English translations of Rumi's poetry available on the market today (with varying quality) are selections from these two works.

Religion of Love

This is the root of the root of the root of religion. Masnavi, 1: Introduction

At the outset of his great work *Masnavi*, Rumi says that the content of his poetry is the very root and core of all religions. In one poem, he even says, "I eat love" (*Divân*: 3999). Rumi's path of spirituality is based on love (*traigat-e eshg*, "the path of love").

Rumi's poems are filled with expressions of love, beloved, friend, mercy, joy, grief, longing, heart, wine, drunkard, selflessness, senselessness, God, separation, and union. Love is a key to understanding Rumi's poetry but it is also important to have a right view of what he means by love. "Love" is a tricky, multi-faceted, and hence a complicated term because it can cover so many different feelings of affection and attachment. Sometimes, we think we love someone but our feeling is actually rooted in our possessive, self-centered desires. Such "love" can thus easily turn into hatred if our ego is slightly hurt, because both feelings are two sides of the same coin – selfishness. The term "love" is also sometimes used for sexual lust, in which case the "beloved" simply satisfies our sexual desires. While, Rumi honors romance, marriage, and warm, affectionate feelings, his poetry also clearly states that superficial, egoistic relationships deprive us of the depth, expanse, and hidden meanings that true love offers.

Love for Rumi was the outcome of his deep meditation on the nature of life and reality. A close reading of his poetry and parables reveals that Rumi's realization of love was based on (1) transcendence from the small self and its endless desires and its dualistic thinking (us versus the rest, this versus that), and (2) union with the Divine attributes of mercy, beauty, goodness, glory, joy, creativity, and peace, and so forth. This union with the Divine is not merely an after-death affair (returning to God); Rumi's poetry expresses it to be also a love-affair of the heart, in this very life and involving the whole of creation. He uses the symbolism of wine and drunkenness to describe selflessness (in contrast to selfishness), realization of oneness with the All, and ecstasy of melting into the mystery and presence of God. Out of this union, an all-inclusive, deep love emerges in the poet's heart. The heart, which appears over and over in Rumi's poetry, is described as a shining sun, a green garden of sacred secrets, a boundless desert or an ocean without shores. Rumi finds the heart to be his true home and the source of his poetry.

In *Man's Search for Meaning*, Viktor Frankl (1905-1997), a Jewish Austrian psychiatrist and Holocaust survivor, describes how those individuals who had a strong sense of meaning in their lives better survived the brutal conditions of German concentration camps during World War II. Frankl suggests that the "will-to-meaning" or what he calls logo-therapy ("meaning-therapy") can actually help to treat certain psychological distresses and anxiety. In this book, he also remarks that "what matters is not the meaning of life in general but rather the specific meaning of a person's life at a given moment." In other words, "One should not look for an abstract meaning of life."[12]

In Rumi's poetry and vision, love is not abstract, metaphysical, aloof or impractical, but alive, rich, and relevant. That is why he refers to God as a beloved on earth or a friend (*doost* or *yâr*) in our life. Rumi's notion of love is accessible on three levels. On a cosmic level, Rumi considers love to be the very matrix of creation and the universe. On a personal level, he views the path of love as the strongest link between humans and God, between the perishable and the eternal. And on a social level, Rumi articulates an organic relationship between our love of God and our love for fellow beings. Because true love, no matter whose and to whom, is a reflection of the Divine in the lover's heart.

Like Adam and Eve, Love gives birth to a thousand forms.
The world is full of its paintings and images,
but Love is not a painted image or an imagined form.　　　　　*Divân*: 5057

Rumi sees the rays of Divine love shining upon all places and ages. This integral view of love makes it possible for humans to tap into this marvelous source "this moment, right here." Socrates has said, "The unexamined life is not worth living." But how can we examine life? Through love, according to

Rumi: *"If you have not been a lover, do not count your days as a life truly lived"* (*Divân*: 10315).

A Poet of Peace

Conflicts among people arise from their attachments to names.
When people go into the meanings, peace prevails.   *Masnavi*, II: 3680

Rumi's poetry (as his life) brings love from an abstract metaphysics into our life and world encompassing our interpersonal, international and interfaith relations. In this sense, he is a planetary poet of peace. He was also a man who lived a peaceful life and died in peace. Rumi passed away on December 17, 1273, aged sixty six. People from diverse religions and ethnicities – Muslims, Christians, Jews, Persians, Turks, Arabs and Greek, rich, poor, elite, uneducated, women, and men – all came to his funeral and mourned the loss of their great sage and poet. Buried in Konya, Rumi's mausoleum (Green Dome, called "Gobbat ul-Khadrâ" in Arabic, "Yâshil Turbe" in Turkish, and "Gonbad-e Sabz" in Persian) has become a shrine for tens of thousands of his lovers, visitors, and pilgrims each year. It is located in a beautiful rose garden that originally belonged to Sultan Alâ'eddin Kaygubâd but the king donated it to Rumi's family upon Bahâ Valad's death. The mausoleum contains the tombs of Bahâ Valad, Rumi and his wife Kerâ and their children and grandchildren, as well as Salâhuddin Zarkub, Husâmuddin Chelebi, Feridoon Sepah-sâlâr, and several other close disciples.

December 17 in Konya is celebrated as *Shab-e Urs* (*Shab-e Arus*), a Persian word meaning "Wedding Night," which symbolizes reunion with the Divine. This ceremony is conducted in the spirit of Rumi's own will that those who come to his tomb should not come to cry and grieve but rejoice in poetry, music, prayer, contemplation, and compassion.

It is interesting to note that Rumi was born on Sunday and died at sunset on Sunday. This symbolism of his birth and death on a day named after the Sun is beautifully consistent with the name of Rumi's beloved friend Shams ("Sun") as well as with the place of Rumi in history. For seven centuries, his poetry has shined like a bright, warm sun upon the minds and hearts of many people. Master Rumi is an enlightening poet for all ages and people.

Rumi in America

A person of God is not of air or of earth.
A person of God is not of fire of water.
A person of God is a boundless ocean.
A person of God rains pearls without a dark cloud.[13]

English translations of Rumi date back to the late nineteenth and early twentieth centuries, notably by two Cambridge University professors of Persian literature, Reynold A. Nicholson (1868-1945) and Arthur J. Arberry (1905-1969). These gentlemen produced literal, scholarly translations of Rumi's poetry which have been used by many students of Sufism and Persian literature for decades. Arberry once remarked, "In Rumi the Persian mystical genius found its supreme expression. Viewing the vast landscape of Sufi poetry, we see him standing out as a sublime mountain-peak; the many other poets before and after him are but foot-hills in comparison ... To the West, now slowly realizing the magnitude of his genius, ... he is fully able to prove a source of inspiration and delight not surpassed by any other poet in the world's literature."[14]

The current fascination with Rumi is due partly to exposure: Free-verse translations of his poetry have made it easier for readers to approach this great poet. A pioneer of this venture is Coleman Barks, a retired professor of poetry and creative writing from University of Georgia, who started his work on Rumi in the late 1970s and has, since then, produced over a dozen volumes of Rumi's poetry. Barks does not read Persian himself, but works from literal translations made by other scholars and tries to offer a flavor of Rumi's poems in modern English. Over the past two decades, several other poets and translators (partly motivated by Barks' success) have popularized Rumi's poetry.[15]

Why is Rumi so popular? Partly also because of the wholeness of his personality: Rumi integrated in his life the learning of a scholar, the insightful and compassionate spirit of a sage, and the literary genius of a poet. Also Rumi's experience and message appeal to our thirst for meaning, warm heart, happiness, love, tranquility, and spiritual solutions to our life problems. Somehow we sense correctly that the spiritual solution heals us wholly and dissolves the root cause of our suffering, rather than tackling the long train of problems one by one. Rumi appeals because, as he believed, each one of us carries a memory (no matter how faint) of our Divine home, and each one of us hears (no matter how infrequently) the celestial bird's singing in the garden of our heart.

This chapter is based on the following articles:

"Master Rumi: A Spiritual Poet for All Ages," *The Payvand Online* (www.payvand.com com), October 2, 2007.

"Moulana Rumi: A Spiritual Poet for All Ages," *Persian Heritage Monthly*, English section, p. 4, October 2007. Also posted under the title "Love is Food" on the website of *Sufi News and Sufi World Report* (htpp://sufinews.blogspot.com), October 4, 2007.

"Poetry of Universal Love: The Journey of the Poet Rumi," *The World and I Online Magazine* (www.worldandi.com), April 2009.

[6]
Rumi's Roots:
The Historical Rumi

Each person, of his own imagination, made me his dear friend.
Alas, none sought my secrets from within me.
My secret is not far from my lament.
But the eye and the ear have no such illumination.

Masnavi, I: 6-7

Despite Rumi's popularity in the West, several aspects about his life, culture, and thinking are less known or misinterpreted in anthologies and translations of his work. This chapter reflects on some of these issues in order to better situate and appreciate Rumi's mind and poetry.

Sufism of Khorâsân

The fact that Rumi's poems reach us across cultures, languages, and centuries is a testimony to his universal love and vision. But it is important to remember that his poetry and ideas were rooted in his historical, geographical, cultural, literary, and spiritual background. Rumi did not emerge in a vacuum; he stood on "the shoulders of giants" spanning centuries before him. Therefore, in the popularization of Rumi and translation of his poetry, we should not uproot him from his cultural soil and transplant him to today's world without recognizing his roots and upbringing. Indeed, it is very interesting to find out what intellectual trajectories helped Rumi embark on a spiritual path and what resources he utilized to articulate a perennial philosophy.

From the hagiographies that Rumi's son, Sultân Valad,[1] and his two disciples, Feridoon Sepah-sâlâr[2] and Shamsuddin Ahmad Aflâki,[3] have left, we know that Jalâluddin Mohammad, later to be known as Rumi, was born on September 30, 1207 and raised in the city of Balkh, which was then a major city in the Persian Kingdom under Mohammad Khârazm-Shah. Balkh together with historical cities of Nishâbur, Mash'had, Marv, and Herat were parts of the Khorâsân Province in northeast Iran (Persia). After Afghanistan was separated from Iran in the nineteenth century (due to British colonial adventures in the region), the Khorâsân Province shrank to its present extent within Iran, and its eastern part, including Balkh, is now located in Afghanistan.

Khorâsân is one of the major centers of religious and mystical thought in history. Its fertile intellectual soil has nurtured Zoroastrian, Buddhist, Manichean, and Islamic traditions. Khorâsân was also one of the two birthplaces of Sufism (the second place being Mesopotamia in present-day Iraq). One of the earliest Sufi masters was Ibrahim bin Adham, who was a prince in Balkh in the eight century A.D., but left his palace (much like the Buddha) in search of spiritual life and enlightenment. Other eminent Sufi masters, poets, and philosophers from Khorâsân include: Bâyazid Bastâmi (804-874), Abul-Hasan Kharagâni (960-1033), Abu-Said Abul-Khayr (967-1049), Abdullah Ansâri (1006-1089), Abu Hâmed Ghazzâli (1058-1111) and his younger brother Ahmad Ghazzâli (1061-1126), Ibn Sinâ (Avicenna, 980-1037), Omar Khayyâm (1048-1123), Sanâ'ie (?-1131), and Attâr (1145-1221). All of these luminaries preceded Rumi.

The Sufism that emerged in Khorâsân should not be understood merely as the mystical dimension of the Arabic or Islamic religion (although it highly reflects that as well), for this would be like regarding Zen Buddhism as merely Indian because the Buddha lived and taught in India. Drawing on its rich mystical and literary heritage, the Khorâsânian Sufism has made great contributions to mystical thought. These are too enormous to be discussed in detail here, but for the purpose of situating Rumi in a historical context, I should briefly mention the following points:

(1) The earliest teaching books on Sufism were produced by Sufi masters from Khorâsân. Some of these books were systematic theoretical treatises, for example, Hujwiri's *Kashf ul-Mahjub* ("The Revelation of the Veiled"). Some were chronicles of Sufi masters, for instance, Ansâri's *Tabagât us-Suffiya*

("Generations of Sufis"). And some were anthologies of parables narrated in poetry, such as Attâr's *Asrâr Nâmeh* ("Book of Mysteries"). Legend has it that Attâr presented a copy of this book to the teenaged Rumi when Rumi's family stopped in Nishâbur on their flight from Balkh to avoid the onslaught of Genghis Khan's brutal army. It was in this tradition of didactic Sufi literature, more specifically writing parables in poetry, that Rumi devoted the last decade of his life to composing the *Masnavi-ye Ma'navi*[4] ("Spiritual Couplets"), and in doing so, he drew from Islamic, Christian, Jewish, Persian, Greek, and Indian sources.

(2) Khorâsânian Sufis also used Persian poetry as their main medium for mystical expressions. Sanâ'ie, Attâr, Rumi, and Jâmi (1414-1492) all fall in this category. In some of his poems, Rumi views himself as heir to Sanâ'ie and Attâr. For example, this line has been attributed to Rumi: *Attâr was the soul, and Sanâ'ie was its two eyes; I have come after them.*[5] Sufi poetry was often used in conjunction with music – a practice called *samâ*, "listening" to music, but which sometimes also included dancing such as the whirling dance developed by Rumi, and later institutionalized by his son Sultân Valad as a major spiritual practice in the Mawlaviyyah (Mevlevi) Sufi Order – hence the so-called "Whirling Dervishes."

(3) Khorâsânian Sufis drew a clear demarcation between the realm of philosophy and science (*elm*) and the realm of esoteric knowledge and mysticism (*erfân*, an Arabic translation of the Greek word "gnosis"). They stated openly that the logic of the head would not properly understand the secrets of the heart. Rumi clearly says this: *"The legs of argumentative logicians are wooden"* (*Masnavi*, I: 2128), implying that philosophical talk is one thing, walking on a spiritual path quite another. That is why Sufis did not seek a "scientific God" (as some philosophers and theologians have tried to do), although Sufis appreciated the function of science in its own realm. As Rumi puts it, *"Water beneath the boat is life-support, but poured into the boat sinks it to death"* (*Masnavi*, I: 985). The word "heart" (*del* in Persian, *qalb* in Arabic), which frequently appears in Rumi's poetry, is not simply a symbolic organ for our emotions, but a faculty of inner knowing; it is the "garden of mysteries."

(4) The Sufis also regarded God, not as an aloof heavenly king, but as their beloved on this earth and in this life. They developed a rich symbolic language, full of feminine terms, to express their adorations and prayers to the Divine. This language was a paradigm shift from the masculine terms by which God has been addressed in some languages like Arabic and English. Despite many translations of Persian Sufi poetry, including Rumi's, a reliable and comprehensive work in the field of Sufi symbolic language in classical Persian poetry is yet be published (*The Triumphal Sun* by Annmarie Schimmel is a good start). Therefore, many of the metaphors and idioms used in the original Persian may not be comprehensible in English translations. For instance, *zolf*, the beautiful long, curved hair of the woman symbolizes the interlinked, chain-like manifestations of the Divine in creation, with beauty within beauty, lines and space within lines and space, and mystery within mystery. Consider these two lines from Rumi (*Masnavi*, V: 1917):

Hundreds of chains, I cut and tear
Except the chain of my Beloved's hair.

"Chain" in the first line refers to the attachments and desires of which the poet – the lover of God – is willing to get rid of; but, holding the chain of the beloved's hair (in the second line) is like homecoming and a love affair. In the latter sense, Rumi recommends enjoying the beauty and mystery of creation, rather than renouncing it. It is akin to the famous saying of Jesus Christ, "Be ye in the world, but not of it." It will be difficult to grasp this couplet (and many others like that) without understanding Rumi's mystical language and background.

(5) Khorâsânian Sufis are famous for their reference to "intoxication" (*sukr* or *masti*) by drinking from the pure Divine wine (*sharâb*, *mey* or *bâdeh*) as a metaphor for a state of mystical love, selflessness and senselessness, or what Sufis call *fanâ* ("extinction", akin to the Buddhist idea of *nirvâna* which similarly means "extinction" in Sanskrit). We often encounter terms like wine, jug, grape, cup, cup-bearer, tavern, drunkard, etc. in the poetry of Omar Khayyam, Rumi, Hâfez, and many other Sufi poets. Such expressions should not be misinterpreted that these poets were alcoholics. They indicate the absence of ego, a relaxed and ecstatic state of the soul, and the mystic's transcendence to oneness.

The Making of Rumi the Poet

Rumi was connected to the Sufi thought and tradition of Khorâsân through several important teachers in his life. The first was his father, Bahâ Valad, who was a Muslim preacher and teacher. Fortunately, we have a collection of Bahâ Valad's discourses and writings, the *Ma'âref-e Bahâ-Valad*,[6] which clearly show his affinities to mystical doctrines as well as his devotion to God and a pious life. The young Rumi was very fond of reading this book.

In 1219, Bahâ Valad along with his family and disciples left Balkh and journeyed westward. Eventually, they settled in the city of Konya in Anatolia (now Turkey), which was then the capital of the Seljuq Kingdom. Bahâ Valad spent his last years teaching in a religious school donated to him by the king, Sultân Alâ'eddin Kaygubâd.

While growing up in Balkh, Rumi had a tutor, Burhânuddin Mohaggeg Termezi, who was himself a disciple of Bahâ Valad. A year after Rumi's father died in Konya in 1231 (at the age of eighty) and left his school to Rumi, Burhân came to Konya and took on the responsibility of training the young Rumi. Again we are fortunate to have an extant book of Burhân,[7] which shows similar strands of mystical thinking as those of Bahâ Valad. On Burhân's orders, Rumi spent several years at Aleppo and Damascus (in Syria) to study with the great Islamic scholars living there. While in Damascus, Rumi probably also attended the discourses of the renowned Sufi master Ibn Arabi, who taught the doctrine of *wahdat ul-wojud*, "the Oneness of Being," which is also the philosophical basis of Rumi's poetry: The One Divine Reality is the source (the Alpha) and return-point (the Omega) of the All.

Rumi was thus highly educated in both Persian and Arabic literature, as well as Islamic law and theology. We also know that Burhân trained Rumi in Sufi practices, such as forty-day solitary retreats (*chelleh*). In this way, Rumi became a reputed teacher and master in Konya, presiding over his father's school.

On November 29, 1244, Rumi, then aged thirty seven, met the third, and perhaps the most important person in his life – a wandering dervish, probably aged sixty, named Shams ("Sun") of Tabriz (a city in northwest Iran). Shams is a mysterious figure – a blunt and difficult person and often believed to be uneducated. So it puzzles Rumi's fans to think how a person like Shams could have transformed the great scholar Rumi into a passionate poet. What went on between these two? Who was the master and who was the disciple? To answer these questions, we need to consider two facts. First, Shams was not an illiterate, beggar dervish. True, Shams was not as educated as Rumi; but he had studied with scholars and Sufi masters, and the extant book of his discourses, the *Maqâlât-e Shams-e Tabrizi*[8] written down probably by Rumi's son, shows him as an insightful and learned man. Second, Rumi was ready for Shams; he had been prepared by his father and teachers to take on the Sufi path of love, enlightenment, and ecstasy. Shams simply opened the mouth of a fiery volcano – Rumi's soul – and Rumi's literary genius poured out in those beautiful, insightful, and ecstatic poems.

Rumi and Shams: The Mystery of Their Relationship

If Shams and Rumi had not met, we would have never heard of Shams, and Rumi's name would have been merely recorded as a Muslim teacher in some obscure books. Such was the significance of the meeting of these two souls; it immortalized both Rumi and Shams. What went on between these two men is enigmatic: What was the nature of their relationship?

We know that after meeting Shams, Rumi began singing his lyric poems collected in the *Divân-e Shams-e Tabrizi*[9] ("Book of Poetry Dedicated to Shams"), also known as the *Divân-e Kabir* ("The Great Book of Poetry"). This poetry book contains about 3,300 sonnets (*ghazaliyât*) and nearly 1900 quatrains (*rubâiyât*), totaling over 44,000 lines. The book is full of passionate love poems, many of which specifically mention Shams by name. Impressed by such poems, one may be tempted to think that Rumi and Shams had a romantic and sexual relationship. This view would, however, be a misunderstanding of Rumi's poetry, and a misinterpretation of the whole spiritual environment which surrounded Rumi and Shams. In pondering the mystery of Rumi's love poems and the nature of the relationship between Rumi and Shams, several points are noteworthy:

(1) Rumi was not the first or the last Persian Sufi poet to compose love poems, and the history of Persian poetry should give us a context in which to analyze this subject. Although, in some of the poems in the *Divân-e Shams*, Rumi expresses adoration and respect explicitly to Shams, he also has many love poems, in which the love expressions are for God, the Creation, the All,

the Soul, and the Beloved (much as in the poems of Persian mystics before and after Rumi). In many poems, Shams' name appears in the last line because this way of ending the *ghazal* with a name is a common practice in Persian poetry; but, while other poets usually use their pen names, Rumi used Shams' name out of his love and devotion. Rumi also has many *ghazal* poems which he ends with the pen-name, *Khamoosh* ("Silent").

(2) There is a Sufi tradition called *soh'bat* ("conversation"): Two seekers, loving and respecting each other, regularly meet and share their experiences and wisdom; the pair could be a master and a disciple, or even two masters. This practice is believed to strengthen the spiritual wayfarers. Rumi treasures Shams as his *ham-soh'bat* ("conversation friend") because a spiritual friend of that caliber is not easy to come by in one's life. Shams also has many sayings in praise of Rumi. These men were like two mighty rivers that flowed and merged in the ocean of love. They were both masters and disciples of each other.

(3) Rumi loved Shams because he was a window through which Rumi could see the inner truth and beauty of existence. Shams opened Rumi's spiritual eye to a realm in which Rumi found his true home. All of those marvelous poems Rumi composed were a verbal residue of what he actually experienced in his heart and what he saw in the rays of Divine light.

(4) The meeting of Shams and Rumi is a rare event in history. Perhaps, the mystery of their meeting and what went on between these two great souls will always be a mystery unless we meet them on their level, in which case, we may not be able to elaborate but remain silent, or sing and write poetry like Rumi did.

A Bird from the Celestial Garden

Rumi died on a Sunday sunset, December 7, 1273, and since then his tomb has been a shrine for his lovers and spiritual pilgrims. The poet known in the West as Rumi (because he lived in "Rūm," the Byzantine Empire in Anatolia) is respectfully called *Mawlânâ* (or *Mowlânâ* in Iran and *Mevlânâ* in Turkey), "Our Master" in the East.

As a final note, I would like to juxtapose two popular images of Rumi in the West. Some view Rumi simply as a poet of love and praise him for his art, much like Shakespeare and Beethoven (as one of Rumi's modern translators once remarked). There are also those who view Rumi as a faithful Muslim and the originator of a Sufi Order, the Whirling Dervishes, and thus far from the ordinary life and cultural environment of the vast majority of world population. In a sense, both approaches are valid if the end result is a true understanding of Rumi's message of love and universal compassion. Therefore, while there are elements of truth in both of these popular images of Rumi, neither is, I believe, how Rumi would have regarded himself exclusively. The first camp looks at the fruit of Rumi's poetry without paying attention to the tree itself, thus ignoring the fact that Rumi was a deeply religious person, a man of faith, who prayed, fasted, and meditated within the Islamic tradition (some may find this surprising given the often negative image of Islam in today's world). The second camp confines Rumi to a particular sect or creed, and thus puts this vast tree inside a labeled box. The spirit of Rumi's poetry is vast and lofty, but also deeply rooted in the rich religious and mystical traditions of the Middle East as well as Persian literature. Rumi's message of universal love was not an abstract, intellectual concept but one that he experienced with his total being. His religious faith was not a rigid, dogmatic, literalist, sectarian conviction but benevolent, compassionate, and inclusive, and it inspired his poetry. The tree of Rumi's poetry has both roots and fruits. And the more we delve into Rumi's roots the better we can connect to the flight of this "bird from the celestial garden" (as he calls himself) in the expanse of the spiritual sky.

An earlier version, "Garden of Secrets: The Real Rumi," was published in *Quest: Journal of the Theosophical Society of America*," Summer 2010, pp. 106-108 & 120.

[7]
Rumi and the Buddha: Correlative Ideas on Spiritual Awakening

The Buddha was an enlightened teacher of the fifth century BC in northern India; Rumi was a Muslim mystic and a Persian poet of the thirteenth century AD, some eighteen hundred years after the Buddha. How can these two different persons and their widely varying cultures, lands, and centuries be correlated? As we explore this question in this chapter, we will encounter interesting lessons for our own spiritual transformation as well.

In recent years during my visit to bookstores in North America, I have noticed the popularity of books on Buddhism and Rumi. And I am not surprised to see this popularity. Born and raised in Iran (Rumi's cultural land) and having lived for years in India (where Buddhism originated) and Japan (where Zen Buddhism blossomed), I have been a student of both Sufism and Buddhism, and have paid special attention to the similarities and differences of these two spiritual and religious traditions. Here I share some impressions about Rumi and the Buddha. I hope that this comparative study of these two great minds, as incomplete and modest as it is in this chapter, may be of interest to interfaith dialogues, and may particularly be informative to Muslims and Buddhists who may not yet recognize the common ground between Sufi and Buddhist teachings. The emphasis of this chapter is on correlative ideas and practices rather than contrasts between Rumi and the Buddha; more specifically, I will focus on the process and attributes of spiritual enlightenment as these two great mystics viewed it. In a broader perspective, this chapter offers a cross-current of thoughts between the Eastern and Western spiritual traditions because Sufism is rooted in the three Abrahamic religions of Judaism, Christianity and Islam, which have been historically prevalent in southwest Asia and the Western world, while Buddhism is a product of the Oriental thought, specifically of Indian, Chinese, and Japanese cultures.

From Bodh Gaya to Konya

The Buddha[1] and Rumi[2] came from different walks of life. Buddha's clan name was Shakyamuni, "a sage from the Shakya tribe" that ruled a kingdom in the foothills of the Himalayas in Nepal and northern India. Siddhartha Gautama (later to be the Buddha) was a prince who had been provided with every material means and comforts in the palace to ensure that he would grow up and take over his father's throne. However, he chose not to do so. Witnessing that life is perishable by illness, old age, and death (as the famous story goes), Siddhartha left his family and palace at the age of twenty nine in search of the truth and meaning of life.

Rumi, on the other hand, came from a family of Muslim scholars. His father, Bahâ Valad, was known as the *Sultân-e Ulamâ* ("king of the scholars") – an entirely different kind of king, for that matter). Bahâ Valad's father, Hossein ibn Ahmad Khatibi, was one of the most eminent Islamic scholars of his age. Bahâ Valad was from Balkh (in today's Afghanistan) but immigrated to Anatolia with his family when Rumi was barely a teenager. Anatolia was part of the historical Byzantine, Rome or "Rūm" in Arabic and Persian. Rumi's given name was Jalâluddin ("glory of religion") Mohammad, and he was trained from childhood by his father and other teachers in matters of Islamic law and theology. After Bahâ Valad died in the town of Konya in Anatolia (present-day Turkey), Rumi, aged twenty four, took over his father's position and seminary, and after a decade of studies, he became a reputed Islamic teachers and leader in Konya. In 1244, Rumi met a wandering dervish, Shams Tabrizi (Shams from the city of Tabriz in northwest Iran), who radically changed Rumi's life from that of an *Âlem* ("learned scholar") and a preacher to that of an *Âref* ("gnostic," or mystic) and a poet. This happened when Rumi was thirty seven. Incidentally, Siddhartha was also enlightened at a similar age – thirty five – while meditating under the banyan (papal) tree in Gaya (now called Bodh Gaya and located in the Indian state of Bihar).

Rumi died in 1273 – aged sixty six – and his tomb has been for centuries a shrine at Konya. The Buddha lived to the age of eighty, and passed away at

Kushinagara (in the modern Indian state of Uttar Pradesh) in 483 B.C. The places where the Buddha was born (Lumbini, in Nepal), enlightened (Bodh Gaya), first preached (Sarnath, close to the city of Banaras or Varanasi in north India), and ultimately passed away (Kushinagara) are all sites of pilgrimage.

Direct Spiritual Experience

Both Rumi and the Buddha adopted a non-philosophical approach in their teachings. The Buddha called it *Dhamma* in his native tongue of Pali (*Dharma* in Sanskrit), which variously means wheel, truth, teachings, doctrine, duty, and law. Rumi's sayings are collected in several volumes of poetry and discourses. A Sufi term for his works is *Ma'âref* ("gnostic teachings").

The teachings and sayings of the Buddha and Rumi have, of course, philosophical implications in a broad sense, but they did not employ the common philosopher's methodology because such verbal arguments and debates, interesting as they may be, do not themselves lead us to spiritual salvation and happiness. Here, I consider four aspects in Rumi's and the Buddha's "non-philosophical" approach to spiritual truth and learning.

(1) Rumi and the Buddha (like the other great spiritual masters in history) used simple words, parables and poetic expressions, rather than a technical, scholastic or philosophical language. Buddhist scriptures (*sutras*) mostly consist of stories (each starting with "Thus I have heard") or verses (called *gâtha* in Sanskrit). The *Dhammapadha* is probably the best-known Buddhist scripture. Rumi's major works include: (1) *Masnavi-ye Ma'navi* ("spiritual couplets"), six volumes of stories and parables narrated in verse; (2) *Divân-e Shams-e Tabrizi*, comprised of lyrical odes (*ghazaliyât*) and quatrains (*rubâiyât*); and (3) *Fihi Mâ Fih*, his book of public discourses which is also rich in poems and parables.

(2) Although Rumi and the Buddha had learned the philosophical knowledge of their time, they found it futile to construct yet another philosophical system because no such system can ever totally describe truth or life in any given moment. Any systematic, philosophical arrangement of the Buddha's

and Rumi's teachings, respectively in the form of Buddhism and Sufism, were made by their disciples and scholars after their death.

(3) Rumi and the Buddha practiced what they preached, and also offered a practical way for their teachings; they were not professional philosophers or academic professors trying to publish books. Edward Conze remarks that in the West "there is an almost complete gap between the theory of philosophers and their practice, between their views on the nature of the universe, and their mode of life ... His greed, hate and attachment remain practically untouched by his philosophical arguments. He is judged by the consistency of his views, not with his life."[3]

(4) Both Rumi and the Buddha placed particular emphasis on direct spiritual experience. No intellectual knowledge can ever replace meditation, prayer, seeing with the spiritual eye, and feeling from the heart.

There is a famous story told by the Buddha that explains the marked difference between the work of a sage and that of a philosopher. Suppose a man is wounded by a poisoned arrow and a physician wants to help him but the man refuses, demanding that first he should find out the name and clan of the person who shot the arrow, and of what material the arrow was made, and so forth.[4]

Similarly, in the *Masnavi* (III: 1380-1385) Rumi tells the story of two men who were quarreling. A slapped B on the neck; as B was trying to hit him back, A said, "Before you hit me, please answer this question: The sound that my slapping produced, was it from my hand or your neck?" B answered, "I am in too much pain to think about such a question."

Both stories point out that irrelevant, remote metaphysical questions or argumentative thinking are not the real answers to our life problems, whether psychological or physical. The heart, love, or inner knowing has its own logic and applicability. *"By the time our little intellect finishes thinking and sorting out,"* Rumi says, *"love has reached the seventh heaven"* (*Divân*: 2031).

The following Zen maxim shows the importance of first-hand spiritual experience in Buddhist practice:

Transmission [of enlightenment] *outside scriptures;*
Not relying on letters;

Pointing directly to one's mind;
Attainment of Buddhahood by seeing into one's nature.[5]

Indeed, there is a story[6] that suggests that Rumi's enlightenment was of a similar nature. One day, Rumi was sitting with his disciples by a pool and with books around him. Shams, then unknown to Rumi, came along, greeted, and sat down. Then pointing to the books, he asked Rumi: "What are they?" Rumi said, "They are some literature (*gâl*) that you would not understand." Shams threw the books into the pool, and then pulled them out one by one from the water; the books were all dry. Rumi was astonished and asked Shams about it, to which he replied, "And this is an inner state (*hâl*) that you would not understand." This story probably did not happen, at least not in the miraculous manner it has been narrated, but we do know that Rumi's reliance on books was greatly reduced after encountering Shams. Therefore, Rumi says:

The book of the Sufi contains no literal knowledge or words;
It is none other than the heart – white as snow.   Masnavi, II: 159

The Buddha's and Rumi's emphasis on direct spiritual experience does not mean that they negated knowledge, science, philosophy or rational thinking in human life and society. In fact, the Buddha recommended that people should not blindly believe what he or others taught but that they should put the teaching to the test and see its truth and goodness. Even a true teaching, according to the Buddha, is like "a raft for crossing over," and not a dogma to be blindly attached to.[7]

Reason has its own place and applications as well as limitations. As Rumi puts it:

Water filling the boat destroys it.
Water beneath the boat supports it.   Masnavi, I: 985

In other words, science and religion have their own places and values. As humans we need both rational thinking and spiritual feeling. They are not contradictory but complementary. For example, it is one thing to scientifically map and investigate our brain images when we pray, meditate, sleep, play or feel loving and compassionate; it is quite another thing to actually experience them. In the same way, no amount of praying or meditation can replace scientific research to understand the physical and chemical processes in the human body or on Earth.

Know Thyself

Buddhists take refuge in three Jewels: the Buddha, Dharma, and Sangha (Buddhist community). To become a Muslim, one must bear "witness" (*sha'hâda*) to two articles of faith: "There is no god but One God, and Muhammad is God's messenger." However, these vows and maxims are only the beginning of a spiritual path. Individual effort, practice, and attention are always needed along the journey.

It has been recorded that the last words of the Buddha at his death bed were: "Work out your salvation with diligence."[8] In a BBC documentary on religions, *The Long Search*, Ronald Eyre asks a Zen master (Roshi) in Kyoto, "What is the most important thing that a man should do with his life?" The Roshi answers, "Of course, to know himself – not only through ideas but through his total being."[9] In his book of *Discourses*, Rumi quotes a famous saying of Prophet Muhammad that "Whoever knows himself also knows God."[10] Rumi then comments that through knowing your true self you also come to recognize your false masks and selves.

According to Islam (as well as Judaism and Christianity), "God created Adam [humans] in His own image" (a famous saying of Prophet Muhammad) or "I [God] have made him [human] and have breathed into him my spirit" (*Quran*, XV: 29). Of course, God has no image, head or breath. As the Islamic scholar Seyyed Hossein Nasr[11] points out the Divine image and breath refer to the Divine Attributes (*sifât*) or the "ninety-nine beautiful names of God" (*asmâ ul-husnâ*) which are inherent in human nature (*fitrat*) to the degree of human capacity.

To put it in Buddhist terms, "All sentient beings have Buddha-nature (*buddhata*)." After quoting this saying from the *Lotus Sutra*, the Vietnamese Zen master Thich Nhat Hanh adds that "with the right conditions, the seed of Buddha nature in us will grow."[12] Islam's emphasis on God and Buddhism's not-mentioning of the word God may appear that they are teaching entirely different concepts, but actually when we go beyond the words and consider what the Divine attributes and Buddha-nature actually mean, we see similar contents, notably the virtues of knowing (*prâjna* in Buddhism; *ma'rifat* in Sufism) and mercy (*karuna* in Buddhism; *rahmat* in Sufism).

From Greed to Suffering

In his first sermon at Deer Park at Sarnath, the Buddha taught the Four Noble Truths: (1) Life is full of suffering and dissatisfaction (*dukkah*); (2) desire (*trishna* in Sanskrit and *tanhâ* in Pali) is the cause of human suffering; (3) suffering can be ceased; and (4) a spiritual path with righteousness, mindfulness and non-attachment leads to salvation and liberation (*muksha*) from suffering.

The Sanskrit word *trishna* (akin to the Persian word *tishna*) literally means "thirst" and implies craving, attachment, and selfish desires. Interestingly, in the opening poem of the *Masnavi*, Rumi has a verse that associates thirst with greed, and greed with our enslavement; he also suggests that contentment and non-attachment are the keys to liberation:

Break off your chains, Man! Be free.
How long will you remain the slave of gold and silver?
Even if you pour the whole sea into a pitcher,
how much water can the pitcher contain?
No more than today's portion.
But the pitcher of the greedy eye cannot be filled.
Lo! The oyster-shell cannot be filled with a jewel
unless it becomes content and closed. *Masnavi*, I: 19-21

Fanâ and Nirvâna

Rumi uses the words *fanâ* ("annihilation") and *fâni* ("subject to annihilation") in two distinct meanings, both of which have Buddhist equivalents.

(1) In numerous poems Rumi describes this world (and all material things in it) as "the perishable world" (*donyây-e fâni*). This Sufi concept is rooted in the Quranic teachings: "Everything perishes except the Face of God" (XXVIII:

88). This notion reminds us of the Buddhist idea of "impermanence" (Sanskrit: *anitya*, Pali: *anicca*): "All conditioned things are impermanent."[13] We all observe the fact of change, decay and death in nature as well as human life, in both animate and inanimate beings. But we often forget this fact and thus live in an illusory world as if things and affairs have a concrete, permanent existence.

If no part or particle of the world has an independent existence, and if everything changes and nothing lasts forever, how does the world continue to exist as the world? In answer to this question, Rumi teaches the notion of "continuous creation." Rumi says that God re-creates the world each and every moment:

The world is like a stream
that appears to be enclosed, but
its water ever flows and comes afresh.
Where does it come from?   *Divân:* 4908

The image of the world as a stream emphasizes the ever-changing nature and flow of the world in time, or as the Greek philosopher Heraclitus put it, "You cannot step into the same river twice." It also refers to the coming into existence of the world every moment from the Realm of the Unseen (*gheyb*). In other words, the existence of this perishable world is contingent on a Great Mystery – whatever we may call it.

(2) Rumi says that the Sufi spiritual path leads to *fanâ* – the annihilation of small ego (*nafs*) and the human mind's dissolution in the Divine attributes:

You are your own shadow!
Become annihilated in the rays of the Sun.
How long will you look at your shadow?
Look instead at the Divine light.   *Divân:* 20395

The Buddha's path ultimately leads to *nirvâna* – a Sanskrit word which means "extinguishing" as when "the wind blows out the fire." (The Pali pronunciation is *nibbbâna*.) *Nirvâna* refers to the extinction of egoistic greed and ignorance which, in turn, brings about tremendous happiness (*sukha*) in life. Here again, we see a parallel concept between Buddhism and Sufism:

From ego (*nafs*) to *fanâ*; from suffering (*dukkah*) to *nirvâna* and happiness (*sukha*). Sufis also emphasize that after *fanâ*, the enlightened person enters *baqâ* ("staying with the Divine"). Rumi says:

I do not remember that wine and how it annihilated me.
In this nowhere-land, I do not know where I am.
Sometimes, I dive into the abyss of a sea.
Other times, I rise to the sky like the sun.   *Divân:* 16055-56

To understand what the mysterious sea and sun mean, let's refer to Rumi's own poems: "*Love cannot be contained in talking and listening; love is a sea whose abyss is invisible*" (*Masnavi*, V: 2728). And "*Divine love is the Sun of perfection; sunlight radiates at the Divine command while creatures appear like shadows*" (*Masnavi*, VI: 983). Therefore, love is "*sometimes manifest as all-pervading sunlight or a bottomless ocean*" (*Masnavi*, VI: 1413). *Fanâ* or *nirvâna* is the transcendence from conflicts and illusions, and melting into this eternal presence through love. Otherwise, we live as dark shadowy forms.

Given the close similarities between *fanâ* and *nirvâna* and the fact that the Buddhist concept is historically older, one may suspect that the Sufi concept of *fanâ* was an influence from Buddhism or Indian thought. This is possible because the eastern part of the ancient Persian Empire, which was a significant birthplace of Sufism, was also a region where Buddhism flourished long before Islam. Even after Persia was invaded by the Arabs in the seventh century and became part of the Islamic world, Muslim thinkers of the eastern Persian region were in contact with India for centuries. Reynold Nicholson (1868-1945), the renowned scholar at Cambridge, once commented that "the Sufi conception of the passing-away (*fanâ*) of individual self in Universal Being is certainly, I think, of Indian origin. Its first great exponent was the Persian mystic, Bâyazid of Bistâm [d. 875], who may have received it from his teacher, Abu Ali of Sind."[14]

While one cannot deny the influence of Indian (as well as Persian, Greek and Christian) thought on the development of Sufism, *fanâ* is not alien to Islamic thought. The *Quran* says that "everything perishes except the Face of God" and there is also a famous saying of Muhammad that "God created human being (Adam) in His own image (attributes)."[11] Meditation on these teachings easily leads to the notions of *fanâ* and *baqâ*. Indeed, this pattern of thinking is readable from the following Rumi poem:

"All things perish except God's Face."   (*Quran*, XXVIII:88)
Do not seek existence in anything except God's Face.
Whoever is annihilated at the sight of God's Face,
"Everything perishes" shall not be his punishment.   *Masnavi*, I: 3052-53

Selfless and No-Self

The Buddha's path from the "impermanent world" to *nirvâna* involves the realization of "no-self" (Sanskrit: *anatman*; Pali: *anatta*). All schools of Buddhism believe in the "Four Dharma Seals" or principles: (1) All composite (conditioned) things are impermanent; (2) all contaminated things are in a state of suffering; (3) all phenomena are empty and self-less; and (4) *nirvâna* is the true peace.[15]

The Buddhist idea of "no-self" means that if we contemplate deeply on the nature of things including what we perceive as our "self" or "I," we note that everything is composed of and dependent on other things, and all things are ever changing; in other words, nothing has a fixed, discrete, independent existence. The Buddha suggested that the human self is an assembly and interplay of five aggregates (*skandha*) – the body, feelings, perceptions, mental formations, and consciousness – none of which has absolute or fixed existence; therefore, we should not be attached to any of them. The Buddha's principle of "no-self" has been debated among Buddhists and Hindus (who believe in the Great Soul, *Brahma*, and Individual Soul, *Âtmân*). I think one reason the Buddha taught the notion of "no-self" was to strike at the very root of desire – even the ego that desires to be spiritual and God-like.

Rumi also talks of "selflessness" (*bi'khoodi* or *bi'khishi* in Persian), but in a somewhat different light. When we melt to Divine presence by drinking from the wine of love, we become intoxicated and lose our selfish senses of "I", life, and the world. And this opens the door of *fanâ*. In Rumi's vocabulary, a "selfless" person is a true "lover" of God:

If you are not drunk,
you lag behind all pilgrims.
When you are selfless,
there is only one step between you and your Mecca.   *Divân*: 9060

In the *Masnavi* (I: 3056), Rumi tells the story of a man who loved a lady and went to see her. He knocked on her door, and she asked, "Who is it?" He answered, "It's me." She said, "Go away! There is no place for you here." The man left the house, wandered and meditated for a whole year. He then returned to his beloved's house. She asked, "Who is it knocking on the door?" This time he answered, "It is *you*." And the door opened.

Rumi also describes the process of selflessness as "dying before the physical death":

Die! Die! Die in this love.
When you die in this love,
you attain the vast spirit.
Die! And don't fear this death!
When you sprout out from this soil,
you attain the high heaven. *Divân:* 6628-29

A seventeenth-century Japanese Zen master, Shido Bunan, has composed a Japanese *waka* poem with a similar message:

Die while alive, and be completely dead.
Then do whatever you will, all is good.[16]

The practice of "no-self" leads us to the "real self;" and the realization of "senselessness" (*bi-hooshi*) awakens us to the "real sense" (*hoosh*) or pure consciousness: "*Only the person who is senseless has the real sense to understand my words*" (*Masnavi*, I: 14).

Transcendence and Unity

A profound quality of the mind that both Rumi and the Buddha associate with *fanâ* or *nirvâna* is the transcendence from duality to unity, although the symbolism that Buddhism and Sufism have developed to express this transcendence differs from each other.

In the last book of the *Masnavi*, Rumi says that the world functions by the interactions of the "opposites" (*azdâd*) or the "wars of opposite particles": Cold and hot, light and dark; up and down; male and female, and so forth. He then points out that from the Divine perspective there are no opposites; it is all unity. When an enlightened person – a lover of God – dissolves into the Divine presence as "a particle melts into the Sun," he or she goes beyond the world of duality (but without denying the opposites, which is the foundation of the physical world):

Since you are my eyes and tongue,
I don't see two; I don't hear two;
I don't chase duality.   *Divân:* 16866

In the history of Islamic thought, Rumi and his contemporary Sufi master Ibn Arabi (1165-1240) are the main proponents of the notion of the "Unity of Being" (*wah'dat ul-wojud*), suggesting that (1) the whole world is a single entity and (2) the world does not have its own independent existence but exists as a "shadow" of God's being. Therefore, only God's being is real; there is only one real being. This should not be mistaken as pantheism ("God is all this, and all this is God") because God is not limited to this world.

There is a commonly-recited Islamic phrase: *Allah-o Akbar.* This is often translated as "God is great." But it actually means that God is greater than whatever we perceive: God is the greatest of all. (This is precisely the God of Abraham, Moses, Jesus, and Muhammad). Rumi, following the teachings of the *Quran,* views the whole of creation is full of Divine "signs" (*âyât*): "Wherever you turn you face, there is the face of God" (*Quran,* II: 115) and "God is nearer to human than his or her jugular vein" (*Quran,* L: 16). God is immanent in his creation but is not limited to it. God is also transcendent – greater than and beyond His creation and whatever we can perceive of Him. Rumi's idea of the "Unity of Being" refers to God's immanence and transcendence together.

In the following poem attributed to Rumi, we see a profound expression of the realization of the Unity of Being, and what it means to live in a state of non-dualistic mind:

What is to be done, O Muslims, for I can't identify myself?
I'm neither Christian nor Jewish;
          neither Zoroastrian nor Muslim.
I'm neither Eastern nor Western;

> *neither of the land nor of the sea.*
> *I'm not from the mines of Earth, nor from the circling heavens.*
> *My place is placeless, my trace is traceless.*
> *This is neither body nor soul,*
> > *for I belong to the soul of the Beloved.*
> *I have put away duality;*
> *I have seen the two worlds as one.*
> *I seek one, I know one, I see one, I read one.*
> *God is the first and God is the last.*
> *God is the inner and God is the outer.*[17]

To Rumi, the realization of the Unity of Being involves transcending the ego and its dualistic judgments, and seeing the Divine in the entirety of creation, and melting into this Divine presence. This realization is the ultimate meaning of *Islam* (which literally means being in "peace" with and "submission" to God) as well as the true faith in *tawhid* ("Divine unity"), which is the fundamental tenet of Islam: There is no god but One God (*lâ ilâha ill'Allâh*). Indeed, the last verse (God is the first, God is the last; God is the inner, God is the outer) in the above-mentioned poem is a direct quote from the *Quran* (LVII: 3).

The renowned Zen teacher Daisetz Suzuki writes: "When an intuitive or experimental understanding of Reality is verbally formulated as All is One and One is All, we have there the fundamental statement as it is taught by all the various schools of Buddhism."[18] Suzuki then adds that in the Mahayana School of Buddhism, transcendence and non-duality is described as "emptiness" (Sanskrit: *shunyâta*) and "suchness" (*tathatâ*). The practitioner comes to the realization that nothing has a fixed or independent existence, everything is interdependent and in flux. I am not me but the whole world, and reality is as it is – beyond our judgement, conceptualization or verbalization. The tradition of sitting-meditation (Japanese: *zazen*) in Buddhism is meant to guide the practitioner from egoistic attachments and thoughts to the realization of non-duality, emptiness, awakening, liberation, and peace. "Our life is shaped by our mind. We become what we think." This is the opening verse of the *Dhammapada*. "He [the practitioner] has reached the end of the way; he has crossed the river of life. All that he had to do is done: he has become one with all of life." This is the last verse in the *Dhammapada*.[19]

Ecstasy and Tranquility

Spiritual enlightenment is called *eshrâg* in Arabic and Persian, *sambodhi* in Sanskrit and Pali, *wu* in Chinese, and *satori* in Japanese. These parallel words and concepts indicate the common roots of spiritual experience in human beings regardless of their countries or centuries. This spiritual commonality is well illustrated in the personalities, words, and works of both the Buddha and Rumi, who were separated from each other by eighteen hundred years and by different languages, cultures, and lands. Of course, one can sense cultural, metaphysical and religious differences between the spiritual paths of the Buddha and Rumi, but the fountainhead of their experiences and the fruits of their teachings were and are similar.

Rumi's thinking was rooted in the Judaic-Christian-Islamic heritage of the Middle East, and thus his expressions and explanations are theistic. Rumi believes in One Absolute God who is the source of creation, power, knowledge, beauty, and love. Rumi's vision is fine-tuned to this Quranic verse: "We are from God and unto God we return" (II: 156). The Buddha, on the other hand, left out the metaphysical notions like God from his teachings altogether. Nonetheless, when we consider the ethical, spiritual, and psychological implications of Rumi's metaphysics and enlightenment, we see strikingly similar processes and results to those of the Buddha's teachings.

Rumi was a faithful Muslim who observed daily prayers, kept fasting in the month of Ramadan, and practiced Sufi meditation. Yet, Rumi was not a dry, dogmatic religious person; he was also a passionate poet engaged in *samâ* (music and dance). Therefore, his language is poetic, romantic, and oftentimes ecstatic. Indeed, Rumi's visualization of the path of love in ecstatic words and images is rarely seen in the works of other mystics and sages. Although love and compassion are at the core of Buddhist practice too, the Buddha does not speak in a language of ecstatic love. Instead, his path of liberation and compassion is primarily through silent meditation, and his language is that of tranquility and calmness. Of course, tranquility and ecstasy are inter-related. Tranquility leads to ecstasy, and ecstasy leads to tranquility. They are two sides of the same coin and two valleys of the same mountain; call it selflessness or transcendence. In regard to "intoxication by the wine of love," Rumi says:

This intoxication
> *is not such that you may wish to be sober and serious later.*
This intoxication
> *awakens your heart and intellect altogether.*

Divân: 12029

One final note. It is interesting that both the Buddha and Rumi are known to the public more by their titles than their given names. The Buddha ("an awakened one") is a general title, but has become the specific name for Shakyamuni Siddhartha Gautama. In the East, Rumi is usually called Mawlânâ (Mowlânâ in Persian and Mevlânâ in Turkish) which means "Our Master." Again, this Arabic word is a general title for any eminent sage or teacher, but has become a proper noun for Jalâluddin Mohammad Balkhi Rumi.

An earlier version of this chapter was published in *Interreligious Insight*, July 2007, pp. 28-38.

[8]
Sufi and Buddhist Teachings:
Views from Rumi's Poetry and Life

In this earth,
in this soil,
in this pure field,
let us not plant any seeds
other than the seeds of compassion and love.   Divân: 1475

This simple poem and this sincere invitation from Rumi captures the essence of both Sufi and Buddhist ethics. Farmers would better appreciate this poem because they know from experience that "we reap what we sow." Moreover, farmers know that in order to grow healthy grains, fruits, vegetables, and flowers we need to plant the right seeds, water the soil properly, take care of the farm, and work diligently.

In his book, *Understanding the Mind*, the Vietnamese Zen teacher Thich Nhat Hanh writes that "our human mind is a field in which every kind of seed (*bija*) is sown – seeds of compassion, joy, and hope, seeds of sorrow, fear, and difficulties."[1] Both Rumi and Thich Nhat Hanh tell us that each person is a farmer of his or her own life, and the world is a vast farmland. A happy or a miserable life, a peaceful or violent world is the result of what we, individually and collectively, plant and grow. This is indeed a poetic expression of the principle of *karma* in Indian religions. The Sanskrit word *karma* and the Persian word *kâr* have the same root, and both mean "action or work". (This should not be surprising because both Sanskrit and Persian belong to the Indo-European family of languages.) Let us not do any work other than the work done with love. Let us not plant any seeds other than the seeds of love.

* * *

Science and spiritualty have fascinated me since a young age. While growing up in my home country, Iran, I was drawn to Persian Sufi poetry. After leaving Iran, I lived in India and Japan for over a decade, and thus also learned about Indian and Buddhist philosophy and spiritual traditions. Sufism (*tasawwuf*) is usually regarded as the mystical and esoteric dimension of Islam. In other words, Sufism is an Islamic spiritual way (*tarigat*) towards the truth (*hagigat*) of life, spiritual enlightenment (*eshrâg*), and esoteric "knowing" (*ma'rifat* or *erfân*, an Arabic-Persian translation of the Greek word "gnosis"). Literature about the spiritual journey and "gnosis" is found in many cultures and in different languages.

Comparative studies of spiritual literature and religions help nations better understand one another and find a common ground of humanity in our divided, violent world. The Dalai Lama often says that all humans, from whatever country or religion, want to be happy. This is so true. We all want a happy life and to live in a happy and peaceful community – in the family, at work, and in our city and country. Ignorance, violence, and suffering go hand in hand. The cross-cultural sharing and understanding of spiritual literature inspires us to create a better, happier life, and a more peaceful, prosperous world for ourselves and for the generations to come. In this regard, Rumi's poetry is a treasury of pearls to be shared. Here, I share some notes on my readings of Rumi's poetry in order to shed light on certain parallels between Sufi and Buddhist teachings. (Of course, these ideas and teachings are also common to other great religions of the world which are not featured here.)

* * *

Rumi was not a poet by profession; rather like the Buddha, he was an enlightened master, mystic, and spiritual teacher. Nevertheless, Rumi was a prolific poet. His two great works, *Divân-e Shams-e Tabrizi* ("Poetry Book of Shams Tabrizi" dedicated to his spiritual teacher Shams Tabrizi) and *Masnavi-ye Ma'navi* ("Rhyming Couplets on Spiritual Matters"), together contain about 70,000 verses (couplets). What is more remarkable is that the vast corpus of his literature has grown in its popularity far and wide through the ages because Rumi created beautiful poetry and a spiritual school around the core principle of love (*eshg*) and its various facets: *mehr* (compassion), *muhabbat* (loving-kindness), *doosti* (friendship), *yâri* (help), *ferâg* (separation), *showg* (longing), and *vesâl* (union). These qualities are also found in Buddhist teachings and principles, notably *karunâ* ("compassion" in Sanskrit) and *mettâ* ("loving-kindness" in Pali).

Every chapter in the *Quran* begins with the phrase "In the Name of God, the Most Merciful (*Al-rahmân*), the Most Compassionate (*Al-rahim*)" because love is the very heart of religiosity. Indeed, the success of any religion in accomplishing its mission for humanity can be measured by how far it has spread and nurtured the seeds of love and compassion, which are the Divine attributes and the foundation of faith in God.

In his interview with His Holiness the Dalai Lama for the 1996 TV series *Search for God in America*, journalist Hugh Hewitt asked whether the Dalai Lama as a Buddhist monk believed in God. The Dalai Lama answered, "In the sense that God is love, yes." This is a profound statement for building a common ground of understanding between Christianity, Islam, Buddhism, and other great religions of the world.

Rumi (like other Sufi masters) believes that human love (a loving feeling toward humans and other beings) is a reflection of Divine love. The source of all true love is one – which is God. Rumi calls it *eshg-e hagigi*, "true source of love." God's love is the foundation and fabric of the entire creation, and its rays (*eshg-e majâzi*, "derivative love") shine everywhere. Sufis have a beautiful parable to illustrate this point: Sunshine is too strong for us to look at the Sun directly, but we can comfortably see the Sun as reflected on a lake. True love intoxicates and illuminates the lover. True love is unselfish, non-possessive, and non-arrogant. All of our true feelings of love toward people (spouses, parents, children, family and friends, etc.) as well as toward nature, beauty, knowledge, goodness, and so forth lead us to the Divine. Rumi says:

Love-madness is different from all other kinds of illness.
Love is the astrolabe of the Divine mysteries.
A lover may be drawn this way or that way.
But, in the end, all devoted lovers are drawn to the King of Love.

Masnavi, I: 110-111

Love, being of Divine nature, has no beginning or end; it is eternal and thus accessible every moment:

Love comes from the beginningless time.
Love will remain for eternity.
And countless are the seekers of love.   Divân: 754

* * *

Both Sufism and Buddhism insist on direct spiritual experience rather than accumulating verbal knowledge or engaging in abstract arguments. "The Buddha," writes the Sri Lankan Buddhist scholar Walopa Rahula, "was not interested in discussing unnecessary metaphysical questions which are purely speculative and which create imaginary problems."[2] Rumi says, *"The legs of argumentative logicians are made of wood"* (*Masnavi*, I: 2128). They talk and play with words, but they do not walk or do real work. One must walk on the path in order to experience and know its truth. A scholastic knowledge of scriptures, important as it may be for research and teaching, is no replacement for practice. "Those who recite many scriptures but fail to practice," warns the *Dhammapada*, "are like a cowherd counting another's cows."[3] In the same vein, Rumi says:

The book of the Sufi contains no letters or words;
It is none other than the heart – white as snow.   *Masnavi*, II: 159

* * *

While living in Japan, I was fascinated by the observation that Zen is associated not only with temples and monastic life but also with various forms of art. These Zen arts, as Daistez Suzuki detailed in his 1959 book *Zen and Japanese Culture*, have, in fact, become an integral part of Japanese culture and society: Poetry (in various styles of *haiku*, *waka* and *tanka*), calligraphy (*shodo*), painting (especially brush painting or *sumiye*), traditional theater shows and dances (*noh* and *kabuki*), green-tea ceremony (*sâdo* or *cha-no-yu*), flower arrangement (*ikebânâ*), indoor pot gardening (*bonsâi*), rock gardens (*sekitei*), architecture, landscape design, and even martial arts and the ethos of the *samurai* class.

    Similar spiritual arts have also been developed in the Sufi tradition, and have been visible features of Persian culture for centuries: Gardens, architecture, painting, poetry, calligraphy, music, and even manners of daily greetings and conversation in Iran have been influenced by Sufi ideals and artistic expressions. In Sufi lodges (*khânigah*), where practitioners conduct meditation (*morâgibah*) and chanting (*zikr*), serving and drinking tea (*chai*, black tea) is a spiritual practice in itself.

* * *

Most people know of Rumi as the founder of the Mevlevi Order – the Whirling Dervishes who dance their way in ecstasy toward the Divine. The word "darvish" (as my Webster dictionary says) first appeared in the English language in the 1580s. But what does it really mean? Darvish is a Persian word which literally means a poor, needy person standing at the door (*dar*). Another related Sufi term is *faqir*, also meaning "poor, needy or beggar;" this word entered English as *fakir* in the early 1600s. "Poor one or beggar" is also exactly the meaning of *bhikkhu* (Buddhist monk) in Pali – the language the Buddha spoke. A dervish (fakir) and a bhikkhu are both wayfarers on the path of spiritual poverty. He may even carry a begging bowl, but his humble begging is out of compassion: He wants to kindle kindness in the hearts of people.

Society, and particularly the individualistic modern society, praises the visible and the material, and thus idealizes money, fame, and power. But when Jesus Christ says, "Blessed are the poor in spirit" (*The Gospel of Matthew*, 5:3), he refers to the genuine spiritual tradition epitomized by Christian mystics, Sufi dervishes, and Buddhist bhikkhus. That we are "poor" is not really a mystery; it is a fact of life: We all are born poor and we all die poor; our life is full of needs and dependent on everything else; we do not own even our own bodies. Sages are conscious of this reality; most of us are forgetful of it. Sages have realized spiritual poverty, live by it, and thus reap its blessings. Of course, we all need money, food, clothing, shelter, family, and material as well as emotional support in life; in fact, we should work diligently to get these necessities of life. Life is sacred; work is noble. But the real wealth is not the materials we collect out of greed, envy, attachment, selfishness, and meanness to other humans or toward nature. The real wealth is what we gain and share, what we learn and teach, and what we contribute and leave behind after we depart from this life. Spiritual poverty means living consciously and knowing that we really do not own anything in this world; in this way we can truly enjoy every moment of life as a gift.

* * *

Muslims worship God (*Allah*) five times a day. Rumi was a pious, faithful Muslim and observed daily worships as well as fasting during the month of Ramadan. As a Sufi, he also practiced meditation (*morâgibah*), contemplation (*fikr*), chanting (*zikr*), and prayer (*wird*). Most people identify meditation practices as a unique feature of the Hindu or Buddhist religions. In reality, meditation and contemplation in various forms are found in the esoteric traditions of other religions as well.

One form of meditation that Sufis often practice is called *zikr* (Persian pronunciation of the Arabic term *dhikr*). It involves the chanting of some sacred word or phrase, often from the ninety-nine names of God. *Zikr* may be conducted in a group or individually; the sacred word may be said verbally or silently in the heart, and oftentimes using a rosary (*tasbeeh*). Literally, *zikr* means "remembrance." Sufis believe that humans are often "forgetful" of God and His graces and gifts; humans are also often unconscious of their own deeds and thoughts. There are, indeed, many distractions in life that make us so unconscious and forgetful. The practice of *zikr* brings us back to our heart, to here-and-now, and to our communion with God; *zikr* keeps us mindful of our life in every situation.

According to the *Quran*, "The hearts receive assurance [trust and comfort] from the remembrance, *zikr*, of God" (XIII: 28). "*Zikr*," Rumi says," *is the rope of union with the beloved*" (*Divân*: 1466). And somewhere else, he says, "*Practice the remembrance of God (zikr-e haqq) until you forget your ego*" (*Divân*: 35585).

Zikr is comparable to the principle and practice of mindfulness in Buddhism: "Mindfulness" (Sanskrit: *smiriti*; Pali: *sati*) is the seventh stage in the Buddha's "Noble Eight-fold Path" that liberates humans from suffering and leads them toward *nirvâna*. Some Buddhist teachers, such as Thich Nhat Hanh, highlight "mindfulness" as the core teaching and practice of the Buddhist path.[4]

* * *

The Sufi path leads to *fanâ*; the Buddhist path leads to *nirvâna*. Both of these terms literally mean "cessation or extinguishing" of egoistic clinging and self-centered desires. In other words, *nirvâna* also means cessation of suffering and ignorance. Sufis believe that after *fanâ*, the seeker enters the stage of *baqâ*

— consciously being with the Divine, much like a ray of light realizing that it is not separate from the sun; it is sunshine itself.

Rumi says:

Other than being a captive or a captor,
there is a third state:
When I am in that state of fanâ,
I lament for both the captive and the captor.   Divân: 18309

Or:

Enter the garden of non-existence (fanâ), and
you will see a paradise existing (bagâ) within your soul.   Divân: 40471

Nirvâna or *fanâ* stands for the liberation, freedom or salvation of the human soul from worldly delusions, attachments, and sufferings. Or as Rumi symbolically expresses in his poems and parables, spiritual enlightenment is like the parrot (*tooti*) breaking out of its cage and flying to the expanse of the sky, or it is like the elephant (*pil* or *fil*) breaking its chains and returning to its homeland in India. This liberation of the soul from the mundane cage is called *moksha* or *mukti* in Sanskrit (*mutti* in Pali). The Islamic call for prayer, which can be heard five times a day from the minarets of major mosques in Muslim cities, includes a line which says, "Come to salvation and success (*falâh*)." Buddhism, Sufism, and other religious traditions have developed practices and pathways so that we live as human beings in the natural habitat of our heart and spirit. That is a successful and accomplished life, but it requires salvation and liberation from the small ego.

* * *

Let's close this chapter with a short prayer from the *Masnavi* (II: 2443-49):

Lord, give us Your hand,
and save us from what our hands may do to us.
Lift the veil before our eyes,
but do not tear the curtain that protects our life.
Save us from this mean ego of ours;

its knife has reached our bones.
Let us turn from ourselves to You,
who are nearer to us than ourselves.
Lord, even this prayer is Your gift and teaching to us.
How else could a rose garden grow from the ashes of our fire.

This chapter is revised and expanded from "Sufi Reflections on Buddhist Thought: Views from Rumi's Poetry," published in *Sufi* [London], Issue 74, Winter 2007, pp. 28-33.

[9]
Jesus Christ in Rumi's Poetry and Parables

Christians and Muslims have much in common. Both Christianity and Islam originated in the Middle East and trace their ancestry through Judaism all the way back to Abraham. Moreover, Jesus Christ is a holy figure in Islam. This is rarely known to the Western public and is often overlooked by the mass media. It is thus saddening to see that some extremist and violent events of the recent years and the mass media's thirst for conflicts and polarization have portrayed an image of anti-Christian Islamic world against the Christian Western world. Such a division does not really exist in the teachings of either Christianity or Islam. Perhaps a very useful portal of entry to understand the sacred position of Jesus Christ in Islam is Mawlânâ Jalâluddin Rumi, the renowned Persian and Sufi poet of the thirteenth century and currently one of the most popular poets in North America. As a person born and raised in Iran (Rumi's cultural land) I have been fascinated with Rumi's poetry for over three decades, and am privileged here to present some facets of Jesus Christ in Rumi's *Masnavi-ye Ma'navi* ("Spiritual Couplets").

* * *

Isâ Masih, in Arabic (also in Persian, Turkish, and Urdu), literally means "Jesus the Messiah." Muslims believe in the "virgin birth" of Jesus Christ. According to the *Quran* (XV: 29; XXXVIII: 72), God (*Allah*) breathed His Spirit into Adam when He created humanity. Sufis extend this quality to the birth of Jesus through Mary (*Mariyam* in Arabic, which is also the title of Chapter 19 in the *Quran*) because they believe that Jesus was born without an earthly father. This is consistent with the Islamic epithet of Jesus as the Divine Spirit (*Ruh ul'lâh*) among the prophets (in a similar vein, Abraham is called *Khalil ul'lâh*, the Loyal Friend of God, and Moses *Kalim ul'lâh*, the Interlocutor and Conversant with God). The Holy Spirit as a medium between the Divine and the world of creation is called *Ruh ul-guds* in the *Quran*. Sufis particularly praise the purity and piety of Mary, and emphasize that the same Holy Spirit does wonders with any human who is devoted to the Divine.

In a long poem in the *Masnavi* (Book III: 3700-3789) Rumi recounts the virgin birth of Jesus. He refers to the story in the *Quran* (XIX: 17-18) that in order to give birth to Jesus, the Holy Spirit was sent by God and appeared to Mary as a very good-looking man, but even then Mary said, "I seek refuge in God." Rumi then continues:

The Holy Spirit said to Mary:
Oh, the exemplar of charity! Do not fear me!
I am the trusty one sent by the Lord.
Don't hide yourself from me;
I am the champion of dignity and honor!
Do not hide yourself from me;
I am the best confidant.
As the Holy Spirit uttered these words,
the rays of pure light sprang from his lips
and shone upon the stars of the sky.
The Holy Spirit continued:
Oh Mary, how can you flee from my presence into the invisible?
I am the king of the unseen world.
The very foundation and residence of my being is the unseen world.
What is present before you is only an image of me.
Oh Mary! Look at me. I am an image hard to come by;
I am the new moon you see up in the sky;
I am the fantasy and vision of your heart.
When such an image as this one settles in your heart,
wherever you go, it is within you.
This is not a delusion or a false dawn
that appears and then disappears before the daylight.
I am the genuine morning light radiated from the Lord.
The darkness of night never gathers around my daylight.

These are poetic words of an eminent, faithful Muslim thinker about the Divine qualities that gave birth to Jesus through the Holy Spirit. Jesus, for Rumi, was "a genuine light at dawn" for the whole of humanity – the light that never goes dark.

* * *

Jesus was a famous healer in his community, and his miracles of healing are credited both in the *Gospels* and in the *Quran*. In the *Masnavi* (III: 298-363), Rumi talks about this aspect of Jesus Christ:

The house of Jesus was the banquet of the "people of the heart."
Oh, the suffering one! Do not quit his door.
From all sides, people used to gather around his house:
Some were blind, some lame, and some insane.
Each morning they went to his door
so that their defects could be healed by Jesus' Breath.
Jesus, that man of the noble path, would say his prayers,
and then would come out to greet the sick and weak people
who, in groups, were sitting and waiting at his door of hope.
Jesus would say: "Oh, the stricken ones!
God has granted your needs and cures.
Go and walk, with no pain and trouble,
toward the blessings and mercy of God."
Like the camel whose chains were lifted from their feet,
the people would then walk freely and joyfully to their houses.
They were all cured by the prayers of Jesus.
And now, you, my friend!
Have you examined your own defects?
Have you found a healthy state of being
in the presence of the masters of the noble path?
Has your lame walking on the spiritual path been cured?
Has your soul been made free from the sufferings and sorrows of this world?

Rumi points out that the sick were cured by Jesus Christ because they were "people of the heart" (*ahl-e del* in Persian), sitting lovingly and faithfully at Jesus' "door of hope", and thus Jesus' presence and prayers were instrumental. Rumi narrates these miracles of Jesus symbolically to suggest that humans suffer because they have developed the illnesses of greed, envy, fear and hatred and that they are chained to their world of illusions. However, when they examine these defects and illusions, they walk on the noble path of the heart and of hope, faith, healing, salvation, joy, and homecoming. All of these are contained in the healing Breath of Jesus.

In Sufi literature, especially in Persian poetry, there are frequent references to the Breath of Jesus (*Dam-e Isâ*) or Messiah's Breath (*Masihâ Nafas*) as possessing a healing power. In the *Masnavi* (I: 528), Rumi says that *"a hundred thousand medical feats of Galen would not be a match to a single Breath of Jesus."* Again, in the same book (I: 794), Rumi, using a beautiful imagery, says:

In the fire of the Divine love, behold,
I saw a whole universe, wherein
each particle possessed a Breath of Jesus.

Despite these words of praise and adorations for Jesus, one cannot deny that Islam's (and Rumi's) perspective Jesus Christ is somewhat different from that of traditional Christian theology. Islam considers Jesus not as God but a human being created by God and one who was blessed by the Divine spirit and was sent to the whole of humanity as a messenger of God to teach truth, goodness, and love. Islam does not subscribe to the Christian theology of the Trinity or Jesus as God or the only begotten Son of God. The *Quran* (V: 116) states that Jesus never said that people should consider him as a being equal to God. Elsewhere, the *Quran* (XIX: 30) quotes Jesus as saying that "I am a devotee and worshipper of God." In a similar vein, the *Gospel of John* quotes Jesus, "By myself I can do nothing; I judge as I hear, and my judgment is just, for I seek not to please myself but Him who sent me" (V:30); "Whoever believes in me does not believe in me, but in the one who sent me" (XII:44); "For I did not speak on my own, but the Father who sent me commanded me to say all that I have spoken" (XII:49).[1]

In his poems, Rumi narrates the sayings and stories of Jesus because he wants the readers to be inspired by Jesus' message and presence. For example, in his references to Jesus and his donkey (which Jesus rode as he entered Jerusalem), Rumi likens the Divine spirit within all humans to Jesus himself and our material desires to the donkey, thus saying that we should not place the heavy burden of this world upon our soul; the donkey should not ride us (*Masnavi*, II: 1850-1861). Or in a reference to Jesus' walking on water (which is again adopted from the *Gospels*), Rumi likens our walking on the dry land as the outward (exoteric) path of life, and Jesus' walking on water as the inner (esoteric) journey of humans toward God (*Masnavi*, I: 570-572).

* * *

Rumi's praise of Jesus is also partly related to the similar temperaments between these two great teachers. It is said of Jesus' disciples that they were simple men – fishermen, tax collectors, and so on. Interestingly, many of Rumi's disciples were also ordinary people. Once, the Prime Minister of Konya remarked that Rumi was a learned and pious man, but his disciples were too ordinary: "Wherever there is a tailor, a cloth merchant, and a grocer, Mawlânâ accepts him as a disciple." Rumi rebutted and said that our great Sufi masters had ordinary professions: Mansur was a "wool-carder" (Hallâj); Shaykh Abu Bakr of Bokhara was a "weaver" (Nassâj), and the other perfect master was a "glass-maker" (Zajjâj). "What harm did their profession do to their spiritual knowledge?" On another occasion, Rumi replied, "If my disciples were better, I would myself have been their disciple."[2]

The *Gospel of Luke* (7:36-50) reports that when Jesus was in the house of a Pharisee for dinner, a prostitute visited him, "As she stood behind him at his feet weeping, she began to wet his feet with tears. Then she wiped them with her hair, kissed them and poured perfume on them." The Pharisee, whose name was Simon and who had hidden behind, saw all this, and said to himself, "If this man were a prophet, he would know who is touching him and what kind of woman she is – that she is a sinner." Jesus noticed it and replied that her love and honesty were superior to that of Simon. And Jesus turned to the woman and said, "Your faith has saved you."[1]

Aflâki reports a similar incident about Rumi. There was a prostitute who was very beautiful and had many girls working for her. One day, Rumi was passing by her house. The woman came out running toward him and fell at his feet and wept. Rumi addressed her, "O, Râbi'a, Râbi'a, Râbi'a!" (Râbi'a, a female, was one of the greatest and earliest Sufi masters.) A prominent man in Konya heard this story and remarked: "It is not proper for such as great person as Mawlânâ to be involved with prostitutes and show them this much compassion." Rumi replied that that honesty and affection of that prostitute is a lesson to be learned. In the end, the woman abandoned prostitution, freed her slave girls, and became a devotee of Rumi's teachings.[3]

* * *

The verses of the *Quran* as well as Rumi's affectionate poetry about Jesus clearly show that Islam is not against Christianity (or other world religions, for that matter) and that Muslims have great respect and adoration for Jesus Christ. The violent actions of a small minority of extremist, misled militant Muslims in the name of Islam against Christians, Muslims and other people do not reflect the true teachings of Islam.[4] In fact, when a Muslim wants to say Jesus' name in Arabic, he or she says: *Hadrat Isâ Maish (sallâlah alay'hi va sallam)*, "His Holiness Jesus Christ (peace be upon him)," which is exactly the same expression they use when they utter the name of Muhammad and other prophets. And this should not come as a surprise; after all, Islam regards its source and inspiration from the very same God that Abraham, David, Moses, and Jesus all believed and took refuge in. In this perspective, Rumi's poetry, seven centuries after his life, perhaps has a new significance to our age and world, calling out to the followers of all religions to unite and cooperate in a loving spirit rather than being divided by the walls of hatred and violence.

An earlier version of this chapter was published in *Interreligious Insight*, April 2008, pp. 22-25.

[10]
Rumi's Poems on Jesus' Breath

In their stories of creation, both the *Torah* (Genesis, 2:7) and the *Quran* (XV: 29) state that God created humankind (symbolized as Adam or the archetypal human) from clay, and then breathed life from his own spirit into Adam. Physically, humans are mammalian animals, and like the other living creatures, their bodies consist of the elements of the earth – carbon, calcium, oxygen, water, and so on – as modern science describes in minute details. Indeed, the Hebrew word *adama* means "soil." However, this same human being, in the Judeo-Christian-Islamic perspective, also possesses a certain quality to which the scriptures refer as the Divine breath of life or "spirit" (Latin, *spiritus*, "breath;" equivalent of *ruh* in Arabic). The Divine spirit, as mentioned in the story of creation, is inherent in all humans, regardless of their gender, race, language, religion or country. Spirit is the faculty by which we appreciate goodness, love, beauty, truth, justice, holiness, and piety. In another scriptural story, God is said to have infused his breath in the creation of a specific human, and that is the virgin birth of Jesus of Nazareth. Both the *Gospels* (Matthew, I: 20) and the *Quran* (4:171, 19:17-26) state that God breathed the Holy Spirit into Mary in order to give birth to Jesus. That is why in Islamic scriptures Jesus is called *Ruh ul'lâh* ("spirit of God").

* * *

The *Quran* has a high regard for Jesus Christ (*Isâ Masih*), who is also a beloved figure in Sufi literature such as in the works of the thirteenth century Persian Sufi poet Mawlânâ Jalâluddin Rumi. This chapter reflects on the term "Breath of Jesus" (*Dam-e Isâ*), which occasionally appears in Rumi's works, including the *Masnavi* (at least five times) and the *Divân-e Shams* (at least thirty three times per my count).

Let's begin with this beautiful poem:

I look upon the world as if it were a mother's womb,
    and I find peace in this fire.
In this fire, I see the whole world,
    wherein each particle possesses the Breath of Jesus.

Masnavi, I: 794-95

A few points need to be mentioned here. First, the Arabic word *rahma*, "compassion or mercy," comes from *rahem*, "womb." In Rumi's poetic purview, the world is like the mother's womb; it is where we are nurtured, and its warmth and nourishment comes from the fire of love or, in other words, from the Breath of Jesus. Interestingly, Jesus also says, "Whoever is near me is near the fire, whoever is far from me is far from the kingdom" (*The Gospel of Thomas*, 82).[1]

The whole world pulsates with love:

If the sky were not in love,
    its chest would not be pleasant.
If the sun were not in love,
    its face would not be bright.
If the earth and mountains were not in love,
    no plant could sprout out from their heart.
If the ocean were not aware of love
    it would have remained motionless somewhere.

Divân, 28369-72

Each and every particle in God's creation carries the loving spirit of Jesus, which has Divine origin. Jesus' Breath is the essence of humankind:

Everywhere in the universe is filled with Jesus;
where then can the garb of an Anti-Christ fit?
When the world is overflowing with pure water,
where can the bitter water of a dark soul fit?

Divân: Quatrain 1081

The world is like Mary's womb pregnant with love and Jesus. Mother Teresa once opined about her humanitarian work in Calcutta: "Actually we are touching Christ's body in the poor. In the poor it is the hungry Christ that we are feeding, it is the naked Christ that we are clothing, it is the homeless Christ that we are giving shelter."[2] In a somewhat different context, Rumi also talks about the baby Jesus within each human being: "*Our body is like Mary, and each one of us carries a baby Jesus within. If we go through birth pains, our Jesus will be born; but if we do not experience pain, the Jesus in us will return to his origin via the hidden road he came, and we will remain deprived of our inner Jesus.*"[3]

Love is fire; it has Divine source. It comes to us as a Breath of Jesus or, in other words, as the pleasant odor of an incense burning in the Realm of the Unseen (*gheyb*).

In the Realm of the Unseen,
  there is a sandalwood burning.
This love
  is the smoke of that incense.

Divân: 31322

Human essence has a ray of God's spirit – full of love, goodness, joy, consciousness, beauty, and creativity. Rumi calls it the Breath of Jesus; Zen Buddhists call it "Buddha-nature" (*bush'sho* in Japanese).

The souls in their essence have the Breath of Jesus.
One breath of you is pain; the other breath is cure.
If the veil is removed from the souls,
each soul would talk like Jesus Christ.

Masnavi, I: 1598-99

Nevertheless, this peaceful, loving, blissful essence cannot be realized without effort and without being matured and ripe through difficult tests in life. Cure is for the wound, so our wounds are also a vehicle for awakening and healing. It is like the process of breathing itself: The first breath provides the life-supporting oxygen, but the process does not end there. We need to exhale the suffocating carbon dioxide from our lungs as well; the second breath provides the cure. The ego (*nafs*) veils our heart, our true nature. Once the veil is removed, the Breath of Jesus moves our tongue and speaks. In the same vein, Jesus says: "Whoever drinks from my mouth will become like me; I myself shall become that person, and the hidden things will be revealed to that person" (*The Gospel of Thomas*, 108).

A verse in the *Quran* (V: 110) reports that one day the young Jesus made a bird from clay and water, and breathed into it, and the clay-bird spread out wings and flew. Rumi is fond of this symbolic story, and here and there in his poetry Rumi equates Jesus' breathing into the clay-bird with a life full of spirit. For example:

O, Breath of Jesus!
I am your bird made from clay.
Breathe into me
I want to fly to the heights of the sky.

Divân: 14962

* * *

Let's conclude this chapter with a poem from Rumi, which perhaps sums up all the points discussed above:

Know that the whirling of the heavens,
    and the wheel of life are all turned by the waves of love.
Without love, the world would freeze and decay.
Without love, how could the minerals disappear
    in order to be incorporated into plants?
Without love, how could the plants be sacrificed
    in order to acquire the human soul?
Without love, how could the soul be that Holy Spirit
    whose breeze made Mary pregnant?

Masnavi, V: 3854-56

This chapter has not been published previously.

[11]
In the Ocean of Rumi

My face is the color of autumn,
    and yours, the color of spring.
Unless these two become one,
    roses and thorns cannot grow.
Roses and thorns appear to be opposites,
but the garden laughs at those
    who see them as opposites.

Divân: Quatrain 886

This short poem beautifully sums up the inspirational and transcendental nature of Rumi's thought and poetry. Rumi, the Persian Sufi poet of the thirteenth century, is presently one of the most widely read poets in North America. His popularity, seven centuries after his death, and in lands and languages different from his own, is not entirely surprising: Rumi's vision goes beyond time and place; his words touch the inner core of our mind and heart. Rumi does not argue or philosophize; he simply shares his own spiritual experience and insights in elegant words and imagery. He excludes no one; his heart is an ocean of love with no shores, which includes the entire Divine creation. Poetry can be therapeutic. In the expanse of Rumi's poetry, one can find clues and cures to our life and social problems.

Like many other young boys raised in Iran (Persia), I was first exposed to Rumi's poems in my textbooks. Since leaving Iran in 1980, I have lived in India, Japan, and now the United States. In all these years, Rumi's poetry has been a rich source of insight, joy, and inner peace for me. I feel privileged to narrate my own inner journey through the ocean of Rumi's poetry and illumination.

Who Was Rumi?

The outcome of my life is no more than these three lines:
  I was a raw material;
  I was cooked and became mature;
  I was baked and burned.[1]

Jalâluddin Mohammad was born on September 30, 1207, in the city of Balkh (now in northern Afghanistan), which was then a major city in the Persian Kingdom. His father was a clergyman with an interest in Islamic mysticism (Sufism), which influenced Rumi from an early age. When Rumi was about twelve years old, his family left Balkh to journey westward, probably to flee the imminent death and destruction of the Persian Kingdom by Genghis Khan. They finally settled in Konya (now in southwest Turkey), where Rumi became an eminent scholar, preacher, and poet.

Rumi died on December 17, 1273, at the age of sixty-six. His tomb in Konya has been a shrine for lovers of his poetry for seven centuries. In Western nations, he is known as "Rumi," because he spent most of his life in Anatolia (Asia Minor), which was historically part of the Byzantine Empire called Rūm (Rome) in Arabic and Persian. People in the East usually call him Mawlânâ ("Our Master").

As long as you are on the endless path of selfish desires,
you will remain farther away from the Beloved's house.
If you are seeking union,
you must work diligently in the desert of longing.   *Divân:* Quatrain[2]

The Alchemy of Love

O God, this love,
    how hidden it is;
    how visible it is.
It's like intoxicating wine;
It's like the luminous Moon.
O God, this love has decorated
    our soul and the universe.   *Divân:* 1059-61

Rumi was a prolific and passionate poet. He composed approximately 70,000 lines of poetry, and they all revolve around love. However, Rumi's expression of love should not be confused with lust. For him, love was the outcome of a profound spiritual encounter with the Divine in the same manner that Jesus Christ said: "God is love" and "Love thy neighbor." Divine love, or what Rumi calls the "true source of love," is manifested in human love (our love for each other) or what Rumi calls the "derivative love". For this reason, Rumi does not draw a rigid boundary between Divine and human love.

Sufis believe that we can realize God's love through our own love and compassion toward fellow human beings and other creatures because God's love is like the shining Sun – too powerful to look at directly, but it can be comfortably seen through its reflection on a lake. In Rumi's poetic language, the words God, love, and light convey closely-related notions. God is love. God is also light, and spiritual awakening is nothing more than seeing things in the Divine light (not through the lens of our self-centered judgements). Rumi's path of love is also a path of spiritual awakening. Through love we gain insight into the hidden reality. A true lover gains existential understanding that cannot be gained through philosophy or reasoning. That is why in Sufism (as in Christian mysticism), the words *erfân* (esoteric knowledge), *eshrâg* (enlightenment), and *eshg* (love) are organically interrelated.

What strikes us most in Rumi's poetry is that he does not address God as a remote, aloof heavenly father who strictly punishes or rewards his children; rather, Rumi calls God a Beloved in life and a Friend on earth. God is to be loved and befriended. This is Rumi's path of love. It is we who should try to be on God's side through our love for God's creation. To see God as "taking sides" in our petty disagreements or greedy wishes would be to confine God to our limited, biased beliefs; Rumi does not consider such a view to be the hallmark of spiritual awakening or true faith. Hatred distances us from God, while compassion brings us closer to Him; compassion is the sweet fruit that grows on the tree of spirituality.

Rumi views love as akin to the force of gravity – something embedded in the fabric of the universe:

If the Sky were not in love,
    its chest would not be pleasant.
If the Sun were not in love,

> *its face would not be bright.*
> *If the Earth and mountains were not in love,*
>   *no plant could sprout from their heart.*
> *If the Sea were not aware of love*
>   *it would have remained motionless somewhere.*   Divân, 28369-72

In Rumi's vision, love is what moves the universe ceaselessly. The relationship between two seemingly opposite things is not necessarily a war in which one side should be destroyed; rather it is a loving relationship between two poles. Flowers and thorns (as Rumi says) are not opposites but parts of the same plant; they originate from the same seed and soil, and are nourished by the same water; they both are products of the same love process. Rumi expresses the "opposites" – winter and summer, fire and water, life and death, man and woman, and so forth in the light of unifying love.

Rumi's love is alchemy. In the alchemy of love nothing is wasted, everything has its own place and use; the opposites are united; conflicts are dissolved:

> *Through love*
>   *bitter things become sweet.*
> *Through love*
>   *bits of copper turn into gold.*
> *Through love*
>   *dregs taste like pure wine.*
> *Through love*
>   *pains are healed.*
> *Through love*
>   *death turns into life.*
> *Through love*
>   *kings become servants.*   Masnavi (II: 1529-31)

Rumi believes that there are two births in life, both of which take place through love. The first is our biological birth, through a mother; and the second is our spiritual birth, in which the person's heart and inner eyes open to the Divine light. For the spiritual birth, one has to "die before death;" that is, to become free from the prison enclosed by the walls of egoistic expectations, delusions, and worldly attachments. Rumi offers rich imagery to illustrate this second death and its subsequent spiritual rebirth: It is like the parrot breaking its cage and flying into the expanse of sky, or it is like the elephant breaking its chains and returning to India (the homeland for both parrot and elephant). From his own experience, Rumi associated spiritual awakening and rebirth with the process of love:

I was dead;
  I became alive.
I was all cries;
  I became laughter.
The glory of love came upon me, and
  I became everlasting glory.   Divân: 14742

The Heart is an Ocean without Shores

The one who is not attached to this world,
  finds a home in the heart.
Nowhere in this universe
  is more spacious than the heart.   Divân: 4477

To comprehend Rumi's poetry, one needs to picture a "spiritual body" with the organs like the heart, eye, ear, hand, foot, etc. Just as we see the outer world through our external sensory organs, we also need to fine-tune our internal sensory organs to comprehend the spiritual universe. But where is this spiritual universe? It is not far out in the remote recesses of the universe; it is everywhere including within ourselves, and the heart (*del* or *galb*), which is a recurring theme in Rumi's poetry, is the organ of its perception.

The notion that the heart is the seat of love and the faculty of spiritual cognition is found in all religious traditions and spiritual literature, and this commonality indeed testifies to the naturalness of spirituality. What is so profound in Rumi's poetry is the rich imagery he has created to show the various facets and functions of this inner heart. A spiritual entity like the heart cannot be seen with our eye or touched by our hand; therefore, we may easily deny or ignore its existence. However, the overwhelming presence of the heart can be felt by its cries, joy, effects, and actions in life and society. In this sense, Rumi's poetry is a valuable map of the heart and spiritual realm. In many of his poems, Rumi says that the heart is like a brilliant mirror reflecting beauty and goodness: it is the source of happiness; it is the gate to paradise; it is the window to light; it is a desert of tranquility with no bounds; and it is an ocean of life without shores. Aflâki, one of Rumi's disciples who recorded the life story of his master, writes that someone once asked Rumi, "You tell us so much about the Place of Placeness. Where is it?" Rumi answered, "Of course, it is the heart of a liberated human."[3]

While Rumi's name is very well known today, not many people know that Rumi's pen-name (as he addressed himself in the last line of many of his lyric poems) was *Khamoosh* ("Silent") because he did not regard his poetry as an intellectual verbalization, but rather something that emanated from his heart. And that is why his poetry, even centuries later, still "settles in our hearts," and serves as a spiritual guide and consolation. This is a remarkable achievement for a poet and a valuable treasure for humanity.

Are you searching for your true self?
Then come out of your own prison.
Leave the little creek and
    join the mighty river that flows into the ocean.
Like an ox, don't pull the wheel of this world on your back;
take off the burden; whirl and circle, and
rise above the wheel of the world:
There is another view.   *Divân*: Quatrain[4]

An earlier version titled "In the Ocean of Rumi: Poetry of Love and Spiritual Awakening" was published in *Pure Inspiration*, Spring 2008, pp. 34-40.

[12]
Love and Life in Rumi's Poetry

Ali Dashti, an Iranian scholar, once remarked, *"Whenever I encounter Rumi in his Divân [poetry book], a sense of awe and wonder engulfs me: What does this man want? What is he seeking? What is he saying? What has he felt? His restless poetry is the reflection of what storm?"*[1] Devoted readers of Rumi eventually face these same questions. One way to approach these questions about Rumi is to explore his views on love and life.

Love (*eshg* in the Arabic-Persian languages) is a common thread that runs through all of Rumi's poems. But what does love mean to Rumi? Relatively less attention has been given to this aspect of Rumi's poetry than to the beauty and imaginative power of his verses. Understanding Rumi's mind not only enriches our reading of his poems but also introduces us to a very rich spiritual tradition in which he lived and was nurtured. Fortunately, Rumi provides us with considerable materials to explore: (1) the six volumes of the *Masnavi-ye Ma'navi* ("Spiritual Couplets"), which narrate hundreds of stories and parables in about 26,000 verses of poetry; and (2) the *Divân-e Shams-e Tabrizi*, a collection of his sonnets (*ghazaliyât*) and quatrains (*rubâiyât*), totaling about 44,000 verses.

* * *

Love cannot be defined in strict words or proven through the logic of the head; it can only be experienced:

Someone asked: What is love?
I said: Don't ask about its meaning.
You will see love when you become like me.   Divân: 29050-51

Persian Sufi poetry is a rare gem among the world's spiritual literature in that it expresses and symbolizes the Divine beauties through the features of the female body and face. The charming *sâgi* ("cupbearer") who dances and serves the wine of love is a recurring image in Rumi's poetry. But none of these should be misinterpreted; Rumi was neither an alcoholic nor a womanizer. Coleman Barks, who has successfully popularized Rumi's poems through rendering them to the modern English style of free verse, reminds us that Rumi's love is not of the kind, "she left me; she came back; she left me."[2] Rumi's love is grounded in his realization of Divine love; it is not a frail feeling rooted in selfishness or lust. Of course, Divine love is inclusive of all types of genuine love.

In the Realm of the Unseen, there is a sandal wood burning.
This love is the smoke of that incense.   *Divân*: 31322

Indeed, of the ninety-nine names (attributes) of God that Sufis have extracted from the *Quran*, one is "*Al-wadud*" (All-Loving), and a host of other names are also related to loving. Every chapter in the *Quran* begins *"In the Name of God, the Most Merciful (Al-Rahmân) and the Most Compassionate (Al-Rahim).*"

Rumi refers to love among humans as Derivative Love (*eshg-e majâzi*) because it is a reflection of the Divine or True Love (*eshg-e hagigi*). In one poem (*Divân*: 336-338), Rumi says that "*the path of Derivative Love leads to True Love*" and that "*the culmination of human love is the love of Al-Rahmân (the kindness and grace of God).*"

Rumi also emphasizes that Divine Love is manifested in the entire creation:

If the Sky were not in love,
    its breast would not be pleasant.
If the Sun were not in love,
    its beautiful face would not be bright.
If the Earth and mountains were not in love,
    no plant could sprout out from their heart.
If the Sea were not aware of love,
    it would have remained motionless somewhere.   *Divân*: 28369-28372

A detailed critique of love in Rumi's poetry can easily fill a whole book.[3] I have personally learned most from Rumi when I have juxtaposed his love poems with real life subjects. Such comparisons and contrasts are more impactful and practical than elaborate philosophical discussions on the idea of love.

There is a Persian word, *jân*, which Rumi often uses, and one of the challenges for Rumi's translators is to find contextually appropriate words in English for *jân* because it means soul, life, heart, love, and dear — often in combination. Even in the modern colloquial Persian, a mother often replies to her child, *jânam*," which means "Yes, my dear (soul, life, love, and heart)." I use this example to illustrate the dynamic nature of love in Rumi's vision.

Love is embedded in the very fabric of human nature and daily life. For this reason, Rumi (perhaps more than any other classical Persian poet) uses simple common words to express his impressions of love:

One night I asked Love: Tell me truly, what are you?
It said: I am life everlasting, I multiply the joyful life.
I asked: Oh you, who are outside of space and time, where is your home?
It said: I am a companion to the heart's fire; I sit beside wet eyes.

Divân: 14851-52

Rumi associates love with both the joys and sorrows of life. But happiness and sadness arising out of love are qualitatively different from those that affect us as consequences of our possessive ego and greedy attachments. Ignorance, greed and attachment bring about fear, conflict, and suffering. Happiness that emanates from love does not make us arrogant; it liberates and uplifts us:

Out of fear, the world is torn apart.
Out of love, the soul flies higher.

Divân: 3524

Of course, the spiritual journey — the journey within the heart — is not a smooth path:

In love, there is union with,
    and separation from the beloved.
The path has ups and downs.

Divân: 29156

Without love we miss precious life as it passes. In fact, according to Rumi, the real span of our life should be the number of the days spent in love:

Do not count those days of your life
as really lived if you were not a lover.   *Divân:* 10315

That is why Rumi says that love is for living humans, not something to be postponed to the after-life.

Life must be spent in love.
The dead are not supposed to do that.
Do you know who is alive?
The one who is regenerated every moment in love.   *Divân:* 8824

* * *

Love is a creative, transformative force; it gives us a new life. And Rumi has a personal experience to tell us – his experience of enlightenment:

I was dead: I became alive.
I was all cries: I became laughter.
The glory of love came upon me.
And I became the everlasting glory.   *Divân:* 1474

One day in late 1244, after years of studying and teaching as a high-rank Islamic scholar in Konya (in present-day Turkey), Rumi met a wandering dervish, Shams of Tabriz. Through conversations (*soh'bat*) and retreats (*khal'vat*) with this sage, Rumi's drastic and pivotal transformation occurred. He then committed himself to the path of Divine love, not through books and intellectual verbalism, but through the heart, compassion, contemplation, beauty, song, and dance. This is how Rumi became a poet of love. And he was prepared for this transformation. Rumi was a dormant volcano which erupted after meeting Shams, and the seeds of an all-inclusive mystical love blossomed in Rumi's soul.

In *The Art of Loving*, Erich Fromm remarks that people often assume that "the problem of love is the problem of an object, not the problem of a faculty. People think that to love is simple, but that to find the right object to love – or to be loved by – is difficult."[4] Rumi also considers love to be an active process, a work to do, and an art and a skill to develop. Love is not something that happens to us passively and accidentally, it is not something that we should consider after we happen to find an object of love. In fact, Rumi takes a step further than Fromm and claims that the reason you are an active seeker of love is because, in actuality, the beloved is actively seeking you. Love is an undercurrent of the soul:

There is no lover seeking union
without a beloved searching for him, too.
A thirsty person cries for fresh water;
while water is groaning: Who is the drinker?   Masnavi, III: 4393-97

* * *

Rumi's poems are full of love because he composed them out of ecstasy and his realization of Divine love. For Rumi love is neither an abstract, philosophical matter nor an exercise of sensual lust. Love (*eshg*) is woven tightly with life and manifests itself as longing (*showg*), seeking (*talab*), the drunkenness (*masti*) and ecstasy (*shoor*) of the soul, joy (*shâdi*), loving-kindness (*muhabbat*), compassion (*mehr*), friendship (*doosti*), and help (*yâri*).

A sectarian love is not real love for Rumi. His feeling of love was directed towards all humans, irrespective of their religion, race or language. He was, in fact, compassionate to all creatures. Ahmad Aflâki, who compiled the life stories of Rumi shortly after his death, records many cases of how Rumi practiced what he preached. In one story,[5] he writes that a female dog had given birth to several puppies but did not want to leave her puppies at risk and danger. So the dog and her puppies were hungry. Rumi used to feed them. (Even though dogs are traditionally considered "dirty" by Muslims.) In another story,[6] Aflâki reports that a Christian monk, who had heard of Rumi's scholarly and spiritual reputation, went to meet him in Konya. Out of respect, the monk prostrated before Rumi, and when he raised his head, he saw that Rumi was returning this deep respect with prostration also.

To sum up: Like his beloved teacher Jesus Christ, Rumi truly believed that the principles of "God is Love" and "Love thy neighbor" either go together or go nowhere. Love for God should be manifested in our life. This view of love has profound implications for solving our grave problems today and for creating a happy, peaceful life – interpersonally as well as internationally.

An earlier version of this chapter appeared in *Persian Heritage*, Summer 2007, pp. 39-40.

[13]
A Map of the Heart in Rumi's Poetry

"I want to share with you the work of a supreme witness of the heart. I want to share with you the work of someone who really understands what has to be done for the heart to become divine and the will to become focused in the Light."

Andrew Harvey[1]

A 1998 US documentary film about Rumi is titled, *Rumi: Poet of the Heart*. What does "Heart" mean to Rumi? What is its place in Rumi's poetry? What role does "Heart" play in his mystical vision? In this chapter, we explore these questions drawing on Rumi's own works: *Masnavi-ye Ma'navi* ("Spiritual Couplets") and *Divân-e Shams-e Tabrizi* ("The Poetry Book Dedicated to Shams Tabrizi" – Rumi's spiritual friend).

"Heart" is a recurring theme in Rumi's poetry, and he uses two words to express it: A Persian word, *del*, and an Arabic word, *qalb*, both of which are used interchangeably. The notion that the heart is the realm of love, feeling and spirit is recognized in many religions and cultures. What is so profound in Rumi's poetry, however, is the rich imagery he has created to describe the various facets and functions of the heart for the wayfarers of spirituality. This imagery, in turn, gives insight into the spiritual states that Rumi himself as a Sufi master experienced in his life journey. Understanding Rumi's views on the heart also helps us to better appreciate his love poems. Indeed, the words which Persian poets use for the Beloved are often associated with the heart: *del-dâr* ("The one who possesses the lover's heart"), *del-bar* or *del-rubâ* ("The one who has charmed or seized the lover's heart"), and *del-ârâm* ("The one who brings tranquility to the heart"). A person who is homesick or longing to see his beloved is *del-tang* ("heart-squeezed").

We sometimes say that people think with their brains and feel with their hearts, or that the brain is the seat of rationality and intellect, while the heart perceives love. All these are, of course, metaphorical. The human body-mind is a single entity. The heart in Rumi's poetry is not the "blood pump" located within our chest; the poetic "heart" is a vital organ of "spiritual physiology," which is not observable to the physical eye or by scientific instruments, but its presence is obvious from its effects, actions, and manifestations in our life, and even in our body. The spiritual heart is connected to all of the organs and cells of the body.

Rumi's poems, which he recited while in retreat, meditation, dance or ecstasy, paint a detailed map of the heart. Here I highlight twenty attributes and functions of the heart mentioned in Rumi's poetry.

(1) The heart is outside of space and time:

Why is the heart a stranger in the two worlds?
Because the quality of "placelessness"
*   keeps it apart from places.*   *Divân*: 28934

(2) The heart is vaster than the universe:

The one who is not attached to this world,
*   finds a dwelling in the heart.*
Nowhere in this universe
*   is more spacious than the heart.*   *Divân*: 4477

(3) The signs of God are everywhere but the closest place we can approach God is in our heart:

Prophet Muhammad said that God revealed this to him:
"I cannot be contained in any place, above or below;
on the Earth, in the Sky, not even on the Divine Throne.
Strangely, however, I am in the heart of the faithful.
If you wish to search for me, seek me in those hearts."
*   Masnavi*: I, 2652-54

(4) The heart is a mirror that reflects the Unseen Realm:

The Sufis have polished their chests
    clean from greed, desire, meanness, and hatred.
The heart is, indeed, a pure mirror,
    for it is receptive of infinite images.
The Sufis possess in their chests the heart's mirror
    that reflects the infinite forms from the Unseen World.
Remember this: The heart's mirror has no bounds.
Therefore, the intellect must remain silent here;
    or else, it will mislead us.
For the heart is with God;
or indeed, God is the heart.   *Masnavi*: I, 3484-3489

The un-tarnished mirror of the heart reflects the Divine attributes. In the very opening poem of the *Masnavi* (I: 34), Rumi says, "*Do you know why your mirror does not shine and reflect light? Because the rust has not been polished from its surface.*"

(5) The heart has been purified by Divine wine:

My chest has opened up.
My heart is crystal clear, full of love.
Because it is God's wine glass.   *Divân*: 2047

(6) The heart is a window to eternal light:

The heart is a window to light.
Our house is bright because of the heart.
The body decays; the heart remains.   *Divân*: 9411

(7) The heart has the quality of fire:

The body – for it came from sperm,
    flows down like water.
The heart – for its origin is fire,
    only goes upward.   *Divân*: 11879

This hearkens to the ancient idea of the Four Elements, in which each element strives to return to its origin: Rocks fall down to the earth; water flows into the ocean; the air rises to the atmosphere; and fire goes to the outer space (heavens). The heart looks heavenward.

(8) The path of the heart is not that of a negative, cynical mind:

The path of argumentation is
    stubbornness, criticism, and justification.
The path of the heart is
    clear vision, joy, and sweet gratification.   Divân: 12187

(9) True intellect is a ladder to reach the heart and see beyond this world:

The heart is so buoyant that it went up – heavenward,
and placed intellect as its ladder.
The heart heard the news of the Beloved's coming.
Overflowing with love, the heart rushed to the rooftop.
Looking for signs of the Beloved,
behold, a world beyond this world came to its sight.   Divân: 29013-15

This imagery becomes more familiar when we know that in the Middle East, people have traditionally gone to the flat rooftops of their houses to chat or view the scenery.

(10) Wash your heart with the water of wisdom:

Wash off the dust from your heart and soul
    with the purifying water of wisdom.
Then your eyes will not be hankered to this mundane world.   Divân: 8049

(11) The heart is by nature silent, and that is why it is the source of songs:

The source of all songs is the heart,
although the sounds are heard in the mountain of the body.
O you who are charmed by the sound,
silently go into the source.   Divân: 2209

Like the heart I am silent.
But the Beloved never sleeps.
So I will be a tongue for my Beloved.
I will sing and dance until dawn.   *Divân*: 973

(12) Only the heart comprehends beauty:

In the bright and warm rays of the heart,
this world of dust and mud
has become a world of beauty, delight, and elegance.   *Divân*: 7386

The face of the heart
    is not like the face of any creature.
For the face of heart
    reflects the beauties of God.   *Divân*: 10570

(13) The heart is the hidden place of God's treasures:

God's treasure is hidden in the ruined heart.
For much treasure is found in the ruins.   *Divân*: 33114

Where there is a ruined place,
    there is hope for treasure.
Why do you not seek God's treasure
    in your broken heart?   *Divân*: 1613

The "ruined heart" (*del-e kharâb*) is our inner space where worldly expectations and desires, which were our prison walls in the first place, are all smashed into pieces. It is in the ruined heart that we find new life, fresh energy, boldness, joy, peace, and light. The Phoenix resides in the broken heart.

(14) The heart is Paradise:

Close the gate of Hell and leave it behind.
Do not stuff your life with greed.
Then open the gate of Paradise,

which is your pure and radiant heart.   *Dívân*: 34717
Even if the whole world is filled with thorns,
the heart of the lover remains an orchard.
Even if the wheel of heaven stops whirling,
the world of the lovers will function fully.
While all others become sorrowful, the lover's soul
is always tender and kind, vivid and delightful.   *Dívân*: 6914-16

(15) The heart is an ocean:

Without You, my face would be only pale.
Without You, the ocean of my heart could not produce any pearl.   *Dívân*: 1581

The ocean of the heart is graceful.
It makes a hundred pearls from a droplet of your mind.   *Dívân*: 6556

(16) Kisses come through the heart's window:

Close the mouth of speech;
     open the window of the heart.
The Moon's kisses
     come only through that window.   *Dívân*: 19863

(17) It is in the heart that the souls meet:

Close your mouth;
     open the window of your heart.
For that is where
     the souls meet and converse.   *Dívân*: 1248

(18) The heart is concealed beneath the tongue (words):

O the Silent one!
Where is the heart hidden?
"Beneath the tongue.
When the words are gone,
the heart is revealed."   *Dívân*: 8408

When the lips are shut tight,
the heart speaks in a hundred tongues.   Divân: 9139

"Silent" (*Khamoosh*) was Rumi's pen name cited at the end of many of his sonnets.

(19) The heart is the garden of secrets:

If I utter words,
what will they understand?
No. I won't talk.
It's better to be silent;
otherwise, the heart will say:
"You can't keep secrets."   Divân: 4822

(20) Spend your time with the "people of the heart (*sâheb del*):"

Oh my heart, sit with a person
    who understands the heart.
Sit under a tree
    which offers fresh flowers.   Divân: 34717

Rumi's poetry paints a map of the heart. Of course, a map is only a map; it is scaled down and uses symbols; it can never present the expanse, majesty or beauty of a landscape. A map can still be useful. Rumi uses words and symbols to guide us into the mysterious, vast, evergreen realm of the heart, which is beyond words and which is within all of us.

An earlier version of this chapter was published in *Persian Heritage*, Winter 2007, pp. 40-41; and *Tiferet: A Journal of Spiritual Literature*, No. 7, 2008, pp. 59-62.

[14]
Rumi's Poetry as a Guiding Light

Guidance is at the heart of existence. Order and comprehensibility of nature constitute the foundation of science. From tiny particles to giant galaxies, the natural world is guided by physical constants, chemical properties, and natural laws. We do not know where these laws, constants, and properties came from; nevertheless, modern science has made great strides in discovering and formulating the principles and processes of nature. One thing, however, is certain: It is because of the laws, constants, and properties embedded in the universe that there are structures, mechanisms, evolution, and life in the world. Guiding light also operates in every moment of our lives. In January 2010, Simran Singh, the editor of the *11:11* magazine, published a special issue on "Guiding Light." In her editorial, she wrote that guidance can only be seen or heard if we become quiet and available for it. This chapter was first published in that issue of the magazine; it presents some illuminating poems from Rumi and brief commentaries and impressions. I hope you enjoy reading it.

Seek the Knowledge of Untying Your Knots

Seek the know-how of untying your knots.
And seek it before life leaves your body.
Leave the nothing that appears to have existence.
Seek the existence that appears to be nothing.   *Divân*: Quatrain[1]

In life we encounter numerous problems, needs, and pains – some of them are real and existential, while others are artifacts of our thoughts and illusions, or products of relationships and expectations. In his 1943 influential article, "A Theory of Human Motivation," the American psychologist Abraham Maslow worked out a scale of fundamental human needs as follows: (1) Physiological needs (air, water, food, sleep and sex), (2) safety and security, (3) love and belonging, (4) esteem and respect, and (5) self-actualization and creativity. More recently, the Chilean economist Manfred Max-Neef, has proposed another, but similar, list: Subsistence, protection, affection, understanding, participation, leisure, creation, identity, and freedom. While all these *needs* are valid, a person's mindset and attitude towards any of them may be twisted and misplaced, and this results in artificial, illusionary *wants*, which, in turn, lead to suffering and pain. Food, for instance, is vital for our survival and health, but one may not have a healthy attitude toward eating: Overeating thus results in overweight, obesity and other health hazards. Participation is a necessity because we are social animals, but in what and how we participate depends on the quality of our mind. In general, if the mind is governed by egoistic, greedy desires, there will be no end for our wants, and whatever we do will actually bring about suffering for us and for others. But if our mind is awake to the reality and has crossed beyond the small self-centered world, we will have the right approach to satisfying our needs. Our thoughts and actions will also yield positive results. This notion is the basis of what Indian religions call *karma*.

As Rumi says we need knowledge to untie the knots in our life. This includes the knowledge of satisfying our real needs as well as the knowledge of avoiding unreal desires and suffering. Moreover, this knowledge cannot be merely intellectual and verbal; it must be practical and existential.

Ignorance and selfishness usually mask what is true and real, and we thus easily forget how precious our life is. Gestalt psychology has demonstrated that human attention is easily drawn to apparent forms and images, and ignores the backgrounds and foundations. For example, if I draw a circle on a white canvas, most people will see the circle but will forget that the seemingly blank canvas or even the pen and ink are actually the basic supports for the circle. In a similar way, an unenlightened mind creates a life of projecting images after images on a white screen and goes on watching these images and games as if they are the reality. But at some point, often toward the end of life, the person suddenly realizes the futility of clinging to the images, and instead yearns to understand and appreciate the vast world and the real life. This is also Rumi's advice: Be aware of what is real and what is illusionary before life leaves your body. This very life is precious.

This Being Human

I died to mineral and became plant.
I died to the plant and became animal.
I died to the animal and became human.
So why fear? When have I been diminished by dying?
Likewise, I should die to this being human and
   fly with the angel's wings.
But I should cross even the angelic river;
"For all things perish save the Divine face."   (*Quran*, XXVIII: 88)
Once more, I shall be sacrificed and die from the angel,
and become that which cannot even be imagined.
I shall become utterly empty.
Nothingness, like an organ, sings to me:
"Verily, unto Him shall we all return."   (*Quran*, II: 151)
               Masnavi, III: 3901-7

In 1897 the French artist Paul Gauguin, then living in Tahiti, painted his masterpiece and entitled it with three questions: "Where do we come from? What are we? Where are we going?" These three questions are closely related to a more personal inquiry: Who am I?

 There is more than one way of answering this question, but, I think we can categorize the answers into three large, end-member positions. The first position is a fundamentally materialistic approach to existence: We are here, in this world of inanimate matter and blind energy, by pure accident; there is no cosmic or special significance for our being or not-being. The second position postpones our real life to another world, after death, and thus renounces this world and this life as unfit, sinful, and undesirable. A common problem with both of these views is a lack of human's spiritual belonging to this world and life. Rumi does not subscribe to any of these views, and instead suggests that we, as humans, have come out of this world in a long (from our standpoint) evolutionary process, and we are on a significant cosmic, spiritual journey. In Rumi's view, existence is sourced in the Divine; the world is sacred; and our life is meaningful and is actually a gift to treasure.

As curious and creative beings, we will always be marveled by questions and discoveries in science and philosophy. But even intuitively we know that we are part of the world; or indeed, we *are* the world: We are minerals, plants, and animals; nevertheless, we are not limited to any of them; we are humans, and according to Rumi, we are traveling on a spiritual journey toward the Divine. The "Angel" is a symbol for purity of the heart and devotion to the Divine. But even the angel is not the final destination for Rumi; the angel too should be transcended because it is not conscious, free or tormented by longing. Being in love and union with the Beloved means living and seeing in the light of the Beloved. Love and union, which run throughout Rumi's poetry, are the climax of the evolutionary spiritual process for human beings.

The Ocean and the Waves

I am a single soul,
    but with a hundred thousand bodies.
It's all me. I am not talking about others.
Like the wave in the ocean, I raise my head.
Look at me carefully!
My head is the same as my body.
Like the wave!   *Divân*: Quatrain 1237

On a seashore, we see a multitude of waves which rise, come forth, and return to the sea. But the waves, no matter how tall or short, are not separate from the sea. In fact, if we dive several feet into the sea, we will see no waves, but a single, vast expanse of water. In the Sufi tradition, Reality is like a shoreless ocean and the myriad manifestations of creation are like ocean waves. As a single wave, we may appear to be separate, one who is born one day and dies another day. But all of us, all creatures, are rooted in a common "ground of being," as the theologian Paul Tillich would say. This is a transcendental view – going beyond dualities and seeing our true nature and our true position in nature. "A hundred thousand bodies," although give a beautiful diversity to existence, all emerge from and return to a single soul –

a common ocean. We are waves on a journey but rooted in the sea. No birth; no death.

Love is Emptiness

Empty bowl you dance on water.
Overfilled you sink into the abyss.   *Divân*: 32544

How can we realize transcendence, peace, joy, and union with the Source? Rumi's answer in his thousands of poems and parables is simply this: Through love. But what is love? We often associate love with an intense liking of a particular person, object or idea. But that feeling is not sufficient because we may like someone or something for our own selfish ends and desires. Love to Rumi is actually the absence of selfishness. In other words, love is "emptiness" – being empty of our self-centered judgments, attachments, lust, and games. In that emptiness, we can truly love because we can be open to participate, share, help, learn, dance, and enjoy.

    There is a beautiful Zen story that illustrates this point. An academic philosopher once went to the monastery of Nan-in, a renowned Zen master in Japan, and requested the master to instruct him on Zen. The Zen master offered his guest green tea, and while serving tea, he continued pouring tea into an already overfilled tea cup. When the philosopher pointed out to the master that the cup was already full, the Zen master replied: This overfilled cup is the state of your mind as a scholar; you have come to me with a mind overfilled with so much history, argument, thought, and judgment. How can I teach you what Zen really is unless your empty your mind?[2]

Fly with Friends

With friends you fly with your wings.
Without friends, you are a single fallen feather.
Flying with your wings you master the wind.
A single feather – the wind blows you in all directions.

                                                            Divân: Quatrain 1872

My fascination with Rumi's spiritual path is partly because it is not one of life negation, cold nihilism or coward escapism. His attitude toward life is optimistic, vivid, and engaging. Life is a springboard for love, insight, and joy. Rumi did not abandon his family in search of enlightenment for himself. He appreciated the company of spiritual community and friends in his own quest and journey, or what he calls "flying with friends."

Humans, Aristotle said, are social animals. An individual cannot do all things necessary for his or her own survival and growth. We need all of society for our material as well as spiritual needs. Life is a caravan, and the spiritual journey goes through deserts, mountains, and storms. Flying with friends, our wings gain more strength, and we can progress. Without spiritual fellowship, we can be easily lost and perish in the desert. Spirituality should be in the midst of social life.

An earlier version of this chapter was published in *11:11 Magazine*, January-February 2010, pp. 32-35.

[15]
Rumi's Poems for Meditation and Life

A poem that arises from the heart lifts off the veils from the hearts.
                                            Divân: 9693

Spiritual traditions around the world have developed various teachings and techniques for what Tibetan Buddhism calls *lojong*, the "training of the mind" or "cleansing of attitudes." In Sufism, there is a similar tradition called *tahdhib ul-akh'lâg* (Persian: *tah'zib-e akh'lâg*), which literally means "cleansing of attitudes" or "purification of ethics." Indeed, the tenth-century Persian Islamic scholar Ibn Miskawayh wrote a book under that title. Over the centuries, Sufism, particularly in its Persian strand, has developed poetry and parables as a powerful tool for this task mainly because spiritual poetry touches the inner core of our consciousness. Rumi is an illustrative case in point. People often think of poetry as something special and detached from daily life, but spiritual poetry can actually orient our life and work in a meditative, mindful way; and in this regard, Rumi's poetry is particularly helpful.

Rumi was not a poet by profession; he was a religious teacher. Nevertheless, he was a prolific poet. He began composing poems in his late thirties, and for the following three decades, until his death in 1273, he composed about 70,000 verses. Unlike many others poets who write down, revise and polish their poems, Rumi did not write down his poems; he spontaneously recited them to his disciples in a state of joy, dance, ecstasy or contemplation. Except for a few lines, his poems are not about his personal memories or past life. He seems to have truly lived in "here and now," in a moment-to-moment awareness of his life, rather than being attached to the desires of becoming or to the regrets of not-becoming.

Rumi's poetry was rooted in dance and music (*samâ*). He is well known as the founder of the Whirling Dervishes. His choice of *samâ* as a source of his poetry is very interesting. Dance and music have this unique quality that they cannot be physically separated from the artist; the performance and the performer are one, in contrast to painting or sculpture in which the artwork and the artist can exist separately. In his *samâ*, Rumi was totally unified with his artistic inspiration and creation. On the other hand, Rumi's choice of poetry as a vehicle of transmitting his art and vision was most generous because a poem can be easily implanted in the reader's or the listener's heart if it is received with attention. A poem can take life in the heart of any person who appreciates it.

Rumi created his poems by living a meditative and simple life. That is partly why his work can transcend linguistic, geographic and historic barriers, and his insight touches our hearts and minds. Poetry can, indeed, be used for meditation.

Meditations on Longing and Love

Anthropologist Loren Eiseley (one of my favorite essayists of all time) often remarked about the loneliness of the human being: "There is nothing more alone in the universe than man."[1] Although we are social animals and have to live in a society, we also feel lonely and may prefer solitude even in the assembly of our fellow beings. There is more than one kind of loneliness and there are many reasons for our feelings of loneliness, but a fundamental reason for our existential loneliness, according to Rumi, is that we have come from a source of love, light and goodness, and desire to live with that source. Or in the words of Eiseley, "Like Odysseus, man seeks his spiritual home and is denied it."[2]

The opening poem of Rumi's *Masnavi* tells the story of the reed-flute that is cut from its reed-bed and laments for reunion:

Listen to this reed-flute,
how it complains, telling the tale of all separations:
Ever since I was cut from the reed-bed,
men and women have cried in my lament.
I seek out a heart that, having been separated,

is shred into pieces;
only then can I describe the pain of longing.
Whoever has gone far from his origin,
seeks to return to the days of his union.

All separations have the same tale. Rumi likens himself to a flute cut from its source (call it God, love, spiritual home, or simply the Beloved); the flute's song takes us on a journey of longing, pain, love, union, peace, and joy. Rumi proposes love as the core of human life. Whether poor or rich, illiterate or highly educated, belonging to this or that religion or nationality, we all feel loneliness, longing, separation, sorrow, happiness, ecstasy, agony, fulfillment and peace; these are various facets of the dynamism of love. Rumi's poems suit all of these situations and are thus reflective meditations on the path of love. Eiseley remarks that "the epic journey of modern science is a story at once of tremendous achievement, loneliness, and terror."[2] Rumi's poetry uncovers and illuminates our lives in the larger context of the metaphysics of love, spiritual home, and belonging.

You are the soul of the soul of the universe.
And your name is love.
Whoever has your wings flies to the greatest heights.   *Divân*: 9522

A spiritual path based on love constitutes the content, core, and vision of Rumi's poetry. Through mystical experience, Rumi realized that love, lover and beloved are all one unity, and that its source is Divine. But his perception of Divine love is not a dry, sad, reclusive or exclusive religious psychology. Divine love, as Rumi sings in his poetry, flows throughout creation and in all moments of life. In other words, the world and the life in it is always fresh, recreated every moment. It is only because of our ignorance, or rather forgetfulness, that we regard the world as dull and dead. We only need to open our spiritual eyes to see the vividness, vitality, beauty, and glory of creation.

Therefore, although Rumi's focus in his poetry may appear to be a mystic's love for God or what he calls "the soul of the soul of the universe," he does not draw a demarcation between Divine love and human love because he believes that genuine human love and compassion for fellow-humans and creatures are merely reflections of Divine love, whether we know it or not. Divine love is like the powerful Sun — too strong for us to look at it directly but we can comfortably enjoy the sunlight through its reflection in the landscape. Indeed, Rumi finds it impossible for a person to have a heart-felt love for God but not for His creation, including human beings. He says:

If you have no beloved,
why do you not seek one?
If you have found your beloved,
why do you not rejoice?   Divân: 9522

In his numerous love poems, Rumi rarely mentions the name of God. In this way he deliberately keeps the boundary between Divine and human love open. For this reason, Rumi's poetry kindles a feeling of love in us, not as a theological doctrine or philosophical inference, but as a meditative experience in our heart. It is thus easier for us to relate his poetry and vision to our lives.

Meditations on Nature

Rumi uses colorful imagery, often from nature, to express his journey of love and enlightenment. Therefore, many of his poems not only invite us to nature but also give depth to that experience. For instance, he invites us to his garden:

The green garden of love has no bounds.
It bears so many kinds of fruit,
        except sorrow and pleasure.
Being in love is beyond sorrow and pleasure
The garden of love is always fresh and green;
        it is beyond the vicissitudes of spring or autumn.
                                                Masnavi, I: 1802-03

Worldly sorrows and pleasures are two sides of the same coin — attachment. The green garden of love is not of duality and conflict, nor of attachments to the projections of the ego, but a garden of eternal greenery and oneness.

Here is another invitation to explore the vast garden hidden in our heart:

The heart is an inner garden; its trees are hidden.
It displays a hundred scenes, but it is one and the same ground.
The heart is like an ocean all around us – with no shores, no bounds.
Each wave creates a hundred waves inside the heart.

Divân: Quatrain 1429

The world flows like a river, but we should not forget its and our eternal source:

Remember this:
The temporal world is a fanciful painting;
    but our true face lies outside of it.
Like a great river, the world is flowing.
And we are standing on the river bank.
What we see on the river are shadows cast by us.

Divân: 3908-10

When I first came across this poem, I was struck by its utter simplicity as well as its deep mystery. It is not hard to remember these few lines; the expression is clear. When we meditate on this poem in various situations in life, each time it spontaneously turns our mind to a great truth: The world flows ceaselessly; we should not take our shadows and images as absolute realities. In this manner, the poem acts like a mental compass to orient us: We have a true face that is unborn and never dies; the faces and images we see in this passing world are like shadows; always remember your true face. This view liberates us from the fantasies and frustrations of the mind, and elevates our daily life to a higher vantage point, where we become more compassionate toward ourselves as well as the world we live in:

In this earth,
in this soil,
in this pure field,
let us not plant any seeds
Other than the seeds of compassion and love.

Divân: 15558

Farmers would better appreciate this poem for they live in an intimate relationship with the soil, water and plants, and they know from experience that we reap what we sow. Compassion is the metabolism of the spiritual body. Rumi says that each one of us is like a farmer in this life and world; let us plant seeds of love and compassion, and create a garden of joy, peace, and goodness for all.

Meditations on Silence

Ulfat Isfahâni, a Persian Sufi scholar of the early twentieth century, noticed that Rumi often used the word *Khamoosh* ("Silent") in the last line of his lyrical odes; he thus suggested that "Silent" was Rumi's pen-name. His idea was corroborated by Badi uz-Zamân Foruzânfar, the former professor of Persian literature at Tehran University, in his classic biography of Rumi.[3] For Rumi, who composed 70,000 verses in the last three decades of his life, the pen-name "Silent" may seem an odd association. But, in fact, silence was the alpha and the omega of his poetry. Rumi's words came from a silent, unseen realm; therefore, his words take us to a realm beyond words. This is meditation at its peak: Silence as inner calmness and pure consciousness expresses the unspeakable. In some of his poems, Rumi characterizes silence in ways that describe his own experience with silence. The following are some examples.

In silence you hear the secrets:

Be silent! Say no more words!
Do not cause fervor and anxiety.
For the Realm of the Unseen
calls out to those souls matured in silence.   *Divân*: 911

In silence you can be a witness of God's light:

In silence, the Sun shines naked – without a veil.
Be silent, for speech is the veil.   *Divân*: 9102

Silence is the prime mover of this world:

Be silent for it is the Silent World
that has caused this World of Sounds.   *Divân:* 1429

Silence is sweet; poetry is an indication of it:

Be silent!
For silence is sweeter than eating honey.
Set fire to words!
Leave only an indication.   *Divân:* 876

* * *

Good poems are always fresh and insightful. Or as Rumi says, "*A poem is like a boat sailing through an ocean of meanings*" (*Divân:* 15985). Rarely a day passes that I do not read a few lines from Rumi, and no matter how many times I read and contemplate any of his poems, I gain something new. His poems are highly meditative and soul nourishing. What exactly is meditation? In his classic book *How to Meditate*, Lawrence LeShan writes that a very satisfactory definition of meditation that he once heard was that "it's like coming home."[4] This is so true. Whenever I read Rumi, it is like a homecoming. And when I am distracted by chores, I start to miss his vast vision and healing words. And this too he knew:

Didn't I say:
    Don't go there; I am the friend who knows you.
    And in this mirage of the world, I am your river of life?
Didn't I say:
    I am the sea, and you are a small fish;
    don't jump onto dry land; I am your sea of comfort?
   Divân: 18057-60

This chapter is largely based on the following two articles: (1) "Rumi's Poetry and Meditative Life: The 800th Anniversary," *Edge Life: A Holistic Journal* (Ramsey, MN), December 2007, p. 15. (2) "Rumi: Poems as Meditation," *Vision: Catalyst for Conscious Living* (San Diego, CA), October 2007, p. 16 & 50.

[16]
Rumi Comes to America

"One can live in the heart. Rumi's odes speak from there and invite us in as though to a galactic residence of interiority. I felt drawn to the vast beauty of that."

Coleman Barks[1]

Three decades ago, few people in the English-speaking world had heard of Rumi, but today Rumi is an icon for poetry of love, world peace, and spiritual life. According to various sources, including *The Christian Science Monitor*,[2] *Time Asia magazine*,[3] the US Department of State's *Washington File*,[4] eminent scholar of religion Huston Smith,[5] and renowned American TV journalist Bill Moyers,[6] Rumi has become one of the most-read and best-selling poets in North America. His poems and portraits are also found on commercial objects – calendars, journals, playing cards, coffee mugs, and T-shirts. Recitations of Rumi's poems, often with music and whirling dance, are popular events. A 1998 CD-recording of Rumi's poems, *A Gift of Love*, by Deepak Chopra and Madonna has been a best-seller. Coleman Barks' versions of Rumi, including *The Essential Rumi* (1995), have sold over half a million copies. An anthology of *Rumi Poems* (edited by Peter Washington, 2006) has been included in the prestigious Everyman Library series. Why has Rumi become so popular in the Western world, particularly in the USA? This chapters explores this question.

Cambridge Professors

Rumi's popularity would not have surprised the three Cambridge professors who first introduced Rumi and his works to the English-speaking world:

Edward G. Browne (1862-1926), Reynold A. Nicholson (1868-1945), and Arthur J. Arberry (1905-1969). According to Browne, Rumi is "without a doubt the most eminent Sufi poet whom Persia has produced, while his mystical *Mathnawi* deserves to rank amongst the great poems of all time."[7] Nicholson, who edited an authoritative version of Rumi's *Masnavi-ye Ma'navi* and translated all of its six volumes into English, also called Rumi "the greatest mystical poet of Persia."[8] Arberry remarked, "In Rumi the Persian mystical genius found its supreme expression. Viewing the vast landscape of Sufi poetry, we see him standing out as a sublime mountain-peak; the many other poets before and after him are but foot-hills in comparison … To the West, now slowly realizing the magnitude of his genius, … he is fully able to prove a source of inspiration and delight not surpassed by any other poet in the world's literature."[9] Elsewhere, Arberry wrote, "Rumi has long been recognized as the greatest mystical poet of Islam, and it can well be argued that he is the supreme mystical poet of all mankind."[10]

Poetry and Spirituality

Rumi was a prolific poet. He composed about 26,000 lines in the *Masnavi-ye Ma'navi* ("spiritual couplets") and 44,000 lines of lyrical odes (*ghazaliyât*) and quatrains (*rubâiyât*) in the *Divân-e Shams-e Tabrizi* (also called the *Divân-e Kabir*). However, Rumi was not a poet by profession; he was a Muslim teacher and Sufi master. He excelled in both spiritual life and poetry, and composed his poems out of ecstasy, often in *samâ* (music and dancing) or during contemplation and public talks. That is why Rumi attracts people who love poetry as well those who are hungry for spiritual teachings. Phyllis Tickle, a contributing editor to *Publishing Weekly*, explains why Rumi's poetry is popular: "It's a matter of our enormous hunger. It's also just beautiful poetry."[2]

In the history of Persian literature over the past twelve hundred years, the Sufi path and poetry have gone hand in hand.[11] The American poet and translator Robert Bly believes that this combination of poetry and spirituality was also once prevalent among the Gnostics in the Christian tradition, but they were discredited as heretics by the Christian church; so Rumi is filling this vacuum.[2, 12] Daniel Ladinsky, a South Carolina poet who is fascinated by the Persian Sufi poets Hâfez and Rumi, opines that "my experience of a poet-saint is that they affect the deepest regions of one's intelligence and heart," and that these poets address our "profound need to make sense out of God. I simply want to get along with the One I have to live with.''"2

Coleman Barks, who was pleasantly surprised by the sudden popularity of Rumi, highlights the spiritual dimension of Rumi's poetry and its implication for modern life: "Rumi celebrates the Presence, he calls it the Friend or the Beloved, that we sense in the beauty outside of us on a rainy day, or in a group of friends fixing food, a horse being saddled, or a child sleeping. All of these things that are obviously beautiful outside of us also touch the beauty inside of us – that jewel-like inner presence that he activates in his poetry."2 Elsewhere he writes, "I don't know why Rumi is so popular in the West now, but I feel it has to do with soul … I can only hope that American culture is beginning to assimilate Rumi's great opening heart, his playfulness, his tremendous grief, and the courage he has to live in pure absence."12

Kabir Helminski, a teacher and translator of Rumi's works, points out three spiritual components in Rumi's poetry that appeal to the Western readers: (1) Rumi is a universal voice calling to us from beyond the concerns of conventional religiosity and limiting beliefs; (2) in Rumi's poetry the boundary between Divine and human love is left ambiguous and thus permeable; (3) the modern world is thirsty for the spiritual ecstasy and joy that are so prevalent in Rumi's poetry.13

The Aesthetics of Imagery in Rumi's Poetry

Rumi's poems in Persian are hugely musical; they are verses rich in rhymes and rhythms. But these characteristics cannot be translated into other languages (just as the rhymes and internal music of Shakespeare's verses cannot be exactly translated into Persian or other languages). Instead, it is the beauty, elegance, and power of images and meanings in Rumi's poetry that attract his English readers.

The visual language and colorful imagery in Rumi's poetry has been discussed by several authors[14] although much work still needs to be done in this field. Perhaps a quotation suffices here. The Iranian scholar Ali Dashti writes that "[Rumi's] *Divân-e Shams* is like an ocean; its calmness is beautiful and its turbulence is ecstatic. Like the ocean, it is full of waves, froth, and storm. Like the ocean, it displays diverse and fresh colors – green, blue, purple, and azure. Like the ocean, it is a mirror reflecting the sky, the stars, sunshine and moonlight; it creates designs of sunrise and sunset. Like the ocean, it is full of motion and life, and under its seemingly calm and clear surface a dynamic and turbulent world lies to be encountered."[15]

Poetry of Love and Transcendence

"Sufism," as the Sufi teacher Javâd Nurbakhsh notes, "is a way to God through love (*eshg*)."[16] And Rumi is undoubtedly one of the world's greatest poets who has expressed the path of love to God – a path that passes through the heart and encompasses the whole of creation and human life. Rumi addresses God not as a distant creator but as our Beloved, Friend, and Heart.

For Rumi, love is not an abstract subject for poetry or philosophy; love is an intimate experience. That is why Rumi's readers can relate his poems to their own lives and psychology. In a preface to *Rumi the Persian* (1965), the American social psychologist Erich Fromm comments, "Rumi was not only a great poet and a mystic and the founder of a religious order; he was a man of profound insight into the nature of man." Reza Arasteh, an Iranian psychologist and the author of *Rumi the Persian*, concludes, "According to Rumi, love is an elixir which transforms all negative feelings, emotional handicaps, and differences into a healthy attitude. To him thinking and reasoning are definite, while life and expression possess indefinite qualities – the characteristics of love alone."[17]

Love in Rumi's perspective is a Divine emanation that manifests itself in various spiritual qualities including beauty (*husn* or *jamâl*), loving-kindness (*muhabbat*), compassion (*mehr*), goodness (*neekee*), friendship (*doosti* or *yâri*), longing (*esh'tiyâg*), and ecstasy (*wajd* or *shoor*). Love is sourced in the Divine and the place of love is place-less (*la-makân*) and metaphysical. Nevertheless, we can experience love by a faculty we call the heart (*del* or *qalb*), which is the ultimate core of our humanness. That is why love has the power to transcend all religions, lands and languages; and yet (if we look closely) it encompasses all of them as well. Love is not limited to a single culture, but is contained in the foundation and fabric of all cultures.

Professor Carl Ernst of the University of North Carolina says, "[Rumi] is such a spokesman for freedom and transcendence that people have found him to be a great literary voice for centuries."[2] Professor William Chittick of Stony Brook University explains Rumi's success in the West in these words: "He brings out what he calls 'the roots of the roots of the roots of the religion,' or the most essential message of Islam, which is the most essential message of traditional religion everywhere: Human beings were born for unlimited freedom and infinite bliss, and their birthright is within their grasp. But in order to reach it, they must surrender to love. What makes Rumi's expression of this message different from other expressions is his extraordinary directness and uncanny ability to employ images drawn from everyday life."[18]

Coleman Barks: Rumi in the Free Verse

Translations of Rumi's poems into English date back to the late nineteenth century, for example E. H. Whinfield's translation of the *Masnavi* (1887) and R. A. Nicholson's *Selected Poems from the Divân-i Shams-i Tabrizi* (1898). In the first half of the twentieth century, Nicholson and Arberry produced the bulk of Rumi translations. Their works were literal and scholarly, and sometimes even in English verse. Nicholson's and Arberry's translations drew attention largely from students of Persian literature or Sufism, and are still very useful to the serious readers of Rumi. What triggered Rumi-mania in North America were free-verse translations of Rumi's poetry, and Coleman Barks is undoubtedly the pioneer of this Rumi movement. "The secret of Rumi's popularity in the United States is Coleman Barks," says James Fadiman, an American scholar. "The publication of Barks' 1995 volume, *The Essential Rumi*, more than any other event, sparked America's interest in the great Persian-language poet."[4] Blurbs and praise for *The Essential Rumi* have come from several eminent scholars of religion – Huston Smith, Seyyed Hossein Nasr, Jack Kornfield, Ram Das, Jay Kinney, and Jacob Needleman. "If Rumi is the most-read poet in America today," writes Huston Smith, "Coleman Barks is in good part responsible. His ear for the truly divine madness in Rumi's poetry is truly remarkable."

Barks was born in Tennessee in 1937 and educated at the University of North Carolina and the University of California at Berkeley. He is a retired professor of poetry and creative writing from the University of Georgia in Atlanta. He lives in Athens, Georgia, and has published about two dozen books of Rumi's poetry, often in collaboration with John Moyne, an Iranian-American professor of linguistics, who supplied Barks with literal translations of Rumi's poems. Barks has also re-worked Nicholson's and Arberry's literal translations. Barks does not know Persian; nonetheless, his modern translations and recitations have drawn a large readership for Rumi. He was awarded an honorary doctorate in Persian literature from the University of Tehran in 2006. Barks has documented his travel to Iran in the *Rumi: Bridge to the Soul*, which was published to commemorate Rumi's 800th birthday.

Other than Barks, several individuals have greatly contributed to the recent translation or popularization of Rumi's poetry in modern English, including the following:

(1) Kabir and Camille Helminski, an American couple, Sufi scholars, and founders of the Threshold Society in the tradition of Mevlevi Order. *The Pocket Rumi Reader* (2001), *The Rumi Collection* (2005), and *The Rumi Daybook* (2011) are among their works.

(2) Nevit Ergin (1928-2015), a native of Turkey and a retired plastic surgeon who, from his base in California, translated the entire *Divân-e Kabir* in twenty two volumes from Abdulbâki Gölpinârli's Turkish translation published in 1957-58.

(3) Andrew Harvey, British author of *Teachings of Rumi* (1999) and *The Way of Passion: A Celebration of Rumi* (2000). Harvey lives in the USA.

(4) Maryam Mafi, a London-based Iranian poet, who in collaboration with Azima Melita Kolin, has published several Rumi volumes, including *Whispers of the Beloved* (2000, republished as *Rumi's Little Book of the Heart*, 2016), *Hidden Music* (2002) and *Gardens of the Beloved* (2004, republished as *Rumi's Little Book of Love*, 2009).

(4) Shahram Shiva, a native of Iran, who lives in New York and conducts Rumi recitations. He has published two translations of Rumi: *Rending the Veil* (1995) and *Hush, Don't Say Anything to God* (1999).

(5) Nader Khalili (1936-2008), an Iranian architect who founded the California Institute of Earth Art and Architecture in California, and translated *Fountain of Fire* (1994) and *Dancing the Flame* (2001).

(6) Jonathan Starr, an American writer, who in collaboration with Shahram Shiva, has published *A Garden beyond Paradise* (1992) and *In the Arms of the Beloved* (1997).

The Future of Rumi in English

One Thousand and One Nights (*Arabian Nights*), *Rubaiyat of Omar Khayyam*, and Kahlil Gibran's *The Prophet* all captured Western attention and imagination when they first appeared in English. Is Rumi going to join this list or will Rumi-mania be extinguished soon? It is hard to predict, but a few points are noteworthy here. First, the above-mentioned books and certain other literary works from the Middle East have not only influenced Western literature but are still in print today. Rumi has already become part of English and American literature, and will continue to remain so. Moreover, Rumi's poetry offers a more comprehensive set of teachings and thoughts; Rumi has a better chance of survival in public literature. Indeed, not all of Rumi's works have been translated into English yet; there is still much room for new translation, interpretation, and popularization of Rumi's poetry and vision.

A more serious question concerns the quality of popular translations of Rumi's poetry. How to make Rumi accessible and comprehensible to Western readers, and yet to retain the intent, meaning, and imagery of Rumi's poetry? Of course, it is impossible to translate poetry exactly (maintaining its music, metaphor, and meaning) into another language, and I agree that free-verse translations make Rumi more accessible to people. However, it is concerning that the relentless re-creation of Rumi's poems could easily result in the translator's own work published under the name of Rumi. In this way, Rumi's own poetry would be lost or diluted by the translator's selection, interpretation, and distortion. Of course, it is justifiable for a poet to be inspired by Rumi (or other poets) and to compose similar poems, but it would be unfair to publish these "inspired" poems as "translated" Rumi poems. (There is a Hemingway Imitation short story writing contest, but those stories are never attributed to Hemingway.) So, Rumi's presence in English literature and public imagination will be deep and long lasting, but how much of that is the real Rumi will depend on the quality of translations and the responsibility of Rumi's translators.

In Persian literature, Rumi is one of the top five poets of all time. Indeed, there is a famous saying that Rumi's *Masnavi* is the *Quran* in the Persian tongue.[19] Back in 1976, when Robert Bly first suggested that Coleman Barks re-translate Rumi, he told Barks, "These poems need to be released from their cages."[20] Now that Rumi's poems are being released into the sky of English literature, it is completely fathomable that Rumi should last for centuries in English (or in other languages for that matter) as he has survived in Persian literature for centuries (and note that Persian literature with a long history and hundreds of poets is very competitive). Of course, we need more translators to bring out the various dimensions, depths and layers of Rumi's poetry, message, and imagery.

Rumi's relevance to our age and world is even more urgent. Coleman Barks writes, "Because of the troubles we're living in, I want to call attention again to Rumi's role as a bridge between religions and cultures."[1] In 2007, when UNESCO issued a medal to commemorate Rumi's 800th birthday, this international organization also released a statement; the following excerpts from UNESCO's statement perhaps summarize why Rumi is so popular in our age: "In their passion, honesty, and gorgeous imagery, the writings of Mawlana have become a means of connecting directly with the Divine ... He offends no one and includes everyone, as a perfect human being who is in search of love, truth and the unity of the human soul ... Let us therefore honour Mawlana Jalal-ud Din Balkhi-Rumi, one of the great humanists, philosophers and poets who belong to humanity in its entirety."[21]

This chapter is based on the following articles:
"Moulana Rumi: The Most Popular Poet in America," *Sufi*, Summer 2007, pp. 34-39.
"Why is Rumi America's Popular Poet? On the Occasion of the 800th Anniversary of Rumi's Birth" [in Persian], *Rahavard: A Persian Journal*, Summer 2007 (No. 79), pp. 53-60.

[17]
Why is Rumi a Best-selling Poet in America?

"Rumi saw the world in new light: everywhere he detected a trace of God's Grandeur and His Grace, listening to the praise of everything created; and he reminded his followers in unforgettable verses that true life is possible only by surrendering to love."

Annemarie Schimmel[1]

In 1968, a year before he died, Arthur Arberry, a professor at Cambridge University and one of the most authoritative Rumi scholars wrote, "Future generations, as his [Rumi's] poetry becomes wider known and more perfectly understood, will enjoy and applaud with increasing insight and enthusiasm the poems of this wisest, most penetrating, and saintliest of men."[2] Arberry's prophecy has been fulfilled. Anthologies of Rumi's poetry are now among the best-selling poetry books in English, and major bookstores carry volumes of Rumi's poetry on a continual basis. The popularity of Rumi's poetry in North America has also been noted by the mass media. For instance, *The Guardian*, *Huffington Post* online, and BBC have each published several articles on Rumi. Some of the articles on Rumi are titled: "Persian Poet Top Seller in America" (*The Christian Science Monitor*, November 25, 1997), "The Mysterious Hold of a 13th Century Mystic" (*Los Angeles Times*, June 18, 1998), "Rumi Rules!" (*TIME Asia Magazine*, October 7, 2002), "Persian Poet Rumi Conquers America" (US State Department's *Washington File*, March 15, 2005), "Can Rumi Save Us Now?" (*San Francisco Chronicle*, April 1, 2007).

While there are numerous English anthologies of Rumi's poems on the market and several books discuss his life and works,[3] relatively less research has been done to analyze the reasons for the recent popularity of Rumi in the West. This subject is part of a larger discourse: How can the Eastern literature of ancient and medieval times be of any help or relevance to people living in twenty-first century Western civilization? Here I discuss how a combination of several factors have made Rumi an influential voice and a popular poet in North America. I hope that this analysis also underscores the vital role that classic literature and ancient wisdom play in the well-being of our life and culture.

The Power of Translation

Sir William Jones (1746-1794), the British father of Orientalism and founder of the Asiatic Society of Bengal in India, was an expert in Persian and Arabic literature. In 1794, he published an article in the *Asiatick Researches* which included the opening lines of Rumi's *Masnavi*, the lament of the reed-flute. In the nineteenth century, European travelers, diplomats, and scholars learned about Rumi's poetry and his Sufi Order (the Whirling Dervishes) and were impressed by the vision of this thirteenth-century mystic. Joseph von Hammer-Purgstall (1774-1856), an Austrian diplomat and scholar, translated some of Rumi's poems into German, and included them in his 1818 book on Persian literature. His student Friederich Ruckert (1788-1866) also translated some of Rumi's poems in a volume published in 1821. These German translations of Rumi won high praise from eminent intellectuals like Hegel and Goethe in Germany and Ralph Waldo Emerson in the US. John Porter Brown, an American diplomat in Constantinople, published the first detailed book on the Sufi teachings of Rumi, *The Dervishes, or Oriental Spiritualism*, in 1868.

Concentrated efforts on English translations of Rumi's poems were made in the late-nineteenth and early-twentieth centuries by several British scholars. Sir James William Redhouse (1811-1892) translated the first book of the *Masnavi* together with selected stories ("The Acts of the Adepts") about Rumi's life from Aflâki's *Manâqeb al-Ârefin* (1881); the latter work was reprinted separately under the title *Legends of the Sufis* (London, 1976). Charles Edward Wilson, a professor of Persian literature at the universities of Cambridge and London, translated the second book of the *Masnavi* (1910). William Hastie (1842-1903), a Scottish clergyman and professor at Glasgow, published *The Festival of Spring from the Divan of Jelaleddin* (1903). Edward Henry Whinfield (1836-1922) translated selections from the six books of

Masnavi-ye Ma'navi (1887, second edition 1898), which was reprinted as *The Teachings of Rumi* (New York, 1973; London, 1994 with a preface by Idries Shah). Frederick Hadland Davis published a small but an influential volume, *The Persian Mystics: Jalaluddin Rumi* (1907), as part of the Wisdom of the East series. Edward Granville Browne (1862-1926) included an informative chapter on Rumi in his magnum opus, *A Literary History of Persia* (volume 2, 1906).

Browne's successors at the University of Cambridge – Reynold Alleyne Nicholson (1868-1945) and Arthur John Arberry (1905-1969) – were largely responsible for introducing Rumi and his works to the English-speaking world. Nicholson published the *Selected Poems from the Divani Shamsi Tabrizi* in 1898 which secured him a teaching position at Cambridge (this work is still in print). He then undertook the massive task of editing a reliable Persian edition of the *Masnavi* (from various manuscripts) as well as translating it into English with detailed notes and commentaries. This work, *The Mathnawi of Jalauddin Rumi*, was published in eight volumes in London from 1925-1940. Nicholson also published several works on Sufism, for example, *The Mystics of Islam* (1914), as well as selections from the *Masnavi*, the *Tales of Mystic Meaning* (1931) and *Rumi: Poet and Mystic* (1950); all of these works are still in print.

Arberry, who chronicled the British contributions to the study of Persian literature and Sufism in his *Oriental Essays: Portraits of Seven Scholars* (London, 1960), was a prolific writer and produced such influential works as the *Rubaiyat of Jalal ul-Din Rumi* (1949), *Classical Persian Literature* (1958, with a chapter on Rumi), *Discourses of Rumi* (1961), *Tales from the Masnavi* (1961), *More Tales from the Masnavi* (1963), *Mystical Poems of Rumi* (volume 1, 1968; volume 2, 1979). All of Arberry's works are still relevant and have been reprinted.

Nicholson and Arberry were path makers, and through their translations, they founded the cornerstone of our knowledge of Rumi in English. Nevertheless, their translations were largely literal and scholastic, which although suited the taste of Victorian and Edwardian English-speaking peoples, were not particularly popular in the second half of the twentieth century. In this manner, Rumi's works, for a long time, were largely confined to the circles of students of Persian literature or Sufism in the West.

Since the early 1980s, new efforts have been made to translate Rumi's poems into the modern style of free verse in English – similar to the poetry of Walt Whitman, Gary Snyder, Mary Oliver, and so on. Coleman Barks (born 1937), a retired professor of poetry and creative writing from University of Georgia, should be credited for pioneering this literary movement. Barks, who is himself a poet, has devoted his life to Rumi's poetry since the late 1970s and is now best known for his versions and recitations of Rumi's poetry. Barks has published dozens of books and audio-recordings of Rumi's poetry. He has often collaborated with John Moyne, an Iranian-American professor of linguistics, who provided Barks with literal translations of Rumi's poems; Barks has also re-translated Rumi from Nicholson's and Arberry's literal works. His anthologies of Rumi's poetry, such as *The Essential Rumi* (1995, 2004), *The Soul of Rumi* (2001) and *Rumi: The Big Red Book* (2010), have sold hundreds of thousands of copies, which is an admirable accomplishment for a poet.

The various translators of Rumi in our time may be categorized into three groups:

(1) Western translators who do not know Persian and thus rely on translations made by others; these include Coleman Barks, Robert Bly, Kabir and Camille Helminski, Nevit Ergin, Andrew Harvey, and Jonathan Starr, many of whom collaborate with Persian-speaking translators or work from Nicholson's and Arberry's translations. Harvey apparently uses French translations of Rumi, and Ergin's works are based on Turkish translations of Rumi's poetry.

(2) Persian-speaking translators who live in the Western world, such as Seyyed Hossein Nasr, Nader Khalili, Shahram Shiva, and Majid Naini in the USA, Maryam Mafi in London, and Leili Anvar in Paris.

(3) Western scholars who know both English and Persian, notably Annemarie Schimmel, William Chittick, Leonard Lewisohn, and Franklin Lewis, who are academic professors of Persian literature, as well as Ibrahim Gamard, a California-based psychologist and self-taught Rumi scholar.

Translations of Rumi's poetry come in various levels of quality and accuracy. Some of them are literal and academic; some are re-translations, inspired versions, or renditions of what Rumi originally composed, and some translations strike a balance between accuracy and accessibility.

Nonetheless, the plain, colloquial style of Rumi translations has undoubtedly contributed to the recent popularity of this poet in North America and Europe. This popularization is not without its critics who point out that some inaccurate, misinterpreted or modernized translations of Rumi's poetry have resulted in a fabricated Rumi, one who is uprooted from his historical, cultural and spiritual environment. While this can be true for certain versions of Rumi, devoted readers of Rumi eventually uncover the depth and truth of Rumi's words and vision no matter how they are first introduced to Rumi. A hidden treasure is not cherished until it is discovered, and this is what free-verse versions of Rumi have done: They have offered some flavor and essence of his poetry. Of course, more work is needed in this genre.

Rumi's Integral Personality

Rumi's thoughts and message are of course products of Rumi's own personality. He integrated in his person and life three important aspects: Philosophical learning, spiritual practice, and poetic skills. All of them to a high degree of refinement.[3]

Rumi was a Muslim preacher, jurist, and scholar (*âlem* in Arabic and Persian) who studied under his father, Bahâ ud-Din Valad (himself a learned Muslim preacher), his tutor Burhân ud-Din Termezi in Balkh and Konya, as well as other distinguished scholars in Damascus and Aleppo. Rumi was also a man of faith, piety, and spiritual practice; he prayed, contemplated, fasted, and was involved in Sufi music and meditation. He was immersed in poetry, both Persian (in particular, the poetry of Sanâ'ie and Attâr) and Arabic (notably al-Mutanabbi). Indeed, among Persians, Rumi is not merely known as a "poet" (*shâ'er*) but also a mystic and sage (*âref*). That is why his poetry is able to express deep philosophical insights, meditative moods, and a compassionate spirit in elegant, ecstatic words.

The Power of Rumi's Poetry

Rumi's poetry was embedded in the rich tradition of Persian literature. And he himself also possessed a rich inner reservoir. Remarkably, Rumi did not write down his poems so he that could revise them later as poets and writers usually do; he recited his poems to his disciples when he was teaching, contemplating, walking, dancing or listening to music. For Rumi, his poems were ecstatic prayers, and he composed them spontaneously. He was (as he himself says) a reed-flute on God's lips.

Rumi's poetic expressions are immensely attractive and beautiful even when his poems, which are densely musical in the original Persian, are translated into other languages. This is because of the vivid imagery and deep meanings contained in his poems. Consider, for instance, the very opening lines of his *Masnavi* (I: 1-4):

Listen to this reed-flute,
how it complains, telling the tale of all separations:
Ever since I was cut from the reed-bed,
men and women have cried in my lament.
I seek out a heart that, having been separated,
*   is shred into pieces;*
only then can I describe the pain of longing.
Whoever has gone far from his origin,
seeks to return to the days of his union.

In this poem, Rumi likens the lover to a reed-flute (*ney*), which is cut from the reed-bed and wishes to return home and to the beloved; therefore, it goes on crying and singing on the lips of people who blow into it. These laments of separation and longing also express the feelings of those who play the reed-flute. The flute sings the soul's nostalgia. At the same time, the reed-flute is a symbol of the "perfect human" (*insân-e kâmil* in Sufi terminology) or even Rumi himself, who realized his true home and beloved but thus awakens and inspires others through his music and poetry.

These opening lines from the *Masnavi* impressed the young Annmarie Schimmel so much that she decided to study Rumi, and became one of the most eminent Rumi scholars of our time. "I remember very well," Schimmel writes, "it was in Berlin in the fall of 1940 – how my revered teacher Hans Heinrich Schader recited to us students the first lines of the Masnavi: Bi-shnau az nay chun hikayat mikunad … (Listen to the reed as it tells and complains of separation …). This was the moment when I decided to study Rumi seriously."[4]

Rumi employs a vast and diverse array of elements in his poetry – animals, birds, flowers, fruits, body organs, human emotions, stars, seasons, and features of the earth, sky and ocean, and so forth. All of these elements take life in his poetry, and as metaphors and symbols they convey profound meanings to the reader. The following is an example (*Divân*: 31168-69)

If you build a house for the chickens in your backyard,
you cannot put a tall camel in it.
The chicken is your small reasoning;
the house is your living body;
and the camel is your beautiful love – grand and exalted.

The richness of Rumi's language is also partly related to the variety of poetic forms he used so skillfully. In the *Divân-e Shams*, which contains his sonnets as well as short quatrains, his language is passionate and visionary with colorful imagery, lofty ideas, and deep meanings. In these poems, Rumi sounds like a mighty river entering an ocean. In the *Masnavi*, which includes hundreds of parables and tales composed in verse, his language is often didactic and wise, yet charming with bursts of turbulent passion here and there. In this book, we encounter a Sun showering rays of light and warmth.

The Sufi Path of Love

There have been mystics and pious sages full of insight and Divine compassion, but they did not possess the passionate tongue of a poet; and there have been poets who have composed passionate poems about their beloved women and men, but they did not have the eyes of a mystic. Rumi integrates wisdom with love, and Divine love with daily life. He was rooted in the Sufi tradition which is essentially the path (*tarigat*) of Divine love (*eshg*). Jesus emphasized that God is love; Rumi's poetry reports on his love affair with God. To Rumi, God is not an aloof heavenly grandpa, but a beloved and intimate friend (*doost, yâr*) here on earth, in this life, and within our heart:

Oh, those who have gone on a pilgrimage to Mecca,
   where have you departed to?
The Beloved is right here. Come here, come back.   *Divân*: 6762

Rumi's poetry of love is an expression of his realization of Divine love. Rumi extends this Divine love, or what he calls *eshg-e hagigi*, "the true source of love," to all of creation, and views human love as a reflection of the Divine; he calls it *eshg-e majâzi*, "love derived from the source." He carries this even further and says that love is the very foundation, fabric, and engine of the universe:

If the Sky were not in love,
    its chest would not be pleasant.
If the Sun were not in love,
    its face would not be bright.
If the Earth and mountains were not in love,
    no plant could sprout from their heart.
If the Sea were not aware of love,
    it would have remained motionless somewhere.   *Divân:* 28369-72

Rumi's poems resonate with his readers because his constituency is the human heart and because he does not draw a rigid boundary between the "religious" love (from God or for God) and the "secular" human love for other humans or nature. The source of heart-felt love is one and the same. As long as our relationship has sincerity, devotion, compassion, joy, and goodness, it is true love.

In fact, for Rumi love is the very essence of being religious, and as such the all-inclusive love is older than all historical religions:

The religion of love is separate from all religions:
For lovers, God is their very religion and nation.   *Masnavi,* II: 1770

Your reasoning mind is not awake.
That is why it is puzzled by the religion of love,
even though you may have studied all religions.   *Divân:* 2610

Indeed, Rumi seems to evaluate the success, richness, and validity of a religious tradition to the degree that it walks on the path of love and how much it kindles love in the heart and life of humanity.

Vast Vision and Peaceful Mind

As we read Rumi more and more, we discover a vast vision, serenity, and a peaceful mind. In his poetry, we gain a glimpse of a pure, beautiful, perfect, and unified world beyond mundane life, beyond heaven and hell, beyond evil and righteousness, beyond attachments and judgments, beyond profits and losses, and beyond suffering and lust. The Iranian scholar Ali Dashti once remarked, "When I delve into the *Divân-e Shams*, it is like orbiting around a distant star and journeying in a world nobler, more inclusive, and more expansive than the atmosphere of this earthly world. In that world, the stars are like living beings talking to you. One gets closer to an eternal and all-inclusive spirit pulsating in the infinite space."[5]

The Indian expression of *Mahatma* ("Great Spirit") for the late Mohandas Gandhi is equally applicable to Rumi: He is inclusive, vast, compassionate, and welcoming. The following poem inscribed at his mausoleum has been frequently cited by many writers and travelers:

Come here, come again, whatever you are:
A non-believer or an idle-worshipper, come again!
Ours is not a house of despair.
Even if you have broken your repentance a hundred times,
Come here, come again![6]

Such capacity and welcoming spirit is of course a fruit of Rumi's journey on the path of love. It is also intimately related to a spiritual experience that Sufis call *fanâ*, "extinction" of the ego (*nafs*) and its attachments and judgements (akin to the Buddhist concept of *nirvâna*). This transcendence takes the wayfarer beyond names and labels, hostility and dualistic views. The mystic thus looks upon the myriad creation of God as droplets of one infinite ocean or rays of light emanating from one Sun. Rumi says:

All images and phenomena are reflections on the stream water.
When you rub your eyes and look well, all that exists is That One.

Masnavi, VI: 3183

There is a famous story in the *Masnavi* (II: 3681-3691) that explains, at least partly, why the world and human life are destroyed by the "wars of seventy-two nations and religions." Four travelers were given a single silver coin to purchase food on their journey. Speaking different languages, they started arguing over what they should buy. The Persian desired "angoor", the Turk "uzoom", the Arab "enab", and the Greek "stafil." They started to quarrel. A learned man, who knew their languages, told them that what they all desired was one and the same thing – grapes. Rumi thus draws our attention to the root of our petty conflicts: First we are selfish, and second ignorant (or vice-versa).

When egoistic desires and their associated sufferings cease, the individual merges with the All and finds peace; it is like a drop of water that flows into the ocean and rests in the bosom of All water. Rumi's words, like a compass, tune us with a unified field and an eternal source of energy; as a result, dualistic divisions and illusions collapse, and myriad forms of creation become our partners and friends. In this journey, transcendence and peace go hand in hand.

Violence is not a healthy state of being; war is a dis-ease. When a person is at ease with himself or herself, with nature, with life, with God, he or she is peaceful and happy, not violent or hysteric. The same is true for social groups. Rumi's poetry offers us peace – inwardly in our own life, and outwardly in society.

Positive Attitude and Joyful Poetry

For Rumi, Sufism or spirituality means the purity, love, and illumination of the heart; it does not mean asceticism or life-negation as some Sufis and monks have practiced. Rumi did not abandon his family, work, and society in order to save his own soul for the merits and benefits of an after-life. Rumi wants people to be in love and rejoice in this very life:

Life must be spent in love.
The dead are not supposed to do that.
Do you know who is alive?
The one who is regenerated every moment in love.   Divân: 8824

Rumi loved music and dance (*samâ* in the Sufi tradition), he appreciated friendship, and he loved to serve people; these were like acts of worship for him. He was in love with all of God's creation. That is why his poetry celebrates life and permeates a sense of immense joy and a positive attitude toward life. Even when Rumi criticizes "the mundane, earthly, perishable world", he does so because he feels that human life is too precious to be wasted by selfishness, greed, conflicts, bloodshed, materialistic energy, and suffering; Rumi wants us to fly higher:

People are deceived and derided by their thoughts.
That is why they are occupied by sorrows,
and their hearts are in pain.
When one is like a high-flying bird,
the small flies of thought do not reach him.　　　　　Masnavi, II: 3559-61

Despite problems and difficulties, Rumi does not subscribe to a life of gloom and doom. He believes in love and light. He also maintains hope: "*Only the person who seeks the flame, finds light.*" (*Masnavi*, III: 3090) In the *Fihi Mâ Fih* (discourse 2), he says: "*Never lose your hope of God. Hope is the entry point for salvation. Even if you are not walking on the path, keep the road entrance open.*"

The Fertile Soil of the Western World

Finally, one should also recognize the present social conditions of the Western world, in which Rumi has become popular. Materialism has dominated our modern lifestyle and society. People are, however, thirsty for a sense of sacredness, inner certainty, balance, healing, and meaning in their lives. In this regard, Rumi's spiritual poetry and insights are helpful and inspirational. Rumi's readers are seekers of spiritual living, love and peace; they feel suffocated in the materialistic, conflict-driven and meaningless life style. Moreover, Western countries enjoy a high degree of democracy and social freedoms, including the freedom of expression, which allow diverse thoughts, arts and books, including Rumi's, to take roots and grow. In contrast, in many parts of the Muslim world, where Rumi comes from, totalitarian ruling, religious fanaticism, and lack of freedom of expression pose restrictions to the teachings of Rumi and other Sufi masters. So the fertile soil of the West is as much responsible for Rumi's popularity as is his poetry. Human rights and freedoms are crucial not only for scientific and technological progress but also social and cultural development.

The Poet Builds a Stream that Flows through the Future

I have discussed several factors that explain the recent popularity of Rumi's poetry in North America and other English-speaking countries. Of these, two factors are external; namely, the free-verse translations of Rumi's poetry, and the particular circumstances in today's Western societies. The other five factors, including Rumi's holistic personality, the elegance of his poetic imagery, his call to the path of love, his spirit of inclusiveness and peace, and his positive, joyful attitude toward life, are all internal and related to the content of his poetry.

Rumi is popular today for the same reasons he was adored and respected during his life time in Konya. When he died on December 17, 1273, people of all faiths, races, and languages in Konya attended his funeral to pay respect to a great soul they felt privileged to have known. Ahmad Aflâki, who compiled Rumi's biography shortly after his death, writes that the Jews loved Rumi because he showed the truth of Moses' teachings to them, the Christians because he taught Jesus' path of love, and the Muslims because he exemplified their religion. Aflâki also quotes a man who came to Rumi's funeral, "Master Rumi was a Sun of truth shining upon all humans, and everybody of course likes sunshine." And a Greek Christian priest said, "Master Rumi is like daily bread and everybody likes to eat it."[7] Rumi's poetry is simply a delicious spiritual food, cooked with love.

Did Rumi, who lived in an age without the printing industry and mass media as we have today, foresee the value of his work for future generations? The following lines from Rumi provide an answer: *"The poet digs a creek in the ground in order to send water to the following ages. Although every age has its own poets and messengers, the words of the by-gone teachers are also helpful."* (*Masnavi*, III, 2537-38). Sometime ago, I was talking with a publisher about Rumi, and he remarked that Rumi has come to America seven centuries after his death, but he is here to stay; now he is an American poet too. This elegantly sums up the value of literary and spiritual heritage of the past, no matter Western or Eastern, for our modern world.

Rumi is an ocean of insightful teachings and healing words. He is more a poet of the future. "In Rumi," Arberry once remarked, "We encounter one of the world's greatest poets. In profundity of thought, inventiveness of image, and triumphant mastery of language, he stands out as the supreme genius of Islamic mysticism. He invites and deserves the most attentive and intensive study, by a succession of devoted scholars, whose combined explorations will vastly improve upon our first halting attempt."[2] Another devotee of Rumi, Annmarie Schimmel, once said, "I can say that for the better part of my life Mawlana Rumi has been my companion, protector, guide, and much more for me. And yet, after reading and rereading his works, after studying the *Divan-i Shams* and the *Masnavi* time and time again, after having translated ever so many of his verses, whenever I come back to him I find new questions, new problems, new ideas."[8]

Parts of this chapter were published in the following journals:
"Why is Moulana Rumi the Best-Selling Poet in America," *Persian Heritage Monthly*, May 2007, English section, p. 1.
"Why is Mawlana Rumi Popular in America?" *Rahavrd: A Persian Journal*, Summer and Autumn 2010 (Nos. 91-92), pp. E37-E45.
"Why is Rumi Popular in America? Eastern Spiritual Literature in the Modern Culture," *Tiferet: A Journal of Spiritual Literature*, No. 17, 2011, pp. 75-81.

[18]
Book Reviews

This chapter includes several Rumi-related book reviews which I wrote for various journals and magazines over the years. They are included here not only to introduce these interesting books but also to enhance the information and discussions presented in the other chapters of this volume. I have slightly revised these book reviews, adding new information or correcting some errors, to better fit in the present volume.

The Garden of Truth

The Garden of Truth: The Vision and Promise of Sufism, Islam's Mystical Tradition by Seyyed Hossein Nasr (HarperCollins Publishers, New York, 2007, Pp. 274).

First published in *Interreligious Insight*, April 2008, pp. 90-91.

This new book on Sufism or Islamic mysticism is a worthy addition to such classic works in this genre as Reynold Nicholson's *The Mystics of Islam* (1914, 1963), Arthur J. Arberry's *Sufism: An Account of the Mystics of Islam* (1950, 1979), Idries Shah's *The Sufis* (1964), Martin Lings' *What is Sufism?* (1975), Annemarie Schimmels' *Mystical Dimensions of Islam* (1975), Titus Burckhardt's *An Introduction to Sufi Doctrine* (1976), and Carl Esin's *The Shambhala Guide to Sufism* (1997). Written by Dr. Seyyed Hossein Nasr, one of the preeminent Islamic and Iranian scholars of our time (a professor at George Washington University since 1984), the book introduces the teachings and the development of Sufism in a lucid language understandable to the general public. Previously, I had read several books of Professor Nasr both in English and in Persian (his native language) and learned immensely from them, but what sets this book apart is the author's direct talk from his heart, rather than merely from a scholastic standpoint; he addresses the readers who want to understand the essence of Sufi teachings regarding the big questions – "Who we are, where we came from, what we are doing here, and where we are going."

The book contains six chapters: (i) What it means to be human?; (ii) Truth; (iii) Love and beauty; (iv) Goodness and human action; (v) How do we reach the garden of truth?; and (vi) Access to the center. It also includes two appendices which provide historical and geographical background: One on the Sufi tradition and Sufi orders, and the other on theoretical Sufism and Islamic Gnosis. Quotations from the *Quran*, the sayings of Prophet Muhammad, and Persian poets, as well as the bibliography and the glossary of technical terms at the end of the book also give a scholarly touch and depth to the book. The title *Garden of Truth* comes from Sufi literature itself. The traditional Islamic and Persian gardens are designed as symbols of Paradise or *Firdaws* in Arabic. Both of these words have been derived from the Persian word, *pardis*, "garden." The highest Sufi garden belongs to the Divine truth.

Sufis, as Nasr explains, believe that there are four aspects in a religion: (1) Practice and law (*shari'a* or *shari'at*) which is like the circumference of a circle; (2) Spiritual path (*tariqa* or *traiqat*) which is like the radius; (3) Truth (*haqiqa* or *haqiqat*), the center; and finally (4) Knowledge of these three aspects (*ma'rifa* or *ma'rifat*). This book is more about the Knowledge of the Path and Truth than of the Practice.

We live in a modern Westernized world in which, as Dr. Nasr remarks, ideas and objects are fast outmoded as the tempo of life has become increasingly fast. So how can contemporary people benefit from the teachings of the centuries-old Sufi tradition? The answer is in the question itself. It is because we live in this kind of the fast-paced stressful world that we need, more than ever, spiritual wisdom like that of the Sufis to give us peace of mind and a balanced life. Or as Dr. Nasr puts it, "In a deeper sense we carry within ourselves the same reality as our ancestors did. Our deepest needs, such as having hope, finding meaning in life, discovering happiness, learning to face tribulations, pain, sorrow, and misery, and being able to confront the reality of death, are the same for us as for men and women who lived in the past." So this book offers Sufi jewels for modern life.

The Fire of Love

Rumi: The Fire of Love by Nahal Tajadod, translated from the French by Robert Bononno (The Overlook Press, New York, 2008, Pp. 320).

First published in *Rain Taxi Review of Books*, Online Edition, Winter 2008/2009.

This book is the first comprehensive historical novel in English about the life and thought of Jalâluddin Rumi, the thirteenth-century Persian mystical poet and currently one of the most-widely read poets in North America.

Nahal Tajadod, born and raised in Iran, has lived and studied in France since 1977; she holds a doctorate in Chinese literature and has researched Manichean texts and Sufi poetry for decades. Tajadod confesses that it took her several years to finish this book, during which she suffered the loss of her mother (Maheen Jahanbeiglou-Tajadod, an Iranian scholar of Persian literature who helped her understand the mystical pomes of Rumi), and celebrated the life of her first-born child (after ten years of trying) – a girl named Kiara, probably after Rumi's wife. During those long years with many interruptions Tajadod was working on this book, her husband (French scriptwriter and actor Jean Claude Carrière) would often inquire about her book on Rumi, and in reply Tajadod would recite one of Rumi's own poems, "For a period of time the *Masnavi* has been delayed." This is the opening line of the second book of the *Masnavi*, which Rumi resumed to compose after a gap of two years. One day, Tajadod writes, while breastfeeding her infant daughter, she opened Rumi's *Masnavi* and noticed that her quoted line continues to say: "Because it takes time for blood to become milk." This is indeed the crux of Rumi's work as well: He used his blood and life to produce pure milk of poetry for all of human generations. This book which sheds light on the life of this spiritual poet is a delight to read.

Rumi was born in 1207 in Balkh (now in Afghanistan), an ancient city in the Persian Kingdom whose history includes the flowering of Zoroastrian, Buddhist and Sufi faiths. His father, Bahâ Valad, was an Islamic preacher, and Rumi's first teacher. Shortly before the Mongols invaded and massacred Balkh and other cities in eastern Iran, Rumi's family migrated westward, and finally settled in Konya (now in southwest Turkey), an important city in Anatolia then ruled by the Seljuq Dynasty. Anatolia was once part of the

Byzantine Empire or Rūm in Arabic and Persian – hence the name Rumi for the poet, known respectfully to the Persians as Mawlânâ or Mowlânâ (Mevlânâ in Turkish), "Our Master." After Bahâ Valad died, Rumi, then aged twenty four, studied under several teachers and spiritual masters. Ten years later, Rumi took over his father's position as an eminent Islamic teacher in Konya. In 1244, Rumi happened to meet a wandering dervish, Shams ("Sun") in a bazaar in Konya. It was Shams who awakened Rumi to esoteric knowledge, mystic love, and union with God. This was a second birth for Rumi; he became a poet of love, or as he himself said: "I was dead; I became alive. I was in tears, I am all laughter."

Rumi treasured friendships and "dialogues" with spiritual friends (a tradition called *soh'bat* in Sufism). Shams was Rumi's first brother in soul. After Shams left Konya in 1248 (or was killed by Rumi's jealous students as some scholars have suggested), Rumi found another friend to converse with, Salâhuddin Zarkub ("goldsmith" by profession) who died in 1258. Rumi's third friend was Husâmuddin Chalabi, to whom he recited the entire book of the *Masnavi* until Rumi's death in 1273. Husâm would die eleven years later. *Rumi: Fire of Love* is thus divided into three parts: Shams, Salah, and Husâm (Tajadod mis-spells it Hesam). This historical novel is written in the first person through Husâm who narrates the story after Rumi had died and Husâm had reached the age of sixty (the same age Shams was when he met Rumi).

Although Rumi's years with Shams were fewer than four, more than half of the book's pages are devoted to the Shams period, not only because Tajadod has squeezed the first half of Rumi's life (before he met Shams) into this part, but also because of the overwhelming impact Shams had on the rest of Rumi's life. Rumi is well known as the originator of "Whirling Dervishes," a Sufi order, institutionalized by Rumi's son Sultân Valad. But how did Rumi discover whirling as a spiritual practice? In the 1998 documentary film *Rumi: Poet of the Heart*, we are told that Rumi turned to whirling dance after Shams left him and Rumi was thus longing for his spiritual friend. But Tajadod's research in this book shows that it was actually Shams who taught Rumi the practice of whirling.

An important aspect of Tajadod's historical novel is that she portrays Rumi not merely as a Sufi master but as an embodiment of ancient wisdom which Rumi had absorbed from Islamic, Christian, Jewish, Greek, Persian and Indian traditions. The book ends with the recalling of Rumi's death at sunset on Sunday in Konya, where his tomb has been a pilgrimage site for centuries. Rumi's funeral was attended by people of various faiths, races, and languages. Rumi's poetry of love is still sweet on the lips of millions of readers seven centuries after his death. This is no small achievement for a poet.

Another significant aspect of this book is that Tajadod knows Persian – Rumi's language – and thus she has used original sources to write this story. These sources include Rumi's own works, including the *Divân-e Shams* ("Book of Poetry dedicated to Shams"), *Masnavi-ye Ma'navi* ("Rhyming Couplets on Spiritual Matters) and *Fihi Mâ Fih* (Discourses), as well as the Discourses of Shams (*Magâlât-e Shams*), The Book of Sultân Valad (*Valad Nâmeh*), and the *Manâqeb ul-Ârefin* ("The Virtuous Acts of Mystics") written by Rumi's disciple Ahmad Aflâki after the master's death.

This book was first published in French in 2004. In 2007, Nahal Tajadod and her husband Jean Claude Carrière released a CD recording of some of Rumi's poems in French (*Chants d'amour de Rumi*) with music by the renowned Turkish composer Kudsi Erguner. Prior to the publication of *Rumi: Fire of Love*, historical novels in English on Rumi's life included Nigel Watts' *The Way of Love* (1998) and Connie Zweigo's *A Moth to the Flame* (2006).

Rumi's Daughter

Rumi's Daughter by Muriel Maufroy (Rider, London, 2006, Pp. 232).

First published in *Kyoto Journal*, No. 66, 2007, p. 85.

With the popularity of Rumi's poetry in the West in recent decades, some writers have turned their attention to Rumi as a subject of fiction and creative writing. Roger Housden's *Chasing Rumi* (2002) and Pico Iyer's *Abandon* (2004) both revolve around the pilgrimage to Rumi's tomb in Konya (in southern Turkey) as an inward journey and on a quest of love. And now a French-British journalist, Muriel Maufroy, in her first novel has tackled one of the lesser known aspects of Rumi's life – the story of his adopted daughter, Kimiyâ.

Rumi, unlike many of his fellow Muslim men in the thirteenth century (or even some today), did not marry four wives. Rumi married his childhood friend, Gowhar Khâtun, in 1224 when he was eighteen. (Khâtun means "Lady.") The couple had two sons – Sultân Valad (the elder), and Alâ'eddin (the younger). Gowhar died of illness, probably within a few years of the marriage in Lâranda (she is not buried in the mausoleum in Konya where Rumi's father, who died in 1231, is buried). Rumi married a widow by the name of Kerâ Khâtun, who had a son (Shamsuddin Yah'yâ) from her first marriage. From their second marriage, Rumi and Kerâ had a son (Muzaffaruddin Amir) and a daughter (Malakeh Khâtun). But we also know of a girl by the name of Kimiyâ who grew up in the house of Rumi and Kerâ. We do not know where she came from. Either Kimiyâ was their adopted daughter or she was from Kerâ's first marriage. The name Kimiyâ means alchemy. In fact, "alchemy" is a corrupted pronunciation of "al-kimiyâ" in the Arabic-Persian languages and was originally derived from the Latin-Greek word "chemeia." Modern chemistry was founded on the Greek-Muslim heritage in alchemy. Kimiyâ, a female name in Persian, also means "rare and exceptional," which is probably as a reference to gold that was the treasured mineral in alchemy. So the little beautiful girl Kimiyâ, who was raised in Rumi's family, could be traced to any ethnic group – Greek, Persian, Turkish and Arab – in thirteenth-century Konya. In her fiction, Maufroy introduces Kimiyâ's mother as a Greek Christian by the name of Evdokia and her father as a Persian Muslim named Farokh. This is possible because these ethnic and religious communities mingled in peace in Anatolia at that time.

Why Kimiyâ came to Rumi's house is unknown. Maufroy mentions the poverty of her parents, who were farmers, as well as Kimiyâ's own desire for learning. Iif so, where better than in the house of a learned scholar such as Rumi? In any case, we know that Kimiyâ was neither a slave girl nor a maidservant; she was treated as a member of Rumi's family. Except for several fictitious names and characters, the rest of Maufroy's novel follows the known history. The climax of the story is deservedly Kimiyâ's marriage to Shams Tabrizi, Rumi's spiritual mentor. Kimiyâ was then a young woman, probably a teenager, and Shams was an old man in his sixties. The marriage was not a happy one. Some historical documents allude that Rumi's son Alâ'eddin was in love with Kimiyâ. Maufroy is silent about this but she does point out Alâ'eddin' contempt for Shams.

Kimiyâ's marriage was indeed brief, only the last quarter of 1247. She died of an illness, after having a quarrel with Shams. I do not want to spoil the joy of reading the novel for potential readers; so I will not say how this happened. Kimiyâ's death was a shock to the whole family. Shortly after, Shams disappeared in early 1248. Some scholars, such as Abdulbâki Gölpinârli, argue that Shams was murdered by Alâ'eddin (out of jealousy and revenge) aided by his friends. Other scholars, such as Franklin Lewis, believe that Shams left Konya on his own because of grief and his difficult situation among Rumi's disciples and because he had accomplished his task of transforming Rumi to the mystical poet we know today. There is a tomb in Konya attributed to Shams but few scholars believe that it is really where Shams is buried. There is another tomb in the town of Khoy in northwest Iran also attributed to Shams. Khoy is en route to the city of Tabriz, from where Shams originally came. Was Shams, then an old man, planning to return to Tabriz after he left Konya? Or was he killed and his body ditched somewhere in Konya? No one knows for sure. Maufroy does not extend her novel to cover this controversial part of the story. Perhaps another novelist will take up this issue.

Several aspects of Maufroy's novel are significant. First, Maufroy has woven together our little and fragmented knowledge of Kimiyâ into a plausible, coherent life story. Second, against the backdrop of this thirteenth-century story we appreciate how greatly women's conditions have improved in our time – thanks to the spread of scientific knowledge, civil liberties, and the women's rights movement. Third, Kimiyâ's story represents a tragic life that many girls experienced throughout history (and some still experience in some parts of our world). Above all, Maufroy's novel shows the power of literature: How can a little known fragment of history be turned into a life story from which we can learn a great deal about the past. Nevertheless, we should not pass a harsh judgement from the vantage point of our time on Shams, Rumi or Kerâ. They lived seven hundred years ago and probably did their best given the culture and circumstances of their time; moreover, we know so little about the story of Kimiyâ. In fact, Maufroy's narrative of Kimiyâ's marriage to Shams is that it was a journey of enlightenment for Kimiyâ and a journey of human love for Shams.

Rumi's Daughter has been translated into Persian twice, indicating the huge interest in Iran about this subject. Another novel related to Kimiyâ is *Kimya Khatun* written by Saideh Ghods, which was first published in Persian in 2004 (Cheshmeh Press, Tehran) and then in English in 2012 (Candle & Fog, London). In 2011, it was reported that a film, *Rumi's Kimya*, was being produced on the basis of Ghods' novel, directed by Dariush Mehrjui and starring Golshifteh Farahani playing Kimiyâ; the film has not yet been released.

Translating Rumi: Three Traditions

Rumi: Bridge to the Soul, new translated poems by Coleman Barks (HarperOne, New York, 2008, Pp. 158).

Rumi: Swallowing the Sun, translated by Franklin D. Lewis (Oneworld, Oxford, 2008, Pp. 226).

Rumi: Say Nothing, poems of Jalal al-Din Rumi in Persian and English, translated by Iraj Anvar and Anne Twitty (Morning Light Press, Sandpoint, ID, 2008, Pp. 174).

First published in *Interreligious Insight*, January 2009, pp. 80-83.

Jalâluddin Mohammad Balkhi Rumi (1207-1273), the renowned Persian Sufi poet, is now a widely-read poet in the Western world, and there are many anthologies of his poetry available in English. Rumi's English translators may be categorized into three groups: (1) American/English poets who rely on original translators to reproduce Rumi's poems in free verse; (2) American/English scholars of Persian literature who know both English and Persian, and (3) those whose first language is Persian (Rumi's language) but also have a working knowledge of English and live in the USA or the UK. The three books, which are the subject-matter of this review, typically represent these three groups of Rumi's translators. Rumi's poetry is not only a powerful expression of love and the human heart but also an elegant bridge across various faiths. For this reason, the art of translating Rumi is too important to be left without evaluation and literary criticism.

The earliest English translations of Rumi's poetry date back to the late nineteenth and early twentieth centuries by British scholars of Persian literature: Sir James William Redhouse (1811-1892), Edward Henry

Whinfield (1836-1922), Edward Henry Palmer (1840-82), William Hastie (1842-1903), Charles Edward Wilson (1858-1938), Reynold Alleyne Nicholson (1868-1945), and Arthur John Arberry (1905-69). For decades, however, these translations appealed only to scholars of Persian literature or serious students of Sufism. The credit of popularizing Rumi in modern English goes to the American poet Coleman Barks (born 1937). Barks, as he has often stated, does not know Persian, and works from literal translations made by Nicholson, Arberry, or supplied by his Iranian/American friend, John Moyne, a professor emeritus of linguistics at the City University of New York. Although Barks and Moyne have published several anthologies of Rumi's poetry, it was their 1995 best-seller *The Essential Rumi* that widely brought Rumi to the attention of the American public.

Rumi: Bridge to the Soul is Barks' latest work, and he has dedicated it to the renowned American poet Robert Bly, the man who first introduced Barks to Arberry's scholarly translation of Rumi's poetry in 1976 and asked Barks "to release these poems from their cages." In 2006, Barks and Bly accepted an invitation from the University of Tehran to travel to Iran. Barks was awarded an honorary doctorate at Tehran. Barks and Bly then visited the historical cities of Shiraz and Isfahan in Iran. In an introductory chapter to this new book, Barks recounts their travel to Iran and discusses how the famous Khâjoo Bridge over the Zâyandeh River in Isfahan (which was built in the seventeenth century) symbolically inspired him to view Rumi's poetry as a bridge across faiths and cultures in the modern world: Both are elegant, durable and stylish bridges connecting people. This book, published to commemorate the 800th anniversary of Rumi's birth, contains ninety lyrical odes (*ghazaliyât*) composed by Rumi, and originally translated by Arthur Arberry (from Persian) or Nevit Ergin (from a Turkish translation) into English.

It is almost impossible to exactly translate a poem from one language to another, but there is a spectrum of how far or how close a translation is to what the poet had originally composed. Reading through Barks' several anthologies of Rumi, including this new one, I can say that Barks' "translations" are not only free verse but also usually free translations, that is renditions, versions and at times summaries of the original, rather than line-to-line accurate translations. Take, for example, the first lines of the poem "Ear-sight" in Barks' new anthology:

Do you want the sweetness of food
or the sweetness of the one
who put sweetness in food?

A complete translation (mine from Persian) would be as follows:

O Friend! Which is sweeter:
Sugar or the one who makes sugar sweet?
And tell me which is more joyful:
The face of the moon or the one who made the moon?

Nonetheless, being in free verse and coming from the mature pen of Barks (who, for three decades, taught English and poetry at the University of Georgia), Barks' anthologies of Rumi are charming and do give some flavor of Rumi to readers. *Rumi: Bridge to the Soul* is subtitled, "Journeys into the Music and Silence of the Heart." And this is indeed a beautiful collection of Rumi's poems centering on music, silence, and the heart.

Dr. Franklin Lewis of the Department of Near Eastern Languages and Civilizations at the University of Chicago belongs to the rare category of Rumi's translators who know both English and Persian. Lewis' 2000 book, *Rumi: Past and Present, East and West* has been hailed as a significant contribution to Rumi studies; it has been translated into Persian twice. His new book, *Swallowing the Sun*, is a collection of Rumi's poems categorized under thirteen topics: Poems of praise and invocation; faith and observance; poetry and music; silence, loss and confusion; disciple to master; master to disciple; master to master; dreams and visions; love and reason; celebrating union; death and beyond; and birthing the soul.

These translations come from Rumi's two major works: (1) *Masnavi-ye Ma'navi* ("Spiritual Couplets"), which is a didactic work of parables in verse, and (2) *Divân-e Shams-e Tabrizi* ("The Poetry Book Dedicated to Shams of Tabriz"), which contains lyrical odes and passionate quatrains. Shams was a mysterious wandering dervish who met Rumi in a marketplace in Konya in 1244, and not only transformed Rumi spiritually but also triggered Rumi's latent poetic talent to blossom. The Arabic/Persian word *Shams* means "the Sun," which also appears in the title of Lewis' book. Persian scholars are fond of saying that Rumi is a vast, deep ocean, and as such, it is impossible to contain Rumi in a single volume. Nonetheless, Lewis' anthology of Rumi offers a rich fragrance of the themes and styles of expression in Rumi's poetry. Lewis has managed to produce verses which both capture the literal meaning of Rumi's poetry and are delightful to read in today's English. Many of these poems first appeared in Lewis' 2000 book on Rumi, but this anthology has its own merits for readers and students who wish to focus on Rumi's poetry rather than his biography and philosophy. There are more than ninety poems in this volume; the original Persian source for each poem is cited, and there are also explanatory notes on poems at the end of the book. Lewis has also written a long introduction to Rumi's Persian poetry and the history of its translation into English. Readers will find this information very valuable in order to better understand Rumi.

In one of his poems (included in this anthology) Rumi says:

I will keep silence from now on.
For in my silence
Truth and error separate
Just like wheat from chaff.

This statement from Rumi may sound strange as he composed 70,000 lines of poems in the last three decades of his life. But there is no contradiction here because all of Rumi's poems poured out of his silence. Indeed, Rumi's poetry was so spontaneous that he did not even write down his poems but only recited them to his son and disciples. In many of his lyrical odes Rumi addresses himself as "the Silent" (*Khamoosh*). In his introductory chapter in *Rumi: Bridge to the Soul,* Barks narrates that someone asked Rumi, "Isn't it strange that you talk so much about silence?" He answered, "The radiant one inside me has never said a word."

With the rising popularity of Rumi in the West in recent years, some Iranian scholars who live in the USA or Europe have also made attempts to translate Rumi directly from Persian into English. *Rumi: Say Nothing* by Dr. Iraj Anvar, an expert on Persian literature and a visiting professor at Brown University, USA, who collaborated with Anne Twitty (an American writer), belongs to this category of Rumi translations. After introductory chapters about Rumi's life and poetry, this volume offers forty-four lyrical odes (*ghazaliyât*) and quatrains (*rubâiyât*) of Rumi, beautifully translated and presented side-by-side with their Persian scripts. Explanatory notes for the poems are also available at the end of the book. This is a small collection but sufficient for a poetry volume.

The title "Say Nothing" comes from one of Rumi's poems included in the book:

I am a slave of the Moon. Talk of nothing but the Moon,
or brightness and sweetness. Other than that, say nothing.

Rumi's Persian poems are all untitled and are usually arranged alphabetically according to the rhymes and meters of the poems. Nonetheless, modern translators find it useful to give a title for each poem.

Rumi was not merely a poet; he was also an eminent thinker and a spiritual master. Rumi's poetry presented in these new anthologies offer a reservoir of timeless wisdom and inspiration, which are needed to transform our divided world and heal our stressed minds. Rumi is an ocean, and we need fine translators with various backgrounds and skills to present his poetry and spiritual vision to our age and generation. Nonetheless, finding a balance between accuracy and beauty in translating Rumi's poetry will continue to pose a challenge.

Rumi's Sun: The Teachings of Shams of Tabriz

Rumi's Sun: The Teachings of Shams of Tabriz, translated by Refik Algan and Camille Adams Helminski (Morning Light Press, Sandpoint, ID, 2008, Pp. xii+442).

First published in *Sufi*, Issue 78, Winter 2009/Spring 2010, p. 51.

Although Mawlânâ Jalâluddin Balkhi Rumi (1207-1273) is a widely-read Sufi poet, his spiritual friend, Shams-e Tabrizi ("Shams of Tabriz") is a less known figure. Shams' name often appears in Rumi's poetry, especially in the *ghazal* poems (lyrical odes) of Rumi's *Divân-e Shams-e Tabrizi* ("Poetry Book of Shams of Tabriz). Shams is an enigmatic figure but a very influential personality in Mawlânâ's life. It was a historical meeting with Shams in 1244 in Konya (in today's Turkey) that transformed Rumi from a preacher to a poet. And yet, were it not for Rumi's poetry, Shams would not have made it into any historical record. During the three years (1244-1247) Shams stayed with Rumi in Konya, he gave short discourses in Persian to Rumi's students and friends. Fortunately, Shams' words were written down by Rumi's son and successor Sultân Valad. His manuscript is still extant: Manuscript #1856 in the library of Vali al-Din Efendi. The *Magâlât-e Shams-e Tabrizi* ("The Sayings of Shams of Tabriz") is far less known than Rumi's poetry books. Even among Rumi's Persian readers this work was not widely known until it was printed in Tehran. The first print in 1970/1350 (Atâ'ie Press, Tehran) was edited by Ahmad Khosh'nevis. Then, in 1990/1369 the Iranian scholar Mohammad Ali Movah'hed published a critically edited and annotated version of the *Magâlât* in two volumes (Khârazmi Press, Tehran). In 2004, Professor William Chittick of the State University at New York translated the *Magâlât* (from Movah'hed's edition) into English: *Me & Rumi: The Autobiography of Shams-i Tabriz* (Fons Vitae, Louisville, Kentucky, 2004). Chittick arranged his translation in an autobiographical scheme that makes it easier for readers to trace the life of Shams. Perhaps for this reason, Chittick's work has been re-translated into Persian (*Man and Mowlânâ*, translated by Shahâbuddin Abbâsi, Morvarid Press, Tehran, 2007/1386).

Now we are fortunate to have a new, complete translation of the *Magâlât* titled, *Rumi's Sun: The Teachings of Shams of Tabriz* by Refik Algan and Camille Adams Helminski, who are respectively a Turkish and an American scholar of Rumi and Sufism. The word "Sun" in the title obviously refers to Shams ("Sun" in Arabic and Persian). The book is highly readable and contains explanatory footnotes added by the translators. This new English translation is based on a Turkish translation of the *Magâlât* by Dr. Mehmet Nuri Gencosman who used the original Persian manuscripts #2144 and #2145 (calligraphed by Ayashli Shakir), which until recent years were at the Mevlana Museum in Konya, but have now been transferred to Ankara for safe-keeping. These two manuscripts are among the six manuscripts that Movah'hed used for his edition of the *Magâlât* (however, Movah'hed gives slightly different manuscript numbers, #2154 and #2155). I compared sections of the new English translation with Movah'hed's Persian edition and found the English translation to be accurate overall, but having a slightly different arrangement of materials mainly because Movah'hed's critical edition relied on several manuscripts and includes the later "additions" to the manuscript in a separate chapter. Algan and Helminski have also given subtitles for the materials, which, although absent in the original manuscript, make it easier to read in English.

The *Maqâlât* of Shams and its English translations are significant for several reasons. First, this book shatters the myth that Shams was an illiterate, unintelligent wandering dervish. Indeed, the book portrays Shams to be a very knowledgeable person who quotes from Arabic and Persian literature, and also a contemplative person who had insight into human nature and the spiritual path. Second, the biographical tales Shams narrates in this book shed light on places he had been and various masters he had studied with before meeting Rumi, which is a valuable source of information for scholars. Third, this book helps us better understand the enigmatic relationship between Rumi and Shams; they were two brothers in soul who held each other in high respect, rather than having had a master-disciple relationship. Fourth, the book contains some stories which are also found in Rumi's *Masnavi-ye Ma'navi* ("Spiritual Couplets") indicating the impact of Shams' conversations on Rumi's spiritual thinking. Finally, the *Maqâlât* itself is an important text in Sufi literature and a literary gem in Persian.

Translation of classic literature demands years of hard work and scholarly commitment. Refik Algan's and Camille Helminski's efforts have resulted in a very valuable contribution to Sufi literature in English. This book is a rich reservoir of ancient wisdom, inspiration and insight. Consider for instance the following saying of Shams: "Sainthood is to have sovereignty over one's self, one's moods, one's quality, one's speech, and one's silence."

The Quatrains of Rumi

The Quatrains of Rumi, Rubaiyat-e Jalaluddin Muhammad Balkhi Rum, translated by Ibrahim Gamard and Rawan Farhadi (Sufi Dari Books, San Rafael, CA, 2008, Pp. xliv+708).

First published in *Sufi*, Issue 78, Winter 2009/Spring 2010, p. 52.

Mawlânâ Jalâluddin Balkh Rumi's poetry is collected into two huge books: (1) the *Masnavi-ye Ma'navi* ("Rhyming Couplets on Spiritual Matters"), which contains hundreds of tales and parables composed in verse, and (ii) the

Divân-e Shams-e Tabrizi ("Book of Poetry Dedicated to Shams of Tabriz"), which contains Rumi's *ghazal* poems (lyrical odes) and *rubâiyât* (quatrains). Rumi's *Rubaiyât* have also been printed separately in the past. In 1949, the Cambridge scholar Arthur John Arberry published the first (abridged) English translation of *The Rubaiyat of Jalal al-Din Rumi: Select Translations into English Verse* (Emery Walker, London) based on an 1896 print in Istanbul and a 1941 print in Isfahan. Arberry's attempt was to provide a verse translation in English, similar to Edward Fitzgerald's translation of the *Rubaiyat of Omar Khayyam* a century earlier. During 1957-67, when the eminent Iranian scholar Badi uz-Zaman Foruzânfar published a critically-edited version of Rumi's *Divân* based on several original manuscripts, he collected 1,983 quatrains in the volume eight of his 10-volume work (published by Tehran University Press, reprinted by Amir Kabir Press in 1976). In recent decades, hundreds of Rumi's quatrains have been translated into English, mostly in the modern style of free verse; for example, *Unseen Rain* (1986) and *Bird Song* (1993) by Coleman Barks; *Rending the Veil* by Shahram Shiva (1995); *Rumi: Whispers of the Beloved* by Maryam Mafi and Azima Melita Kolin (1999); *Dancing the Flame* by Nader Khalili (2001); and *The Rubais of Rumi* by Nevit Ergin and Will Johnson (2007).

This new translation, *The Quatrains of Rumi*, is a ground-breaking work for several reasons: (1) It offers the English translations of all of Rumi's quatrains together with their Persian scripts from Foruzânfar's edition; (2) it provides English translations of Rumi's Arabic quatrains as well (note that Foruzânfar did not attempt to translate Rumi's Arabic poems into Persian); (3) explanatory notes given under each poem are very informative; (4) the English translations are literal and accurate rather than being interpretive, distorted or abridged; (5) the authors have painstakingly compiled a list of previously translated quatrains with cross-references to their new work; (6) the Introduction and the Bibliography in the book are very useful for readers who do not know much about Rumi as well as for those who want to learn more.

While in Persian editions, it is customary to arrange Rumi's poems alphabetically according to the last letter of their rhymes, this new English translation has categorized Rumi's quatrains into five thematic chapters: (1) Some themes of Mawlânâ's life; (2) Love of the human beloved; (3) Metaphorical love becoming real love; (4) Divine love; and (5) Advice to the disciple and aspirant. Each chapter is further subdivided into different themes. This classification is, in its own way, very helpful to understand various themes expressed in Rumi's *Rubâiyât*.

Both Ibrahim Gamard, an American who converted to Sufism and knows Persian, and Rawan Farhadi, an eminent Afghani scholar, are experienced scholars in the field of Rumi's poetry and Sufism. Dr. Gamard, who is a psychologist in California, maintains the website *Dar al-Masnavi* (www.dar-al-masnavi.org) and previously translated an anthology of Rumi's works, *Rumi and Islam* (Sky Light Paths Publishing, 2004). Dr. Rawan Farhadi studied with the famed scholar Louis Massignon in Paris, taught Persian literature at the Sorbonne and UC-Berkeley, and served as Afghan ambassador to France and United Nations.

This is an important publication that will serve Rumi's fans for generations to come. Given its merits, I will not be surprised (rather, will be delighted) if this book is re-translated into Persian. While I do not think that this book puts an end on the art of translating Rumi's *Rubaiyat* (we need various translators), it will definitely set an important yardstick to evaluate to what degree the past and future translations of Rumi's *Rubaiyat* are faithful to Rumi's own version.

[Appendix I]
A Chronology of Rumi's Life & Family

Compared to the other classical Persian poets, we have much information about Rumi's life and family – thanks to his son, Sultân Valad, and his disciples Feridoon Sepah-sâlâr and Ahmad Aflâki, who compiled the biography of Rumi as well as his father and his teachers and spiritual mentors. But still there are some unknown aspects or contradictory reports which make it difficult to prepare a detailed and precise chronology of Rumi's life and his family. The following is based on the most authoritative research works in this field.

Note that the first year cited is A.D. (of the Western calendar) and the second year in parenthesis is A.H., according to the Islamic/Arabic calendar. The Lunar Islamic (*Hijri*) calendar begins in 622 A.D., marking the year Prophet Muhammad migrated (*hijra*) from Mecca to Medina on the Arabian Peninsula. According to this calendar, Rumi's birthday on 30 September 1207 corresponds to 6 Rabi al-Awwal 604 A.H., and his death on 17 December 1273 corresponds to 5 Jamâdi al-Âkhar 672 A.H. (*"after hijra"*).

1207(604)	Jalâluddin Mohammad (Rumi) was born on September 30, Sunday, in Balkh to Bahâuddin Valad and Mo'meneh Khâtun (Bahâ Valad's last wife). He was the youngest child of his parents. This is the reported date and place for Rumi's birth in the historical and biographical records. Some scholars, based on circumstantial evidence from the readings of certain texts, believe that Rumi was born in the town of Vakh'sh (now in Tajikistan), and several years before 1207.

1219-1221 (616-618)	Bahâ Valad, his family and disciples (with a caravan of 300 camels) left Balkh and journeyed westward. They stayed in Nishâbur, Baghdad, Mecca (for pilgrimage) and Damascus, and finally moved to Anatolia (now Turkey), then ruled by the Seljuq Dynasty.
1221 (618)	Mongols invaded and massacred the Persian cities of Balkh and Nishâbur.
1222 (619)	Bahâ Valad and his family in the town of Lâranda (now called Karaman in southwest Turkey).
1224 (621)	Rumi married his childhood friend Gowhar Khâtun (Gevher Hatun in Turkish). Gowhar Khâtun was the daughter of Khâja Sharaf'uddin Lâlâ of Samarqand (a historical city in today's Uzbekistan); her mother was a disciple of Bahâ Valad. She and her family were part of Bahâ Valad's caravan that left Balkh for the safety of Anatolia. Gowhar Khâtun gave birth to two sons; she probably died shortly later in Lâranda (her tomb, as far as we know, is not in the mausoleum in Konya where Rumi and his family members are buried). Nevertheless, some scholars (for example, Zarrinkub) suggest that Gowhar Khâtun and even her mother were living in Konya and taking care of Rumi's two sons, when he was studying in Syria during the 1230s. Zarrinkub places Gowhar Khâtun's death in 1242 (640), implying that she died after Rumi's return to Konya. If this is true, Rumi's second marriage to Kerâ Khâtun took place in about 1243 (641).
1224? or 1229? (621? or 626?)	Rumi's mother Mo'meneh Khâtun died. She is buried in the town of Lâranda (Karaman). Rumi's grandmother (Bahâ Valad's mother), Rumi's mother-in-law (Gowhar Khâtun's mother), and Rumi's older brother also probably all died in Lâranda within a few years of each other.

1225 or 1127 (622? or 624?)	Birth of Rumi' son Alâ'eddin. Named after Rumi's elder brother Alâ'eddin Mohammad who died in Lâranda. He was about two years older than Rumi.
1226 (623)	Birth of Rumi's son Bahâuddin Mohammad Sultân Valad (Veled in Turkish). Named after Rumi's father.
1229 (626)	Bahâ Valad and his family settled in Konya at the request of the Seljuq king Alâ'eddin Kaygubâd. A religious school was donated to Bahâ Valad to hold his classes in Konya; this school was later inherited by Rumi.
1230? (627?) 1243? (641?)	Rumi married Kerâ Khâtun from Konya, a widow with a small boy (Amir Shamsuddin Yah'yâ) from her first marriage to a man named Mohammad Shah.
1231 (628)	Bahâ Valad died in Konya at age 80.
1232 (629)	Burhânnudin Mohaggeg Termezi, Rumi's childhood tutor from Balkh and Bahâ Valad's disciple, arrived in Konya to train Rumi.
1233-1237 (630-634)	Rumi studied in Aleppo and Damascus, and then returned to Konya. In 1237 the Seljuq king Alâ'eddin Kaygubâd died and was succeeded by his son Ghiyâsuddin Kay-khosrow II.
1241 (638)	Burhân Termezi died. He is buried in Geysariyah (Kayseri in southern Turkey, about 300 km northeast of Konya). Rumi inherited his library.
1244 (642)	Shamsuddin (Shams) Tabrizi (aged about sixty) arrived in Konya and met Rumi on November 29. Rumi started composing lyric poems (collected in the *Divân-e Shams-e Tabrizi*) and continued it for the rest of his life.

1246 (643)	In March, Shams left Konya for Damascus (in Syria) in protest to the mistreatment and hostility he had received from Rumi's students. Rumi wrote several letters to Shams, and finally dispatched his son Sultân Valad to bring Shams back to Konya.
1247 (644)	In April, Shams returned to Konya, and a few months later, he married Kimiyâ, Rumi's adopted daughter. The marriage took place in the autumn and lasted for a brief period only as Kimiyâ died of illness later that year.
1248 (645)	Late in 1247 or early in 1248, Shams disappeared; he was either killed by Rumi's angry disciples or left Konya on his own for good. During 1248-1250 (645-647), Rumi took two trips to Damascus in search of Shams but to no avail. There is a tomb in Konya attributed to Shams-e Tabrizi, but its authenticity is highly questionable.
1250 (647)	Rumi chose Salâhuddin Zarkub (a goldsmith in Konya) as his spiritual friend. Both Rumi and Zarkub were students of Burhân Termezi. Sometime later, Sultân Valad, Rumi's son, married Fâtemeh Khâtun, Salâhuddin Zarkub's daughter. In the years to follow, Fâtemeh Khâtun gave birth to one son and two daughters. Sultân Valad also married two other women and had three other sons from them.
1258 (657)	Salâhuddin Zarkub died. The Mongols overthrew the Abbasid caliphate in Baghdad and took over the entire Middle East.
1260 (658)	Rumi chose Husâmuddin Chelebi as his spiritual friend. He was from the chivalry class in Konya and was on good terms with Shams-e Tabrizi. Rumi started composing the *Masnavi-ye Ma'navi* at Husâm's request, and Husâm wrote it down every evening up until Rumi's death.

1262 (660)	Alâ'eddin, Rumi's son, died. We have no information about the names of his wife or children. Husâmuddin Chelebi's wife died. The composition of the *Masnavi* was interrupted for two years; the second book of the *Masnavi* began in 1264 (662).
1272 (670)	Rumi's first grandchild, Jalâluddin Ulu Âref Chelebi, was born to Fâtemeh Khâtun and Sultân Valad.
1273 (672)	Rumi died on December 17, Sunday, and was buried in Konya after a well-attended funeral.
1277 (676)	Mozaffaruddin Amir Âlem Chelebi, son of Rumi and Kerâ Khâtun, died. He was a treasurer at the Seljuq court in Konya.
1284 (683)	Husâmuddin Chelebi died at age 61. Sultân Valad became the Guide (*Shaykh*) of the Whirling Dervishes (the Mevlevi Order).
1292 (691)	Kerâ Khâtun died and was buried next to Rumi.
1304 (703)	Malakeh Khâtun, daughter of Rumi and Kerâ Khâtun, died. She was married to Shahâbuddin Gunawi, a merchant in Konya.
1312 (712)	Sultân Valad died. By then, he had institutionalized the Mawlaviyah (Mevlevi) Order of Sufism based on his father's teachings and practice. Sultân Valad also composed several books of poetry, in the style of Rumi; his works are, however, less known and have not been translated into English. His descendants (the Chelebi family) still live in Turkey and continue Rumi's family lineage.
1320 (719)	Jalâluddin Ulu Âref Chelebi, son of Sultân Valad, died.
1338 (739)	Shamsuddin Amir Âbed Chelebi, son of Sultân Valad, died.

1342 (742)   Husâmuddin Vâjed Chelebi Akbar, son of Sultân Valad, died.

1343 (743)   Shamsuddin Zâhed Chelebi Akbar, son of Sultân Valad, died.

Rumi, his father, his second wife and their children, Sultân Valad and his children as well as Rumi's spiritual friends Salâhuddin Zarkub and Husâmuddin Chelebi are all buried in the same mausoleum in Konya. This mausoleum (now called the Mevlana Museum) is situated in a rose garden that was donated by the Seljuq king Alâ'eddin Kaygubâd to Rumi's family upon Bahâ Valad's death in 1231. After Rumi died in 1273, a building with a green dome was constructed with funds provided by Alam u-Din Geysar (a military commander in Konya) and Princess Gorji Khâtun (daughter of Ghiyâsuddin Kay-khosrow II and wife of Prime Minister Mo'eenuddin Parvâneh). Its architect was Badruddin Tabrizi (from the city of Tabriz in northwest Iran where Shams also came from). The mausoleum is called "Gobbat ul-Khadrâ" (Arabic), "Yâshil Turbe" (Turkish), and "Gonbad-e Sabz" (Persian), which means Green Dome. It has been a gathering place of Rumi's fans and disciples (the Mevlevi Sufi Order) and a pilgrimage site and tourist attraction for centuries.

Sources for this chronology include: (1) *Zendegâni-ye Mowlânâ Jalâluddin Mohammad* ("Biography of Mowlânâ Jalâluddin Muhammad") by Badi uz-Zamân Foruzânfar (Zavvâr, Tehran, 1333/1954, reprinted several times) in Persian. (2) *Pelle Pelle Ta Molagât-e Khoda* ("Step by Step toward Meeting God") by Abdul Hossein Zarrinkub (Elmi, Tehran, 1373/1994, reprinted over a dozen times), in Persian; translated into English, *Step by Step Up to Union with God*, by M. Keyvani (Persian Heritage Foundation, New York, 2009). (3) *Rumi: Past and Present, East and West* by Franklin Lewis (Oneworld, Oxford, 2000). (4) Franklin Lewis, "Towards a chronology of the poems in the Divan-i Shams," in *The Philosophy of Ecstasy: Rumi and the Sufi Tradition*, edited by Leonard Lewisohn (World Wisdom, Bloomington, IN, 2014), pp. 145-176.

[Appendix II]
Glossary and Transliteration

Transliteration and pronunciation of words and terms related to Rumi's biography, poetry, and religion pose a challenge to every author as there is no universal consensus on a particular system of transliteration and pronunciation of Arabic and Persian words. The problem arises from several factors. First, a given term may have different pronunciations in Arabic and Persian. For example, *dhikr* (Arabic) and *zekr* (Persian); scholars use both of them in their writings. The prefix *al* ("the"), which in Arabic is added to make a noun definite is usually dropped in Persian; for example, *Al-Shams* ("the Sun") in Arabic is simply *Shams* in Persian. Then, even in the Persian language, a given word may be pronounced differently in its various dialects –Tehrani, Isfahani, Dari/Afghani, Tajiki, etc. Rumi spoke a Persian dialect that was prevalent in the Khorâsân province of eastern Iran during the thirteenth century. Although his language is perfectly understandable to people who speak Persian today, his pronunciation of certain words may have differed. For example, "Listen," the first word in the *Masnavi*, is pronounced *besh'no* in Iran, but *besh'naw* in the Dari and Tajik dialects (the latter is probably close to how Rumi pronounced it because Khorâsân in Rumi's time included much of today's Afghanistan and Tajikistan). Moreover, a word in Arabic may be written differently from the way it is pronounced. For example, Rumi's name is written *Jalâl al-Din* but pronounced *Jalâluddin*. The Turkish language has borrowed a large number of Arabic and Persian words through centuries of contact with these languages; however, the Turkish pronunciation may slightly differ; for example, *Shams* is pronounced *Shems* in Turkish. Finally, transliteration of a given word may differ even among the European languages. For example, *Darvish* (English) and *Darviche* (French), or *Jalal* (English), *Djalal* (German) and *Çelal* (Turkish).

The following glossary contains selected words and terms related to the history and literature of Sufism, together with their meanings and their pronunciations in Arabic, Persian, and Turkish. For more information on the transliteration and meaning of "terms and symbols in Rumi's poetry" refer to my previous book, *Rumi: The Art of Loving* (2012).

Agl. Arabic word meaning "intellect or reasoning mind." Also used in Persian. *Akil* in Turkish. In Sufi literature, *agl* (the small, calculating mind) is criticized when it rejects the path of love (*eshg*) and the heart (*galb*, *del*). However, *agl* as consciousness and intellect emanating from God and governing the universe, or as a faculty of wisdom, scientific reasoning, responsible living, and right decision making is highly respected.

Akhi (Arabic, "my brother"); ***Fati*** (Arabic, "young"); ***Javânmard*** (Persian, "young man"). Title for a person from the chivalry class.

Âlem, Âlim (plural: ***Ulamâ***) Arabic word, "knowledgeable, learned." Someone who possesses *elm* (*ilm*), "knowledge, learning." A title, also used in Persian and Turkish, for an eminent scholar and scientist.

Allâh. Arabic name for "The God;" also used in Persian; *Állâh* in Turkish. *Allah* is etymologically related to the Hebrew word *Elohim* and the Aramaic word *Alaha* (which was used by Jesus of Nazareth) because all of these three languages belong to the Semitic family.

Âref, Ârif (plural: ***Urafâ***) Arabic word, "gnostic." A title, also used in Persian and Turkish, for a mystic or sage. Someone who possesses *erfân* (*irfân*), "esoteric knowledge."

Al-insân ul-Kâmil. Arabic, "Perfect or Completed Human Being;" it refers to an enlightened sage who has completed the spiritual journey (with the various stages of the Sufi path) and who manifests the Divine attributes (trutfullness, compassion, etc. within human capacity) in his being and life. *Insân-e Kâmil* in Persian.

Al-Asmâ ul-Husnâ. Arabic, "beautiful names." It includes the ninety-nine names (attributes) of God that Sufi masters have extracted from the verses of the *Quran*. Persian: *Asmâ-e Husnâ*.

Bagâ. An Arabic Sufi term meaning "remaining, staying or survival." Also used in Persian, it refers to the final stage (succeeding the *fanâ*) of the spiritual path, in which the seeker lives mindfully in the presence of God, and thus reflects holiness (Divine vibe, so to speak) in his personality. Turkish: *Beka*.

Chelebi (Çelebi), Chalabi. A Turkish surname or title meaning "gentleman." Rumi's descendants from the line of Sultân Valad have this surname.

Chelle, Chelleh, Chella. Persian word meaning "forty days." It refers to the Sufi practice of forty-day retreat (*khal'vat*) and meditation. Also used in Turkish.

Darvish. Originally a Persian word (beggar at the door, *dar*) for a poor wandering Sufi. Also used in Arabic. *Dervish* in Turkish. See also *Fakir*.

Del (Persian), ***Galb*** (Arabic). "Heart." It also means "center, essence, and innermost." Turkish: *Kalp*.

Dhikr. Arabic word, literally "remembrance." It refers to the Sufi practice of reciting short prayers or from the names (attributes) of God. The recitation may be silent or a group chanting. Pronounced *Zekr* or *Zikr* in Persian (same also in Turkish). A person performing *Zekr* individually may use a string of prayer beads (rosary) to count the sayings, usually ninety-nine times (same number as the names of God in Sufism). The rosary may be a short string with thirty-three beads or a full string of ninety-nine beads.

Divân, Diwân. Persian word for the "book of poetry" composed by a given poet. The *Divân* is usually named after the poet's name, but Rumi's work is named after his spiritual teacher Shams-e Tabrizi (*Divân-e Shams-e Tabrizi*), also called *Divân-e Kabir* (The Great Divân). This word is also used in Arabic and Turkish.

Erfân, Irfân. Arabic word for "gnosis" (esoteric way of knowing); also used in Persian and Turkish.

Eshg, Ishg. Arabic word meaning "love." Also used in Persian. *Ashk* in Turkish. The word *ishg* does not appear in the *Quran*, but a word with a similar meaning, *hubb* (love, liking) and its derivatives (*habib*, "dear friend," *mah'boob*, "beloved," *muhebb*, "lover"), often appear in the verses of the *Quran*. According to Sufism, love is the basis of God's creation.

Eshrâg, Ishrâg. Arabic word for "Illumination" or "Enlightenment;" also used in Persian.

Fakir. Arabic word *fagir* (also in Persian) means "poor one." *Fakir* in Turkish entered the English language in the early seventeenth century. See also *Darvish*.

Falsafa, Falsafah. Arabic word for "philosophy," originally derived from the Greek *philosophia* ("love of knowledge"). Also used in Persian (*Falsafeh*) and Turkish (*Felsefe*). *Failasuf* (or *Filsuf* in Persian) means "philosopher."

Fanâ. An Arabic and Sufi term meaning "annihilation or cessation." Much like the Buddhist concept of *nirvâna*, it refers to the final stage of the Sufi path in which selfish attachments and greedy desires become extinct. After that, the seeker enters the stage of *Bagâ*. Also used in Persian; *Fenâ* in Turkish.

Fekr, Fikr. Arabic word meaning "thought." It refers to the Sufi practice of contemplation. Also used in Persian and Turkish.

Fig'h. Arabic word for Islamic law and jurisprudence. Also used in Persian. *Fagih*, an expert in Islamic law. Rumi was an eminent *fagih*.

Fitra, Fitrah. Arabic word for "nature, essence, pure state of humans created by God." *Fitrat* in Persian.

Ghazal (plural: ***Ghazaliyât***). (*gh* as in French **r**; for example, Française.) Arabic word for lyric ode or sonnet; it literally means "talking with the beloved." A form of classical Persian poetry in which each couplet (two lines) end with the same rhyme. The whole *ghazal* (usually having six to sixteen couplets) follows the same meter. Rumi's *ghazals* are collected in the *Divân-e Shams-e Tabrizi*.

Gheyb. Arabic word meaning "the unseen realm, metaphysical or divine secret." In Rumi's poetry, it is from the *Gheyb*, the unseen mysterious realm, that this world of phenomena and objects is manifest, and to which all creatures return. Somewhat similar to the Buddhist concept of "emptiness" (*shunyata*).

Hadith. Arabic word (literally, "news, saying, narrative") for the sayings of Prophet Muhammad as reported orally and then collected in several books. *Hadis* in Persian; *Hedis* in Turkish.

Hagg. Arabic word for "Truth," implying "God" in Sufi literature. *Hagg* also used in Persian; *Hâk* in Turkish.

Hagiga, Haggigah. Arabic word for "Truth." *Hagigat* in Persian; *Hâkikat* in Turkish.

Hajj. Islamic ritual of pilgrimage to Mecca. *Hajj* also used in Persian, Turkish, and other languages in the Muslim world. The person who performs this pilgrimage is called *Hâji* (male) and *Hâjiyah* (female), which is sometimes added as an honorific title before the person's name. The annual *hajj* is held from the eight to twelfth of *Dhul Hijjah* (the last month in the lunar Islamic/Arabic calendar).

Hâl. Arabic word meaning "state, situation, condition." In Sufi literature, it has two meanings: (1) "Feeling from the heart" in contrast to the "learning from words or speech" (*Gâl*, "speech"). (2) An intense transformational feeling (rapture) that comes to the seeker spontaneously on his spiritual path and search; this is different from *Magâm* ("station") or a stage in spiritual search that is achieved by the seeker as a result of his or her own effort and practice.

Hekma, Hikmah. Arabic word, "wisdom or philosophy." *Hekmat* in Persian. *Hakim*, sage or philosopher.

Khalwa, Khalwah. Arabic word (literally, "being empty or void") for the Sufi "retreat, seclusion, solitude." *Khal'vat* in Persian; *Helvet* in Turkish.

Khânigâh. Persian word for a Sufi lodge for gathering, meditation, and study. Another word is *Tekiya* (*Teke* in Turkish). *Zâwiya* in Arabic.

Khâtun. A Turkish word for "lady" or "wife of a Khan ("Sir")." Also used in Persian and Arabic; pronounced *Hatun* in modern Turkish.

Konya (Turkish), ***Guniyyah*** (Persian). A historical city in southwest Turkey. It was the capital of the Seljuq Dynasty during the twelfth century. Rumi spent most of his life in Konya and his tomb in that city is a pilgrimage site. Konya was called *Ikónion* in Greek and *Iconium* in Latin. Today it has a population of 1.2 million people.

Imâm. Arabic title for a religious leader or clergyman in the Islamic faith. Also used in Persian and Turkish. In Sunni Islam, it is a general title for an Islamic expert who preaches and leads the communal prayers in a mosque. In Shi'a Islam, it is also a specific title for the successors of Prophet Muhammad (according to the Shi'a belief) starting with Ali (the Prophet's cousin and son-in-law) and continuing through his two sons and their descendants (up to the fifth, seventh or twelfth generation depending on each Shi'a sect).

Islâm. Arabic word meaning "submission, surrender *(sallam)*" Historically, it refers to the religion founded by Prophet Muhammad in Arabia in the seventh century. Today, Islam has 1.6 billion followers, roughly twenty-two percent of the world's population and is world's second largest religion after Christianity. According to the *Quran*, *Islam* ("surrendering to God") is the name of all revealed religions, and Muhammad is one in the line of prophets that goes back to Abraham, Moses, and Jesus. *Muslim* (English: Moslem) is a follower of Islam. Islam from the root word *salm* means "peace."

Jalâluddin. Rumi's given name was Jalâluddin Mohammad. Jalâluddin (also written Jalâl al-Din) is an Arabic word meaning "glory or splendor of religion." Pronounced Jelâleddin (Çelaleddin) in Turkish.

Ma'rifa, Ma'rifah. Arabic word meaning "knowing, awareness, familiarity, cognition." A body of spiritual knowledge and teachings. *Ma'refat* in Persian. Plural: *Ma'ârif (Ma'âref).*

Magâm (plural: ***Magâmât****).* Arabic word "station, stage, position, standing place, dwelling." Sufi teachers and masters have described various "stations" *(Magâmât)* for the wayfarers which they need to reach by practice and effort. *Magâm* also used in Persian; *Makam* in Turkish.

Masjid. Mosque. Arabic word meaning "place of prostration." *Masjid* is also used in Persian, Turkish, Urdu, and other languages in the Muslim world.

Mawlânâ. Arabic title meaning "our master." Also pronounced *Mowlânâ* in Iran and *Mevlânâ* in Turkey. The title is usually given to an eminent scholar, teacher or sage. It has become a specific title for Jalâluddin Rumi. In Persian, he is also called *Mowlavi* ("my master").

Mathnawi. Arabic word meaning "couplet." Pronounced *Masnavi* or *Masnawi* in Persian and *Mesnevi* in Turkish. A form of classical Persian poetry, usually used for composing stories and parables in verse, in which the two lines of each couplet share the same rhyme. The rhyme changes from one couplet to another, however, the meter of the poem remains the same throughout. Many Persian poets have composed *Masnavi* books, but Rumi's *Masnavi-ye Ma'navi* is so famous that it is simply called the *Masnavi.*

Morâgiba. Sufi meditation. Arabic word meaning "watching over, inspection."

Mecca. Arabic *Makkah.* A holy city on the western part of the Arabian Peninsula where Prophet Muhammad was born and raised, and where the annual Muslim pilgrimage *(Hajj)* is held. It is home to Islam's most sacred mosque, *Al-Masjid al-Haram,* at the center of which is a cubic-shaped building called *Kaaba (Kabah)* (literally, "cube"), believed to have been built by Abraham. Muslims all over the world pray toward the *Kaaba*; the direction toward the *Kaaba* is called *Gibla*. During the *hajj*, the pilgrims circumambulate the *Kaaba* seven times.

Nafs. Arabic word for "soul, self, psyche, and ego" (depending on the context). Hebrew equivalent is *nefesh*. Also used in Persian; *Nefs* in Turkish. It often refers to the carnal self and greedy ego.

Quran. Arabic word (properly pronounced *Gur'ân*; literally, "recitation") for the name of the holy scripture in Islam which was revealed to Prophet Muhammad during the years 609-632 AD. It consists of 114 chapters (*sura*), arranged roughly in the order of their decreasing length, not in the chronological order of revelation. Each chapter consists of verses (*âyât*). Rumi's *Masnavi* has a large number of references to the verses, stories, and teachings of the *Quran*.

Persian. The language Rumi spoke and in which he wrote his poetry. Called *Fârsi (Pârsi)* in Iran, *Dari* in Afghanistan, and *Tajiki* in Tajikistan. Persian is an Indo-European language but has borrowed a large number of Arabic words (after Islam spread in Persia) and uses a modified Arabic script (which itself was derived from Aramaic-Syriac scripts). Modern Persian dates back to the ninth century AD, and encompasses a large number of classical prose and poetry books. Today about 100 million people speak Persian, but its historical influence covers a much wider region from Anatolia (now Turkey) to India.

Ramadân. The ninth month in the lunar Islamic/Arabic calendar during which the faithful Muslims fast from sunrise to sunset. *Ramazân* in Persian (also used in Turkish).

Rubâ'ie (plural: **Rubâiyât**). Arabic word for "quatrain." This shortest form of classical Persian poetry consists of two couplets (four lines) in which the first, second and fourth lines have the same rhyme. In Persian it is also called *do-beyti* ("two couplets"). The most famous work in this category is the *Rubaiyat of Omar Khayyam*, the work of an eleventh-century Persian poet and scientist which was popularized in English by Edward FitzGerald in the late nineteenth century. Rumi's *Rubâiyât* are collected in the last section of the *Divân-e Shams-e Tabrizi*.

Salât. Arabic word for the ritual Muslim prayer (five times a day and on some other occasions). *Namâz* in Persian (also used in Turkish).

Samâ. Arabic word meaning "audition or listening." In the Sufi tradition, it is a practice of listening to music, sometimes, accompanied with dance, as in the whirling dance in Rumi's Sufi Order. Also used in Persian; pronounced *semâ* in Turkish.

Sawm. Arabic word for the ritual Muslim "fasting" in the month of Ramadan. *Roozeh* in Persian (also used in Turkish).

Seljuq (Turkish), ***Saljug*** (Persian). The name of several Turco-Persian dynasties that ruled parts of Central Asia, Iran, and Turkey during the eleventh and twelfth centuries. One particular Seljuq Dynasty that is relevant to Rumi's life is the *Saljugiyân-e Rūm* (the Seljuqs of Rūm or Byzantium) that ruled Anatolia from 1077 to 1308 AD.

Shaykh, Sheikh. An honorific Arabic title meaning "leader, elder, noble, master" used for religious teachers and Sufi masters. *Shaykha* is feminine form. *Murshid* ("Guide") is another Arabic term for a Sufi master. The equivalent Persian words, *Pir* and *Bâbâ*, are also widely used in the Islamic world.

Sirr, Serr. Arabic, "secret, mystery." Plural: ***Asrâr.*** Also used in Persian and Turkish. ***Râz*** in Persian has the same meaning.

Shams. Arabic word meaning "Sun." Hebrew equivalent is *Shemesh*. Also used in Persian; pronounced *Shems* in Turkish. Shamsuddin Mohammad of Tabriz (a city in northwest Iran) was the spiritual mentor and friend of Rumi. Rumi also used *Shams* as a pen-name in many of his poems.

Shâ'er, Shâ'ir. Arabic word, "poet." Also used in Persian and Turkish.

Shahâda, Shahâdah. Arabic word meaning "bearing witness, testimony." Declaration of faith in Islam includes the following phrase: "There is no god but God, and Muhammad is a messenger of God" (*lā ilāha illā-llāh, muhammadun rasūlu-llāh*). *Shahâdat* in Persian; *Shahâdet* in Turkish.

Sharia, Shariah. Arabic word (literally "path to the river water") for "religious laws, rituals and regulations." *Sharia* and *Shariat* also used in Persian.

She'r. Arabic word, "poem or poetry." Also used in Persian and Turkish.

Soh'ba, Soh'bah. Arabic word meaning "conversation, companionship," particularly a spiritual dialogue and fellowship among Sufis. *Soh'bat* in Persian; *Sohbet* in Turkish.

Sufism. English translation of the Arabic word *tasawwuf* ("becoming a Sufi"), the mystical dimension of Islam. A spiritual tradition developed over the centuries in the Islamic world which, although rooted in Islam, also borrowed many concepts and practices from Christian, Persian, Greek and Indian traditions. The word *Sufi* has several meanings, including "pure" (heart) and "wool wearer" (with reference to the woolen garments that Sufis traditionally wore).

Traig, Tariga, Traigah. Arabic words meaning "path," usually a spiritual path. *Tarig, Tariga* and *Tarigat* are also used in Persian. *Tarik* in Turkish.

Tawhid. Arabic word meaning "oneness, unity, union." The oneness of God is the central doctrine of Islam. Also pronounced *Towhid* in Persian and *Tevhid* in Turkish.

Wah'dat al-wojud. Arabic words meaning "the unity of being" or "the oneness of existence." A central concept in the Sufi teachings of Ibn Arabi (1165-1240) and Rumi. Persian: *vah'dat-e vojud*. It states that God's existence is the only one reality; the created universe does not have its own independent existence and is simply a shadow of His existence. Sufis believe that this concept best describes *Tawhid*.

***Wird*, *Verd*.** Arabic word for a "phrase or prayer" (usually from the verses of the *Quran*) recited daily by Sufis. Also used in Persian and Turkish. See for example, *The Mevlevi Wird: The Prayers recited daily by Mevlevi Dervishes*, translated by Camille Helminski and Mahmoud Mostafa (Threshold Society, 2000).

***Zekr*, *Zikr*.** See *Dhikr*.

***Ziyâra*, *Ziyârah*.** Arabic word (literally "visitation") for "pilgrimage." *Ziyârat* in Persian; *Ziyâret* in Turkish. *Zâ'er* or *Zâ'ir*, "Pilgrim."

[Appendix III]
Rumiyât: A Guide to Rumi Studies

I sometimes receive requests to introduce reading or audiovisual material about the poetry, thought, and biography of Rumi. These requests come from English-speaking as well as Persian-speaking fans of Rumi. There are, of course, numerous books in this field, and they come in different categories, levels and quality. Selecting a few books from this vast genre is a difficult and an admittedly subjective task. Nonetheless, here I introduce some books and audiovisual sources based on my own limited experience and readings, but which, I hope, will be useful to readers. The numbering in each category is from introductory to advanced level. This bibliography is not meant to be comprehensive or exhaustive; nor is it an endorsement of the publications and websites mentioned here; the bibliography should serve as some suggestions for your own exploration.

Books about Rumi (Life and Thought)

- In English:

(1) Annemarie Schimmel, *I Am Wind You Are Fire: The Life and Work of Rumi* (Shambhala, Boston, 1992). Republished as *Rumi's World: The Life and Works of the Greatest Sufi Poet* (2001).

(2) William Chittick, *The Sufi Doctrine of Rumi: Illustrated Edition* (World Wisdom, Bloomington, IN, 2005).

(3) Andrew Harvey, *The Way of Passion: A Celebration of Rumi* (J. P. Tarcher/Putnam, New York, 1994).

(4) Eva de Vitray-Meyerovitch, *Rumi and Sufism,* translated from the French by Simone Fattal (Post-Apollo Press, Palo Alto, 1987).

(5) Afzal Iqbal, *The Life and Work of Jalaluddin Rumi* (Oxford University Press, Karachi, 1965, seventh impression, 1999).

(6) Annemarie Schimmel, *The Triumphal Sun: A Study of the Works of Jalaloddin Rumi* (State University of New York Press, 1993).

(7) Franklin Lewis, *Rumi: Past and Present, East and West* (Oneworld, Oxford, 2000).

(8) William Chittick, *The Sufi Path of Love: The Spiritual Teachings of Rumi* (State University of New York Press, 1983).

- In Persian:

All of the English books mentioned above have been translated into Persian.

(1) Abdul Hossein Zarrinkub, *Pelle Pelle Ta Molagât-e Khoda* ("Step by Step toward Meeting God"), (Elmi, Tehran, 1373/1994, reprinted over a dozen times). An excellent introduction to Rumi's life. English translation, *Step by Step Up to Union with God*, by M. Keyvani (Persian Heritage Foundation, New York, 2009). According to Franklin Lewis, this book would make for a good film script.

(2) Mohammad Jafar Mosaffâ, *Bâ Pir-e Balkh* ("In the Company of the Master of Balkh"), (Parishân, Tehran, 1380/1991, second edition) offers enlightening commentaries on several stories from the *Masnavi* through a psychological lens and modern outlook.

(3) Badi uz-Zamân Foruzânfar, *Zendegâni-ye Mowlânâ Jalâluddin Mohammad* ("Biography of Mowlânâ Jalâluddin Muhammad), (Zavvâr, Tehran, 1333/1954, reprinted several times). A scholarly research that has served as the foundation for all the other biographies of Rumi both in Persian and English.

Rumi in English Translations

This category includes hundreds of books available on the market (online sellers and bookstores). Many of these books are not original translations from the Persian but re-translations, renditions, and inspired versions of Rumi's poems. The following are among the books that have achieved popularity among the general readers or reputation from the scholars.

- Anthologies:

(1) Coleman Barks, *The Essential Rumi* (HarperSanFrancisco, 1995; HarperOne, New York, new expanded edition 2004) has remained a best seller not only among the Rumi books but also in the overall category of poetry in the USA.

(2) Jonathan Starr, *Rumi: In the Arms of the Beloved* (J. P. Tarcher/Putnam, New York, 1997).

(3) Coleman Barks, *A Year with Rumi: Daily Readings* (HarperOne, New York, 2006).

(4) Kabir and Camille Helminski, *The Rumi Daybook: 365 Poems and Teachings of the Beloved Sufi Master* (Shambhala, Boston, 2011).

(5) Kabir Helminski, *The Rumi Collection* (Threshold Books, Putney, VT, 1998; Shambhala, Boston, 2005).

(6) Franklin D. Lewis, *Rumi: Swallowing the Sun* (Oneworld, Oxford, 2007 hardcover, 2013 paperback).

(7) Peter Washington, *Rumi Poems* (Everyman's Library Pocket Poets, New York, 2006).

- *Divân-e Shams-e Tabrizi (Divân-e Kabir)*

(1) Coleman Barks, *Rumi: The Big Red Book* (HarperOne, New York, 2010).

(2) Arthur Arberry's *Mystical Poems of Rumi, First Selection, Poems 1-200* (The University of Chicago Press, 1968) and *Mystical Poems of Rumi, Second Selection, Poems 201-400* (Westview Press, Boulder, CO, 1979) are accurate prose translations. These two books combined in one volume was republished as *Mystical Poems of Rumi* (The University of Chicago Press, 2009).

(3) Reynold A. Nicholson, *Selected Poems from the Divân-e Shams-e Tabrizi*, English translation along with the original Persian and scholarly notes (Cambridge University Press, 1898, reprinted several times, most recently by IBEX Publishers, Washington D.C., 2001).

(4) Nevit O. Ergin, a Turkish scholar of Rumi, translated the *Divân-e Kabir* into English in 22 volumes; his work is based on a complete Turkish translation of the *Divân-e Kabir* by the late Abdulbâki Gölpinârli, published in Istanbul, 1956-57 (see the late Nevit Ergin's website for the Society for Understanding of Mevlana based in California: http://sfumevlana.org).

- *Masnavi (Mathnawi)*

(1) Philip Dunn and Manuela Dunn Mascetti, *The Illustrated Rumi: The Treasury of Wisdom from the Poet of the Soul*, a new translation based on R. A. Nicholson's version (HarperSanFransisco, 2000 hardcover; HarperOne, New York, 2010 softcover) is a coffee-table book and contains many inspiring stories enhanced by illustrations.

(2) Coleman Barks, *The Soul of Rumi* (HarperOne, New York, 2002).

(3) Alan Williams, *Spiritual Verses, The First Book of the Masnavi-ye Ma'navi*, (Penguin Classics, London, 2006).

(4) Arthur J. Arberry, *Tales from the Masnavi* (tales 1-100) and *More Tales from the Masnavi* (tales 101-200), (George Allen & Unwin, London, 1961 and 1963) are easy-to-read English prose.

(5) *A Rumi Anthology*, selected and translated by Reynold A. Nicholson (Oneworld, Oxford, 2000) contains two books previously published as: *Rumi: Poet and Mystic: Selections from His Writings* (George Allen & Unwin,

London, 1950) and *Tales of Mystic Meaning, being selections from the Mathnawi of Jalaluddin Rumi* (Chapman & Hall, London; Frekerick A. Stokec Co., New York, 1931).

(6) *The Teachings of Rumi: The Mathnawi*, abridged and translated by E. H. Whinfield (Octagon Press, London, 1994; originally published in London, 1887).

(7) Jawid Mojadeddi, a renowned Sufi scholar from Afghanistan and professor of religion at Rutgers University, has been translating the six books of the *Masnavi* into English verse. So far, the first three books have been published: *The Masnavi, Book One* (2008); *The Masnavi, Book Two* (2008), and *The Masnavi, Book Three* (2014), all published by the Oxford University Press.

(8) Of course, the most complete and scholarly edition is that of Reynold A. Nicholson's *The Mathnawi of Jalaluddin Rumi*, which includes the Persian edition, English translation, and scholarly commentaries (eight volumes, Messers Luzac & Co., London, 1925-1940). The English translation has been republished in three volumes (Gibb Memorial Trust, London, 2001).

- Quatrains (*Rubâiyât*) of Rumi

(1) Maryam Mafi and Azima Melita Kolin, *Rumi: Whispers of the Beloved* (Thorsons, London, 1999). Republished as *Rumi's Little Book of the Heart* (Hampton Roads, Newburyport, MA, 2016).

(2) Maryam Mafi and Azima Melita Kolin, *Rumi: Gardens of the Beloved* (Element, London, 2003). Republished as *Rumi's Little Book of Love* (Hampton Roads, Newburyport, MA, 2009).

(3) Shahram Shiva, *Rending the Veil: Literal and Poetic Translations of Rumi* (Hohm Press, Prescott, AZ, 1995).

(4) Rasoul Shams, *Rumi: The Art of Loving* (Rumi Publications, Salt Lake City, 2012).

(5) *The Quatrains of Rumi* (Ruba'iyat Jalaluddin Muhammad Balkhi), translated by Ibrahim Gamard and Rawan Farhadi (Sufi Dari Books, San Rafael, CA, 2008) is the most complete and scholarly translation of Rumi's quatrains.

- *Fihi Mâ Fih* (Discourses of Rumi)

(1) *Discourses of Rumi*, translated by Arthur J. Arberry (John Murray, London, 1961).

(2) *Signs of the Unseen: The Discourses of Jalaluddin Rumi*, translated by W. M. Thackston (Shambhala, Boston, 1999).

Rumi's Poetry & Works in Persian

Rumi's works in Persian (his native language) include the *Divân-e Shams-e Tabrizi* (*Divân-e Kabir*), the *Masnavi-ye* (*Mathnawi*) *Ma'navi*, the *Fihi Mâ Fih* ("literally, "In it what is in it," or his "Discourses"), the *Majâlis-e Sab'a* ("Seven Sermons"), and the *Maktubât* ("Letters"). The first three have been translated into English. The Persian editions of these books are described below. The *ganjoor* website (http://ganjoor.net) contains the Persian versions of many classical poetry books from Iran.

(1) *Divân-e Shams-e Tabrizi* (also called *Divân-e Kabir* or *Kulliyât-e Shams-e Tabrizi*) includes Rumi's lyrical odes (*ghazaliyât*) (about 3,300 poems) and quatrains (*rubâiyât*) (nearly 1900 quatrains), totaling over 44,000 verses of poetry. *Divân* means "poetry book'; *Kulliyât* means "collected works"; *Kabir* means "great"; and *Shams-e Tabrizi* (Shams of Tabriz) was the name of Rumi's spiritual friend who was responsible for Rumi's transformation to a poet of love and light.

The authoritative printed version of Rumi's *Divân* is the one edited by the late Badi uz-Zamân Foruzânfar (1900-1970), professor of literature at the University of Tehran. This work was published in ten volumes with glossary and indices (University of Tehran Press, 1336-1346/1957-1967); a second edition was brought out by Amir Kabir Press in Tehran (1355/1976; reprinted several times). Since then, several publishers in Tehran have printed single-volume editions of the *Divân* based on the Foruzânfar edition.

Foruzânfar's edition is largely based on the oldest manuscripts of the *Divân*, including that at the Mevlana Museum (Rumi's mausoleum) in Konya.

However, one particular edition (*Kulliyât-e Shams-e Tabrizi*), published by Amir Kabir Press in Tehran in 1341/1962 (and reprinted numerous times) needs caution. That book contains an introductory chapter on Rumi's life adopted from Foruzânfar's biography, but the poetry book was not edited by Foruzânfar, and instead was largely taken from a nineteenth-century Indian print of the *Divân* which includes some poems and lines not found in the oldest manuscripts of the *Divân*. Unfortunately, many English translators of Rumi in recent decades have relied on this edition mistakenly assuming that it is the authentic Foruzânfar's edition, and in this way, some poems (especially quatrains) have become popular in the name of Rumi, but which were probably added to the *Divân* by the scribes in later centuries. In this book, wherever such poems have been cited, they are specified as poems "attributed to Rumi."

Gozide-ye Ghazaliyât-e Shams ("Selections from the Odes of Shams") is a popular anthology of Rumi's lyrical odes (*ghazaliyât*) by the noted Iranian scholar Mohammad Reza Shafi-ye Kadkani (Sokhan, Tehran, first published in 1352/1973, and recently revised and expanded to two volumes, 1388/1999).

(2) *Masnavi-ye Ma'navi* ("Rhyming Couplets on Spiritual Meanings") is a six-volume book of stories and parables in verse which Rumi composed during the last decade of his life and narrated it to his disciple and spiritual friend Husâmuddin Chalabi (Chelebi). *Mathnawi* (Arabic), *Masnavi* (Persian) or *Mesnevi* (Turkish) means "rhyming couplet," and it is a form of classical Persian poetry used for composing stories in verse. Rumi's *Masnavi* has nearly 26,000 verses. The former professor of Persian literature at Cambridge University, Reynold A. Nicholson (1868-1945) devoted three decades of his life to produce a critically edited Persian version from various manuscripts, an accurate English translation, and scholarly commentaries; his work titled, *The Mathnawi of Jalauddin Rumi*, was published in eight volumes ("Gibb Memorial Series," Luzac, London, 1925-1940). A single-volume Persian version based on Nicholson's edition was published by Amir Kabir Press (1336/1957) and has been reprinted numerous times (by Amir Kabir and other publishers in Tehran). The English translation of the *Mathnawi of Jalaluddin Rumi* (six books in three volumes) has been recently

reprinted (Gibb Memorial Trust, London, 2001). Dozens of scholars, poets and mystics have written commentaries on the *Masnavi* in Persian, Turkish, and English. Here, I mention two of them in Persian: *Shar'h-e Jâme-e Masnavi-ye Ma'navi* by Karim Zamâni in six volumes (Ettela'ât Press, Tehran, 1372-1377/1993-1998), and *Masnavi* in seven volumes edited by Mohammad Este'lâmi (Zavvâr, Tehran, 1389/1990, second edition), which is actually a new edition of the *Masnavi* based on the oldest manuscripts kept at the Konya (Mevlana) Museum.

(3) *Fihi Mâ Fih* ("In It What Is In It"), Rumi's seventy-one informal talks written down by his disciples, notably by his son Sultân Valad. Edited by Bad uz-Zamân Foruzânfar (Tehran University Press, 1330/1951; reprinted by Amir Kabir Press, Tehran, 1348/1969).

(4) *Majâles-e Sab'a* ("Seven Sermons"), edited by Ahmad Ramzi, Valad Chelebi, and Feridoon Nâfezbek (Istanbul, 1937); edited by Towfig H. Sob'hâni (Tehran, 1365/1996).

(5) *Maktubât* ("Letters"), edited by Ahmad Ramzi and Feridoon Nâfezbek (Istanbul, 1937); edited by Towfig H. Sob'hani (Iran University Press, Tehran, 1371/2002, second edition). English translations of seventeen of Rumi's letter are available in *This Longing: Poetry, Teaching Stories, and Selected Letters of Rumi* by Coleman Barks and John Moyne (Threshold Books, Putney, VT, 1998; Shambhala, Boston, 2000), pp. 81-107.

Rumi: Journal

Mawlana Rumi Review, published annually since 2010, is an academic journal devoted to the life, thought, poetry, and legacy of Rumi. Edited by Dr. Leonard Lewisohn, it is published by The Center for Persian and Iranian Studies at the University of Exeter in collaboration with The Rumi Institute (Nicosia, Cyprus), and Archetype Books, Cambridge, UK.
Website: http://mawlanarumireview.org

Rumi Poetry: Recitations in English

Spirit of Rumi, Vision II (Angel Records, 1997).

A Gift of Love, Deepak Chopra & Friends Present Music Inspired by the Love Poems of Rumi (Rasa, 1998).

Rumi, Fountain of Fire, translations by Nader Khalili and recited by Qalbi (1999).

When Days Have No Night: Rumi's Songs, music by Mischa Rutenberg (MorPerm, 2000).

Rumi: Lament of the Reed, Seyyed Hossein Nasr and Suleyman Erguner (Asr Media, 2000).

Say I Am You, W. A. Mathieu (Cold Mountain Music, 2003).

Rumi & Strings, W. A. Mathieu (Cold Mountain Music, 2005).

The Way of the Heart: Ecstatic Poetry and Stories of Rumi, compiled by Andrew Vidich, narrated by Tamir with music by Amir Vahab (Amrit Production/Oasis, 2005).

True Love Rumi, Sina recites poems translated by Nader Khalili (2006).

Rumi: Where Everything is Music, Reshad Feild recites poems translated by Coleman Barks with music extemporized on the violin by Andrea Helesfai (Chalice Guild, 2008).

Rumi Symphony, Andrew Harvey and music by Hans Christian (Allemande Music, 2011).

Just Being Here: Rumi and Human Friendship, Coleman Barks and music by David Darling (Sounds True, 2011).

Rumi: Lovedrunk, Shahram Shiva (Racing Shiva Records, 2009, 2012).

Rumi: Voice of Longing, Coleman Barks (Sounds True, 2013).

Like This! Hear the love poems of Rumi in English (Jack Hirschman) and Persian (Mahnaz Badihian) (One Little Indian, 2016).

Rumi: Recitations and Songs in Persian

Rumi, Aqnazar (Buda Mystic, 2003).

The Passion of Rumi, Shahram Nazeri and Hafez Nazeri (Quartertone Productions, 2007).

Rumi: The Beloved is Here, Dariush, Ramesh and Faramarz Aslani (Dbf Records, 2008).

Through Eternity: Homage to Molavi Rumi, Dastan Ensemble with Shahram Nazeri (Sounds True, 2010).

In the Footsteps of Rumi, Rumi Ensemble and Salar Aghili (Talik, 2012).

Rumi Symphony Project: Untold, Hafez Nazeri (Sony Masterworks, 2014).

Rumi: Documentary Films

Rumi: Poet of the Heart, directed by Hayden Reiss, narrated by Debra Winger, 90 minutes (1998).

Rumi: The Wings of Love, directed by Shems Friedlander, 34 minutes (2002).

Rumi: Turning Ecstatic, directed by Tina Petrova and Stephen Roloff, 48 minutes (2007).

Rumi Returning: The Triumph of Divine Passion, produced by Heaven on Earth Creations, 57 minutes (2008).

Rumi: Poesie Des Islam, Poet of Islam, directed by Houchang Allahyari and Tom-Dariusch Allahyari, 87 minutes, German and English (2009).

Rumi-related Websites

http://mevlanafoundation.com
The Chalabi (Çelebi in Turkish) family, Rumi's descendants in Turkey, have formed the International Mevlana Foundation. "The current Celebi, Faruk Hemdem is the 20th great-grandson of Mevlana (22nd generation descendant) and he is the 33rd Celebi to occupy the post." The Foundation's president is Farkuk Hemdem Celebi and the vice-president is Mrs. Esin Celebi Bayru (22nd great grand-daughter of Rumi).

www.mevlana.net
"Çelaleddin Bakir Çelebi, the 21st grandson of Mevlana Celaleddin Rumi died on 13 April, 1996 in Istanbul, Turkey. This site is dedicated to him by his family."

www.hayatidede.org
The Mevlevi Order of America, based in Honolulu, continues the tradition of the Konya Sufi master Suleiman Hayati Dede (1904-1985) through his son Postneshin Jelaleddin Loras. The group offers *samâ* and *zikr*.

www.rumiforum.org
Rumi Forum for Interfaith Dialogue, founded in 1999 and based in Washington D.C., aims to "foster interfaith and intercultural dialogue" in the spirit of Rumi's thought and poetry. Its honorary president is the Turkish Islamic scholar Fetullah Gülen. In 2007, the Rumi Forum began the annual Rumi Peace and Dialogue Awards.

www.mawlanarumireview.com
Website of *Mawlana Rumi Review*, an annual academic journal devoted to Rumi studies (first volume published in 2010). Editor: Dr. Leonard Lewisohn, University of Exeter, UK. Printed and distributed by Archetype Publishing (www.archetype.uk.com).

www.sufism.org
Threshold Society, in the tradition of Mevlevi Order, was founded by Kabir (Edmund) Helminski and his wife Camille Adams Helminski. Based initially in Vermont, then California, and currently in Louisville, Kentucky. Influenced by Suleiman Dede of Konya and Dr. Çelaleddin Çelebi of Istanbul, the couple have published books and recordings, and offer lectures and retreats.

https://rumiscircle.com
The London-based Rumi's Circle is closely associated with the Helminskis' Threshold Society.

www.dar-al-masnavi.org
Managed by Ibrahim Gamard, an American psychologist, a self-taught speaker of Persian, Rumi scholar and a Muslim; the website contains a vast collection of Rumi's work in English.

http://sfumevlanamorg
Society for Understanding of Mevlana founded in 1992 by Dr. Nevit Ergin (1928-2015), a native of Turkey and a retired cosmetic surgeon in California. He translated Rumi's *Divân-e Kabir* (from a Turkish translation by the late Abdulbâki Gölpinârli) in 22 volumes.

www.colemanbarks.com
Website of Coleman Barks in Georgia, a retired English professor, who has successfully popularized Rumi's poetry in North America through rendering the literal translations into the modern English style of free verse.

www.calearth.org
Nader Khalili (1936-2008), an Iranian architect and a Rumi translator, who founded the Californian Institute of Earth Art and Architecture (Cal-Earth) in 1986, inspired by Rumi's poetic imagery.

www.rumi.net
Shahram Shiva, an Iranian-American translator of Rumi, who also conducts Rumi poetry recitation and whirling sessions. He lives in New York.

www.rumionfire.com
"A tribute to Rumi" by Shahriar Shahriari, an Iranian mechanical engineer, writer, and translator of classical Persian poetry, from his base, first in Canada and later in Los Angeles.

www.maryammafi.com
Website of Maryam Mafi, an Iranian translator of Rumi, based in London.

www.naini.net
Majid Naini, a native of Iran and a former electrical engineer and computer scientist, has (since 2002) devoted his life to Rumi's vision of universal love through lectures and translations. Naini lives in Florida.

www. rassouli.com
Renowned painter Freydoon Rassouli, a native of Iran, lives in California. Many of his works are inspired by the mystical Persian poems. Rassouli is the translator and author of *Rumi Revealed: Selected poems from the Divan of Shams* (2015).

www.rumipoetryclub.com
Website of Rumi Poetry Club in Salt Lake City founded in 2007 by Rasoul Shams.

www.khamush.com and www.rumi.org.uk
Created in 2000 by the Greek-born Rumi fan Nihat Tsolak in the UK. A great resource of Rumi's poetry in English.

www.mevlana800.info
"International Sufi Path." In English and Turkish.

http://mevlana.com
In Turkish language.

Notes & References

Chapter 1. Introduction: Why Rumi Matters

1. Mary Oliver, *A Poetry Handbook* (Harcourt, San Diego 1994), p. 11.

2. See the following documents on UNESCO's website:
http://unesdoc.unesco.org/images/0014/001481/148150e.pdf
http://unesdoc.unesco.org/images/0014/001473/147319e.pdf

3. Unless otherwise indicated, translations of Rumi's poems in this book are made by the author from the following Persian prints of Rumi's books:
[*Divân*] *Kulliât-e Shams-e Tabrizi: Divân-e Kabir*, ten volumes, by Mowlânâ Jalâluddin Mohammad Balkhi Rumi, edited by Badi uz-Zamân Foruzânfar (Tehran University Press, 1336-1346/1957-1967; republished by Amir Kabir Press, Tehran, 1355/1976).
[*Masnavi*] *Masnavi-ye Ma'navi* (six books), by Mowlânâ Jalâluddin Mohammad Balkhi Rumi, edited by Reynold A. Nicholson (Amir Kabir Press, Tehran, 1336/1957). This is the single-volume Persian print of Nicholson's edition, originally published in eight volumes including English translation and scholarly commentaries: *The Mathnawi of Jalaluddin Rumi* ("Gibb Memorial Series," Luzac, London, 1925-1940).

4. Learning about the art and craft of poetry helps us better appreciate and enjoy the reading and writing of poems. The following books on this subject are very useful:
A Poetry Handbook by Mary Oliver (Harcourt, San Diego, 1994).
Why Poetry Matters by Jay Parini (Yale University Press, 2008).
Poetry As Spiritual Practice by Robert McDowell (Free Press, New York, 2008).
Letters to a Young Poet by Rainer Maria Rilke, translated by M. D. Herter Norton (W.H. Norton, New York, 1954).
Nine Gates: Entering the Mind of Poetry by Jane Hirshfield (Harper, New York, 1997).
How to Read a Poem by Edward Hirsch (Harcourt, San Diego, 1999).
The Art of Poetry: How to Read a Poem by Shira Wolosky (Oxford University Press, 2008).

Chapter 2. Inspiration: Be Like Melting Snow

1. Loren Eiseley, *The Immense Journey* (Random House, New York, 1957), p. 15.

2. The full poem can be found in Arthur Arberry's *Mystical Poems of Rumi* (The University of Chicago Press, 2009), p. 279; and Coleman Barks' *The Essential Rumi* (HarperOne, New York 2004, p. 13.) The translation here is mine.

3. D. T. Suzuki, Erich Fromm, and Richard de Martino, *Zen Buddhism & Psychoanalysis* (Grove Press, New York, 1960), p. 14.

4. Lao Tzu, *Toa Te Ching: The Richard Wilhelm Edition* (Arkana, London, 1985), No. 43, p. 47.

5. This is a famous quote from Tagore cited frequently (for example, http://www.tagorefoundationinternational.com), but I have not seen a source from Tagore's works for the quote.

6. Linnie Marsh Wolfe, *John of the Mountains: The Unpublished Journals of John Muir* (University of Wisconsin Press, 1979, second edition).

Chapter 4. Master Rumi: The Path to Poetry, Love, and Enlightenment

1. Alexander Marks, "Persian Poet Top Seller in America," *The Christian Science Monitor*, November 25, 1997.

2. Ptolemy Tompkins, "Rumi Rules!" *TIME Asia Magazine*, October 7, 2002.

3. Steve Holgate, "Persian Poet Rumi Conquers America," US Department of State's *Washington File*, March 15, 2005.

4. The oldest sources of information on Rumi's life, all in Persian, include:
(i) *Valad Nâmeh* ("The Book of Valad"), edited by Jalâl Humâ'ie (Igbâl, Tehran, 1316/1937; reprinted by Humâ Press, Tehran, 1389/2010), a narrative poetry by Rumi's eldest son Sultân Valad (1226-1312 AD); yet to be translated into English.
(ii) *Risâle-ye Sepah-sâlâr* ("The Treatise of Sepah-sâlâr"), edited by Sa'id Nafisi (Igbâl, Tehran, 1324/1945; reprinted 1995), written by Rumi's disciple Feridoon Sepah-sâlâr (?-1319 AD); no English translation of this book is available, either.

(iii) *Manâqeb ul-Árefin* ("The Virtuous Acts of the Mystics"), edited by Tahsin Yazici (Yazichi), two volumes (Ankara, 1951 & 1961, second edition 1976 & 1980; reprinted in Tehran, 1983), compiled by another disciple Ahmad Aflâki (?-1356 AD). Partial English translations of this book include James Redhouse's *Legends of the Sufis* ("The Acts of the Adepts," London, 1881, reprinted by Theosophical Books, 1976); Idries Shah's *The Hundred Tales of Wisdom* (Octagon Press, London, 1978). A complete translation is John O'Kane's *The Feats of the Knowers of God* (Brill Academic Publishers, Leiden, 2002). Excerpts from the book have also recently been published as *Rumi and His Friends: Stories of the Lovers of God* by Camille Adams Helminski and Susan Blaylock (Fons Vitae, Louisville, KY, 2013).

5. Among the modern authors who have researched Rumi's life in detail are:
(i) The Iranian scholar Badi uz-Zamân Foruzânfar (1900-1970), author of *Risâleh dar Ahvâl va Zendegâni-ye Mowlânâ Jalâluddin Mohammad* ("Treatise on the Life of Master Jalâluddin Mohammad") [in Persian] (Zavvâr, Tehran, 1954, second edition).
(ii) The Turkish scholar Abdulbâki Gölpinârli (1900-1982), author of *Mevlana Celaleddin, Hayati, Felsefesi, Eserleri, Eserlerinden Secmeler* ("Mevlana Jalaluddin: His Life, Philosophy, Works and Anthology") [in Turkish] (Istanbul, 1959), translated into Persian, *Mowlânâ Rumi*, by Towfiq Sob'hâni (Tehran, 1984).
(iii) The Pakistani scholar Afzal Iqbâl (1919-1994), author of *The Life and Thought of Maulana Jalaluddin Rumi* (Oxford University Press, Karachi, 1956, 1999).
(iv) The German-American scholar Annemarie Schimmel (1922-2003), author of *The Triumphal Sun: A Study of the Works of Jalaluddin Rumi* (London, 1978; State University of New York Press, 1993, second edition), and *I Am Wind, You Are Fire: The Life and Work of Rumi* (Shambhala Press, Boston, 1992; republished as *Rumi's World: The Life and Works of the Greatest Sufi Poet*, 2001).
(v) The American scholar Franklin Lewis, *Rumi: Past and Present, East and West* (Oneworld, Oxford, 2000).

6. Mowlânâ Jalâluddin Mohammad Balkhi Rumi, *Masnavi-ye Ma'navi*, edited by Reynold Nicholson (Amir Kabir Press, Tehran, 1957) [in Persian]. Nicholson's scholarly-edited Persian version, English translation and commentaries of *The Mathnawi of Jalaluddin Rumi* were published in eight volumes by Luzac & Co., London, 1925-1940. Partial English translations of the *Masnavi* include: E. H. Winfield's *Masnawi Ma'nawi: Spiritual Couplets* (London, 1881, reprinted as *Teachings of Rumi: The Masnavi* by Octagon Press, London, 1994) and A. J. Arberry's *Tales from the Masnawi* (George Allen & Unwin, London, 1961) and *More Tales from the Masnawi* (George Allen & Unwin, London, 1963).

7. Mowlânâ Jalâluddin Mohammad Balkhi Rumi, *Kulliyât-e Shams-e Tabrizi (Divân-e Kabir)*, ten volumes, edited by Badi uz-Zamân Foruzânfar (Tehran University Press, 1957-1966; republished by Amir Kabir Press, Tehran, 1976) [in Persian]. No complete English translation of this work from the Persian is available. Partial English translations include: Reynold Nicholson's *Selected Poems from the Divân Shams Tabrizi* (Cambridge University Press, 1898, reprinted several times, most recently by IBEX Publishers, Washington D.C., 2001), and A. J. Arberry's *Mystical Poems of Rumi: First Selection, Poems 1-200* (University of Chicago Press, 1968) and *Second Selection, Poems 201-400* (Westview Press, Boulder, 1979). The most extensive English version is a 22-volume work by Dr. Nevit Ergin who re-translated the *Divân-e Kabir* from the Turkish translation by Abdulbâki Gölpinârli published in Istanbul in 1957-58. Ergin's publications are available from the Society for Understanding Mevlana in California; www.sfumevlana.org.

8. Mowlânâ Jalâluddin Mohammad Balkhi Rumi, *Kitâb-e Fihi Mâ Fih*, edited by Badi uz-Zamân Foruzânfar (Tehran University Press, 1330/1951; Amir Kabir Press, Tehran, 1348/1969, second edition) [in Persian]. Three English translations are available: *Discourses of Rumi* by A. J. Arberry (John Murray, London, 1961); *Signs of the Unseen: The Discourses of Jalaluddin Rumi* by W. M. Thackston (Threshold Books, Putney, VT, 1994; Shambhala, Boston, 1999); *Mirror of the Unseen: The Complete Discourses of Jalaluddin Rumi*, version by Louis Rogers (Writers Club Press/iUniverse, 2002).

9. This famous line attributed to Rumi is probably derived from a similar line in his *Divân* (18521): *"The outcome of my life is no more than these three words: I burned; I burned; I burned."*

10. Bahâ Valad, *Ma'âref* ("The Teachings of Bahâ Valad") two volumes, edited by Badi uz-Zamân Foruzânfar (Ministry of Culture, Tehran, 1955 and 1959; Tahuri Press, Tehran, 1973, second edition) [in Persian]. Two partial translations are: "Mystical Moments" in Arthur J. Arberry's *Aspects of Islamic Civilization* (The University of Michigan Press, 1967), pp. 227-255; and *The Drowned Book: Ecstatic and Earthy Reflections of Bahauddin, the Farther of Rumi* by Coleman Barks and John Moyne (HarperSanFrancisco, 2004). Fritz Meier's biographical research *Bahâ-i Valad: Grundzuge seines Lebens und seiner Mystick* was published by E. J. Brill, Leiden in 1989. Its Persian translation by Mehr Âfâg Bâibourdi was published in Tehran in 1993; no English translation of Meier's work is available.

11. Abdul Rahmân Jâmi (1414-1492), *Nafahât ul-Uns* ("The Fragrances of Fellowship"), edited by Mehdi Towhidipour (Mahmudi, Tehran, 1957; Elmi, Tehran, 1996) [in Persian].

12. Shamsuddin Mohammad Tabrizi, *Maqâlât-e Shams-e Tabrizi* ("The Discourses of Shams of Tabriz"), two volumes, edited by Mohammad Ali Movah'hed (Aryâmehr University, Tehran, 1977; Khârazmi, Tehran, 1990) [in Persian]. English translations include: (i) William Chittick's *Me and Rumi: The Autobiography of Shams-i Tabrizi* (Fons Vitae, Louisville, KY, 2004) based on Movah'hed's Persian edition and arranged chronologically; (ii) Coleman Barks' abridged and paraphrased version from Chittick's translation, *Rumi: Soul Fury: Rumi and Shams on Friendship* (HarperOne, New York, 2014); (iii) *Rumi's Sun: The Teachings of Shams of Tabriz*, translated by Refik Algan and Camille Adams Helminski (Morning Light Press, Sandpoint, ID, 2008) from a Turkish translation; and (iv) *Shams-e Tabrizi: Rumi's Perfect Teacher*, translated by Farida Maleki (Science of the Soul Research Center, New Delhi, 2011), selections from the Movah'hed's edition arranged thematically.

13. The story of the first encounter between Shams and Rumi is given in Sepah-sâlâr's *Risâleh*, Aflâki's *Manâqeb ul-Ârefin* as well as the *Maqâlât-e Shams*. For more information refer to Franklin Lewis' *Rumi: Past and Present, East and West* (Oneworld, Oxford, 2000), chapter 4; and *Me and Rumi: The Autobiography of Shams-i Tabrizi*, translated by William C. Chittick (Fons Vitae, Louisville, KY, 2004).

14. Coleman Barks, *Rumi: The Book of Love* (HarperSanFrancisco, 2003), p. xxii.

15. This famous poem is not in Foruzânfar's edition of the *Divân*, but it is found in some nineteenth-century manuscripts, and is also included in Reynold Nicholson's *Selected Poems from the Divân Shams Tabrizi* (1898).

Chapter 5. Rumi's Life and Spiritual Journey

1. "Secretary-General's remarks at the Rumi commemoration," New York, June 26, 2007, available on the UN's website: http://www.un.org/sg/STATEMENTS/index.asp?nid=2636

2. These lines are from a famous and long sonnet attributed to Rumi. The poem is not included in the oldest manuscripts of Rumi's *Divân* (nor in Foruzânfar's edition of the *Divân*), but it is found in some later manuscripts. A version of it, titled "Who says words with my mouth?" forms the opening poem in *The Essential Rumi* by Coleman Barks.

3. *The Feats of the Knowers of God*, translated by John O'Kane (Brill Academic Publishers, Leiden, 2002).

4. Badi uz-Zamân Foruzânfar, *Risâleh dar Ahvâl va Zendeghâni-ye Mowlânâ Jalâluddin Mohammad* ("Treatise on the Life of Master Jalâluddin Mohammad") (Zavvâr, Tehran, 1954, second edition) [in Persian]. No translation is available but authors referenced below (5-9) have all extensively utilized this source.

5. Abdul Hossein Zarrinkub, *Pelle Pelle ta Molâgât-e Khodâ* ("Step by Step to Meet God") (Sokhan, Tehran, 1990) [in Persian]. English translation, *Step by Step Up to Union with God*, by M. Keyvani (Persian Heritage Foundation, New York, 2009).

6. Abdulbâki Gölpinârli, *Mevlana Celaleddin, Hayati, Felsefesi, Eserleri, Eserlerinden Secmeler* ("Mevlana Jalaluddin: His Life, Philosophy, Works and Anthology") (Istanbul, 1959) [in Turkish]. Persian translation, *Mowlânâ Jalâluddin*, by Towfig Sob'hani (Tehran, 1995).

7. Afzal Iqbâl, *The Life and Thought of Maulana Jalaluddin Rumi* (First edition 1956; seventh edition 1999, Oxford University Press, Karachi).

8. Annemarie Schimmel, *The Triumphal Sun: A Study of the Works of Jalaluddin Rumi* (London, 1978, State University of New York Press, 1993, second edition); *I Am Wind, You Are Fire: The Life and Work of Rumi* (Shambhala Press, Boston, 1992; republished as *Rumi's World: The Life and Works of the Greatest Sufi Poet*, 2001).

9. Franklin D. Lewis, *Rumi, Past and Present, East and West* (Oneworld, Oxford, 2000).

10. Mowlânâ Jalâluddin Mohammad Balkhi Rumi, *Kulliât-e Shams-e Tabrizi* (*Divân-e Kabir*), ten volumes, edited by Badi uz-Zamân Foruzânfar (Tehran University Press, 1957-1967; republished by Amir Kabir Press, Tehran, 1976) [in Persian].

11. Mawlânâ Jalâluddin Mohammad Balkhi Rumi, *The Mathnawi of Jalaluddin Rumi*, eight volumes, a critically-edited Persian version with English translation and scholarly commentaries by Reynold Nicholson ("Gibb Memorial Series," Luzac, London, 1925-1940). The Persian edition was later published in a single volume by Amir Kabir Press, Tehran, 1957, and reprinted numerous times. Note that the *Mathnawi* (*Masnavi*) consists of six books.

12. Viktor E. Frankl, *Man's Search for Meaning* (Pocket Books, New York, 1963), p. 171-172.

13. These lines are from a poem attributed to Rumi. The poem is not found in the oldest manuscripts of Rumi's *Divân* (nor in Foruzânfar's edition of the *Divân*), but it

is found in some later manuscripts, and is also included in Reynold Nicholson's *Selected Poems from the Divân Shams Tabrizi* (Cambridge University Press, 1898).

14. Arthur J. Arberry, "Introduction" to Reynold A. Nicholson's posthumous book, *Rumi, Poet and Persian* (George Allen & Unwin, London, 1950).

15. Some modern free-verse translations and renditions of Rumi's poetry include: *The Essential Rumi* by Coleman Barks and John Moyne (1995, 2004); *The Soul of Rumi* by Coleman Barks (2002); *Rumi: The Big Red Book* by Coleman Barks (2010); *The Rumi Daybook* by Kabir Helminski and Camille Helminski (2011); *In the Arms of the Beloved* by Jonathan Starr (1997); *Rending the Veil* by Shahram Shiva (1995); *Rumi: Fountain of Fire* (1994) and *Rumi: Dancing the Flame* by Nader Khalili (2001); *Whispers of the Beloved* (2000), *Hidden Music* (2002), and *Gardens of the Beloved* (2004) by Maryam Mafi and Azima Melita Kolin; *The Forbidden Rumi* by Nevit Ergin and Will Johnson (2006); *Swallowing the Sun* by Franklin Lewis (2008).

Chapter 6. Rumi's Roots: The Historical Rumi

1. Sultân Valad, *Valad Nâmeh* ("The Book of Valad"), edited by Jalâl Humâ'ie (Igbâl, Tehran, 1316/1937; reprinted by Humâ Press, Tehran, 1380/2010) [in Persian]. No English translation is available to my knowledge.

2. Feridoon Sepah-sâlâr, *Risâleh dar Ahvâl-e Mowlânâ Jalâluddin Mowlavi* ("Treatise on the life of Master Jalâluddin Mowlavi"), edited by Sa'id Nafisi (Igbâl, Tehran, 1324/1945; reprinted 1995) [in Persian]. No English translation is available.

3. Shamsuddin Ahmad Aflâki, *Manâqeb ul-Ârefin* ("The Virtuous Acts of the Mystics"), two volumes, edited by Tahsin Yazichi (Ankara, 1976 and 1980, second edition; reprinted in Tehran, 1983) [in Persian]. Partial English translations include: James Redhouse's *Legends of the Sufis* ("The Acts of the Adepts," London, 1881, reprinted by Theosophical Publishing House, 1976), and Idries Shah's *The Hundred Tales of Wisdom* (Octagon Press, London, 1978). A recent complete translation is: *The Feats of the Knowers of God* by John O'Kane (Brill Academic Publishers, Leiden, 2002); but its price tag of $231 will keep many readers away. Excerpts from the book is recently published as *Rumi and His Friends: Stories of the Lovers of God* by Camille Adams Helminski and Susan Blaylock (Fons Vitae, Louisville, KY, 2013).

4. Mowlânâ Jalâluddin Mohammad Balkhi Rumi, *Masnavi-ye Ma'navi*, based on Reynold Nicholson's edition (Amir Kabir Press, Tehran, 1957) [in Persian]. Nicholson's edition of the *Mathnawi of Jalaluddin Rumi* together with English

translation and scholarly commentaries were first published in eight volumes by Luzac & Co., London, 1925-1940.

5. Annemarie Schimmel, *The Triumphal Sun: A Study of the Works of Jalâloddin Rumi* (State University of New York Press, 1993), p. 37.

6. Bahâ Valad, *Ma'âref* ("The Teachings of Bahâ Valad"), two volumes, edited by Badi uz-Zamân Foruzânfar (Tahuri, Tehran, 1973, second edition) [in Persian]. Two partial translations are: "Mystical Moments" in Arthur J. Arberry's *Aspects of Islamic Civilization* (The University of Michigan Press, 1967), pp. 227-255; and *The Drowned Book: Ecstatic and Earthy Reflections of Bahauddin, the Farther of Rumi* by Coleman Barks and John Moyne (HarperSanFrancisco, 2004).

7. Burhânuddin Mohaggeg Termezi, *Ma'âref* ("The Teachings"), edited by Badi uz-Zamân Foruzânfar (Ministery of Culture, Tehran, 1961) [in Persian]. No English translation is available. (Franklin Lewis and Hassan Lâhuti are reportedly working on an English translation of this work.)

8. Shamsuddin Mohammad Tabrizi, *Magâlât-e Shams-e Tabrizi* ("The Discourses of Shams Tabrizi"), two volumes, edited by Mohammad Ali Movah'hed (Khârazmi, Tehran, 1990) [in Persian]. A partial, chronologically-arranged translation is William Chittick's *Me and Rumi: The Autobiography of Shams-i Tabrizi* (Fons Vitae, Louisville, KY, 2004). A complete English translation (from a Turkish translation) has also been published: *Rumi's Sun: The Teachings of Shams of Tabriz*, by Refik Algan and Camille Adams Helminski (Morning Light Press, Sandpoint, ID, 2008). Coleman Barks has also published a paraphrased version, *Rumi: Soul Fury: Rumi and Shams on Friendship* (HarperOne, New York, 2014), selected from Chittick's translation. Another translation is: *Shams-e Tabrizi: Rumi's Perfect Teacher*, translated by Farida Maleki (Science of the Soul Research Center, New Delhi, 2011), selections from the Movah'hed's edition arranged thematically.

9. Mowlânâ Jalâluddin Mohammad Balkhi Rumi, *Kulliyât-e Shams-e Tabrizi (Divân-e Kabir)*, ten volume, edited by Badi uz-Zamân Foruzânfar (Tehran University Press, 1957-1966; republished by Amir Kabir Press, Tehran, 1976) [in Persian]. No complete English translation of this work from the Persian is available yet. Partial translations include Reynold Nicholson's *Selected Poems from the Divân Shams Tabrizi* (Cambridge University Press, 1898, reprinted by IBEX Publishers, Washington D.C., 2001), and A. J. Arberry's *Mystical Poems of Rumi* (University of Chicago Press, reprinted in 2008). The most extensive English version is a 22-volume work by Dr. Nevit Ergin who re-translated the *Divân-e Kabir* from the Turkish translation by Abdulbâki Gölpinârli published in Istanbul in 1957-58.

Chapter 7. Rumi and the Buddha: Correlative Ideas on Spiritual Awakening

1. Karen Armstrong's *The Buddha* (Viking Penguin, New York, 2001) is a best-seller and highly readable book on the biography of the Buddha. More detailed biographies are: *The Historical Buddha* by H. W. Schumann, translated from the German by M. Walshe (Arkana/Penguin, London, 1989), and *The Buddha: A Beginner's Guide* by John Storng (Oneworld, Oxford, 2009).

2. For Rumi's biography, I recommend Annemarie Schimmel's *I Am Wind You Are Fire: The Life and Work of Rumi* (Shambhala, Boston, 1992; republished as *Rumi's World: The Life and Works of the Greatest Sufi Poet*, 2001). A more recent and detailed biography is Franklin Lewis' *Rumi: Past and Present, East and West* (Oneworld, Oxford, 2000).

3. Edward Conze, *Buddhism: Its Essence and Development* (Harper, New York, 1959), p. 20.

4. Walpola Rahula, *What the Buddha Thought* (Grove Press, New York, 1959, 1974), p. 14.

5. Abbot Zenkei Shibayama, *A Flower Does Not Talk: Zen Essays*, translated by Sumiko Kudo (Charles Tuttle Co., Tokyo, 1980), p. 19.

6. This story has been narrated by the fifteenth-century Persian poet Abdul Rahmân Jâmi in his book *Nafahât ul-Uns* ("The Fragrances of Fellowship"), edited by Mehdi Towhidipour (Elmi, Tehran, 1996) [in Persian].

7. Walpola Rahula, *What the Buddha Thought*, pp. 8-11.

8. Edward Conze, *Buddhism: Its Essence and Development*, p. 16.

9. Ronald Eyre, *The Long Search* (Collins, London, 1979), p. 128.

10. Mowlânâ Jalâluddin Mohammad Balkhi Rumi, *Kitâb-e Fihi Mâ Fih*, edited by Badi uz-Zamân Foruzânfar (Amir Kabir, Tehran, 1969, second edition) p. 56 [in Persian].

11. Seyyed Hossein Nasr, *Ideals and Realities of Islam* (Allen & Unwin, London, 1979), p. 18.

12. Thich Nhat Hanh, *The Heart's of the Buddha's Teaching* (Broadway Books, New York, 1999), p. 187.

13. This phrase can be found in many Buddhist sources including the *Dhammapada* (verse 277). This is part of the last words the Buddha uttered at his death bed: "All conditioned things are impermanent. Work out your salvation with diligence." Edward Conze, *Buddhism: Its Essence and Development*, p. 16; Maurice Percheron, *Buddha and Buddhism* (Longman, Green & Co., London, 1957), p. 37.

14. Reynold A. Nicholson, *The Mystics of Islam* (Routledge & Kegan Paul, London, 1963), p. 17.

15. Tenzin Gyatso, the Fourteenth Dalai Lama, *The Buddhism of Tibet and the Key to the Middle Way* (Harper & Row, New York, 1975), p. 53. This is a famous Buddhist saying recorded in many books, for example, *The Dhammapada*, verse 277.

16. Abbot Zenkei Shibayama, *A Flower Does Not Talk: Zen Essays*, p. 46.

17. The full text and translation of this poem is given in *Selected Poems from the Divân-e Shams-e Tabrizi*, translated and introduced by R. A. Nicholson. The translation of the poem in this article is mine.

18. Daistest Suzuki, *The Awakening of Zen* (Prajna Press, Boulder, CO, 1980), p. 54

19. *The Dhammapada*, translated by Eknath Easwaran (Niligiri Press, Tomales, CA, 1985).

Chapter 8. Sufi and Buddhist Teachings: Views from Rumi's Poetry and Life

1. Thich Nhat Hanh, *Understanding Our Mind* (Parallax Press, Berkeley, 2006), p. 25.

2. Walopa Rahula, *What the Buddha Taught* (Grove Press, New York, 1959, 1974), p. 12.

3. *The Dhammapada*, translated by Eknath Easwaran (Nilgiri Press, Tomales, CA, 1985), p. 80.

4. Thich Nhat Hanh first popularized the Buddhist mindfulness in *The Miracle of Mindfulness* (1975) which has been reprinted several times. In his book, *The Heart of the Buddha's Teaching* (Boradyway Book, New York, 1989), Thich Nhat Hanh writes, "Traditionally, Right Mindfulness is the seventh on the path of eight right practices, but it is presented here third to emphasize its great importance" (p. 64).

Chapter 9. Jesus Christ in Rumi's Poems and Parables

1. *Holy Bible: New International Version* (Zondervan, Grand Rapids, MI, 2011).

2. Shamsuddin Ahmad Aflâki, *Manâqeb ul-Ârefin* ("The Virtuous Acts of the Mystics"), two volumes, edited by Tahsin Yazichi (Ankara, 1976 and 1980, second edition; reprinted in Tehran, 1983) 3/64, p. 151; 3/46; p. 129 [in Persian].

3. *Manâqeb ul-Ârefin*, 3: 542, p. 555.

4. *Jesus in the Eyes of the Sufis*, by Javâd Nurbaksh (London, 1983); *The Muslim Jesus: Sayings and Stories in Islamic Literature* edited and translated by Tarif Khalidi (Harvard University Press, 2001).

Chapter 10. Rumi's Poem on Jesus' Breath

1. *The Gospel of Thomas*, translated by Marvin Meyer (HarperSanFrancisco, 1992).

2. *Mother Teresa: Essential Writings*, selected with an introduction by Jean Maalouf Maryknoll (Orbis Books, New York, 2001), p. 46.

3. Mowlânâ Jalâluddin Mohammad Balkhi Rumi, *Kitâb-e Fihi Mâ Fih*, edited by Badi uz-Zamân Foruzânfar (Amir Kabir, Tehran, 1969) p. 21 [in Persian].

Chapter 11. In the Ocean of Rumi

1. This famous line attributed to Rumi is probably is derived from a similar line in his *Divân* (18521): *"The outcome of my life is no more than these three words: I burned; I burned; I burned."*

2. This quatrain is not found in the oldest manuscripts of the *Divân-e Shams* (nor is it included in Foruzânfar's edition of the *Divân*), but it is found in some later manuscripts and is included in the 1962 Amir Kabir print of *Kulliyât-e Shams-e Tabrizi* (quatrain 1948).

3. Shamsuddin Ahmad Aflâki, *Manâqeb ul-Ârefin* ("The Virtuous Acts of the Mystics"), two volumes, edited by Tahsin Yazichi (Ankara, 1976; 1980, second edition; reprinted in Tehran, 1983) 3/417, p. 451 [in Persian].

4. This quatrain is not found in the oldest manuscripts of the *Divân-e Shams* (nor is it included in Foruzânfar's edition of the *Divân*), but it is found in some later manuscripts and is included in the 1962 Amir Kabir print of *Kulliyât-e Shams-e Tabrizi* (quatrain 62).

Chapter 12. Love and Life in Rumi's Poetry

1. Ali Dashti, *Seyri dar Divân-e Shams* ("A Journey through the Divân-e Shams") (Jâvidân Press, Tehran, 1337/1958) p. 16. [In Persian]. This book has been translated into English by Dashti's daughter living in the US: *A Voyage Through Divan-e Shams*, translated by Sayeh Dashti (Ketâb Sarâ, Tehran, 1382/2003).

2. Coleman Barks, *Rumi: The Book of Love* (HarperSanFrancisco, 2003), p. xxii.

3. William Chittick is one of few authors who has conducted pioneering research on the subject of love in Rumi's poetry. See his book, *The Sufi Path of Love: The Spiritual Teachings of Rumi* (Albany: State University of New York, 1983) and more recently *The Divine Love: Islamic Literature and the Path of God* (Yale University Press, 2013).

4. Erich Fromm, *The Art of Loving* (Harper and Row, New York, 1956), p. 2.

5. Shamsuddin Ahmad Aflâki, *Manâqeb ul-Ârefin* ("The Virtuous Acts of the Mystics"), two volumes, edited by Tahsin Yazichi (Ankara, 1976 and 1980, second edition; reprinted in Tehran, 1983) 3/702, p. 376 [in Persian].

6. Aflâki, *Manâqeb ul-Ârefin*, 3/292, p. 360.

Chapter 13. A Map of the Heart in Rumi's Poetry

1. Andrew Harvey, *The Way of Passion: A Celebration of Rumi* (Tarcher/Putnam, New York, 2000), p. 303.

Chapter 14. Rumi: Poetry as a Guiding Light

1. This quatrain is not found in the oldest manuscripts of the *Divân-e Shams* (nor is it included in Foruzânfar's edition of the *Divân*), but it is found in some later manuscripts and is included in the 1962 Amir Kabir print of *Kulliyât-e Shams-e Tabrizi* (quatrain 106).

2. Paul Reps, *Zen Flesh, Zen Bones* (Penguin Books, London, 1986 reprint), p. 17.

Chapter 15. Rumi: Poetry for Meditation and Life

1. Loren Eiseley, *The Star Thrower* (Harvest/HBJ, San Diego, 1978) p. 37.

2. Loren Eiseley, *The Unexpected Universe* (Harcourt, Brace & World, New York, 1969), p. 4.

3. *Zendegâni-e Mowlânâ Jalâluddin Mohammad* ("Biography of Mowlânâ Jalâluddin Muhammad), by Badi uz-Zamân Foruzânfar (Zavvâr, Tehran 1333/1954, reprinted several times) [in Persian].

4. Lawrence LeeShan, *How to Meditate* (Bantam Books, New York, 1974), p. 1

Chapter 16. Rumi Comes to America

1. Coleman Barks, *The Essential Rumi* (new expanded edition) (HarperOne, New York, 2004), p. xvii.

2. Alexander Marks, "Persian Poet Top Seller in America," *The Christian Science Monitor*, November 25, 1997.

3. Ptolemy Tompkins, "Rumi Rules!" *TIME Asia Magazine*, October 7, 2002.

4. Steve Holgate, "Persian Poet Rumi Conquers America," US Department of State, *Washington File*, March 15, 2005.

5. Huston Smith's interview in the documentary film, *Rumi: Poet of the Heart* (1998).

6. Bill Moyers, *Fooling with the Words* (PBS documentary film, 1999).

7. Edward G. Browne, *A Literary History of Persian* (Cambridge University Press, 1906, volume 2), p. 515.

8. Reynold A. Nicholson, *Rumi: Poet and Mystic* (George Allen & Unwin, London, 1950) p. 17.

9. Arthur J. Arberry, Introduction to R.A. Nicholson's *Rumi: Poet and Mystic*, pp. 25-26.

10. Preface to the *Discourses of Rumi*, translated by A. J. Arberry (John Murray, London, 1961), p. ix.

11. Annemarie Schimmel (*Triumphal Sun: A Study of the Works of Jalâloddin Rumi*, State University of New York Press, 1993, p. 5) writes: "Persian poetry, from its very beginning – e.g. from the 10th century onwards – had been influenced by Sufi thought; the first author to use Persian for his poetical orisons was Abdullâh Ansâri (death 1089), the patron saint of Herat."

12. Coleman Barks, *The Soul of Rumi* (HarperSanFrancisco, 2001), p. 389.

13. Kabir Helminski, "Rumi in English" in *The Rumi Collection* (Shambhala, Boston, 2000) pp. xiii-xxi.

14. The best source in English on the symbols and imagery in Rumi's poetry is Annemarie Schimmel's *Triumphal Sun* (1993). This work has also been translated into Persian. Another good source in Persian is Seyyed Hossein Fâtemi's *Tasvirgari dar Ghazaliyât-e Shams* ("Imagery in the Lyrical Odes of Shams") (Amir Kabir, Tehran, 1986).

15. Ali Dashti, *Seyri dar Divân-e Shams* ("A Journey through the Divân-e Shams"), (Jâvidân Press, Tehran 1337/1958), p. 28-29 [in Persian]. This book has been translated into English by Dashti's daughter living in the US: *A Voyage Through Divan-e Shams*, translated by Sayeh Dashti (Ketâb Sarâ, Tehran, 1382/2003).

16. Javâd Nurbaksh, *In the Tavern of Ruin: Seven Essays on Sufism* (Khaniqâh Nimatullâhi Publications, New York, 1978) p. 23

17. Reza Arasteh, *Rumi the Persian: Rebirth in Creativity and Love*, with a Preface by Erich Fromm (Ashraf Press, Lahore, 1965), pp. 160-161

18. Preface by William Chittick to Nader Khalili's *Fountain of Fire* (Burning Gate, Los Angeles, 1996)

19. Arthur J. Arberry (*Tales from the Masnavi*, 1961, p. 11) and Annmarie Schimmel (*Triumphal Sun*, 1993, p. 369) quote the fifteenth-century Persian Sufi Poet Jâmi that Rumi's *Masnavi* is the *Quran* in the Persian tongue. Hassan Lâhuti, who translated Schimmel's work into Persian (*Shokooh-e Shams*, Tehran, 1988, p. 847), remarks that

he could not find that quote in Jâmi's works, but that the following lines have been attributed to Shaykh Bahâ ud-Din Âmeli (1547-1621): "I am not saying that His Excellency (Rumi) is a Prophet, but he does have a Book: The spiritual couplets of Master Rumi (*Masnavi-ye Ma'nav-ye Mowlavi*) is the *Quran* in the Persian tongue."

20. Barks has said this story in several places, including in his interview in the documentary film *Rumi: Poet of the Heart* (1998), and in his books, *The Essential Rumi* (2004, p. 363) and *The Soul of Rumi* (2001, p. xv).

21. "Medal in Honor of Mawlana Jalaluddin Balkhi Rumi" by UNESCO Executive Board, 175th session (October 3, 2006, Paris); full text is available at UNESCO's website: http://unesdoc.unesco.org/images/0014/001473/147319e.pdf

Chapter 17. Why Is Rumi a Best-selling Poet in America?

1. Annemarie Schimmel, *The Triumphal Sun: A Study of the Works of Jalâloddin Rumi* (State University of New York Press, 1993), p. xviii.

2. Arthur J. Arberry, *Mystical Poems of Rumi, First Selections, Poems 1-200* (The University of Chicago Press, 1968), p. 5-6.

3. For reviews of Rumi's life and works, I recommend the following: Annemarie Schimmel, *Rumi's World: The Life and Works of the Greatest Sufi Poet* (Shambhala, Boston, 2001); Franklin D. Lewis, *Rumi, Past and Present, East and West* (Oneworld, Oxford, 2000).

4. Annemarie Schimmel, "Mawlana Rumi: yesterday, today, and tomorrow," in *Poetry and Mysticism in Islam: The Heritage of Rumi*, edited by Amin Banani, Richard Hovannisian, and Georges Sabagh (Cambridge University Press, 1994), p. 6.

5. Ali Dashti, *Sayri Dar Divân -e Shams* (Jâvidân Press, Tehran 1958), p. 20 [in Persian]. This book has been translated into English by Dashti's daughter, Sayeh Dashti: *A Voyage Through Divân-e Shams: Celebrating Rumi* (Los Angeles: Ketab Sara, 2003).

6. This quatrain often attributed to Rumi is not actually his poem; it is not found in the reliable manuscripts or print editions of any of his works. The poem has also been attributed to other Persian Sufi masters including Abu Saeid Abul-khayr (967-1049), Khâja Abdullâh Ansâri (1006-1088), and Bâbâ Afzal Kâshâni (?-ca. 1214).

Nevertheless, its inscription at Rumi's mausoleum by his disciples indicate its conformity with Rumi's teachings.

7. Shamsuddin Ahmad Aflâki, *Manâqeb ul-Ârefin* ("The Virtuous Acts of the Mystics"), two volumes, edited by Tahsin Yazichi (Ankara, 1976; 1980, second edition; reprinted in Tehran, 1983) p. 592 [in Persian]. See also Franklin Lewis, *Rumi, Past and Present, East and West*, p. 224.

8. Annemarie Schimmel, "Mawlana Rumi: yesterday, today, and tomorrow," in *Poetry and Mysticism in Islam: The Heritage of Rumi*, p. 8.

Index of Names

Abraham (Ancient Semitic Prophet): 68, 80, 85, 170, 172

Abul-Khayr, Abu-Said (967-1049; Persian Sufi): 50, 203

Aflâki, Shamsuddin Ahmad (d. 1360; Biographer of Rumi): 37, 39, 50, 84, 95, 100, 131, 141, 147, 159, 191, 193, 195, 199, 200, 204

Aghili, Sâlâr (1977-; Iranian singer): 185

Alâ'eddin (d. 1262; Rumi's son): 148, 149, 161, 163

Alâ'eddin (Rumi's older brother): 161

Algan, Refik (Turkish Sufi teacher): 154, 155, 156, 193, 196

Al-Mutanabbi, Abu at-Tayyib (915-965; Arab poet): 31, 134

Amir Shamsuddin Yah'yâ (Rumi's stepson): 148, 205

Ansâri, Khâja Abdullah (1006-1089; Persian Sufi): 50, 202, 203

Anvar, Iraj (US-based Iranian scholar): 150, 153

Anvar, Leili (Iranian-French scholar): 133

Arasteh, Reza (1927-1992; Iranian scholar): 125, 202

Arberry, Arthur John (1905-1969; British scholar): 47, 123, 126, 127, 130, 132, 133, 142, 143, 151, 157, 179, 181, 190, 191, 192, 195, 196, 202, 203, 205

Aristotle (384-322 BC; Greek philosopher): 114

Armstrong, Karen (1944-; British scholar): 197

Arnold, Matthew (1822-1888; English poet): 12

Attâr, Sheikh Farid ud-Din (1145-1221; Persian Sufi poet): 28, 30, 31, 40, 41, 50, 143

Bâbâ Afzal Kâshâni (d. ca. 1214-; Persian Sufi): 203

Bahâuddin Âmeli (Shaykh Bâha'ie) (1547-1621; Islamic scholar at the Safavid court in Persia): 203

Bahâuddin Valad (1152-1231; Rumi's father): 30, 40, 41, 53, 58, 134, 146, 159, 160, 161, 191, 196

Ban Ki-moon (UN Secretary-General): 38

Barks, Coleman (1935-; American poet and Rumi translator): 34, 38, 47, 97, 122, 124, 126, 127, 129, 132, 133, 150, 151,

Index of Names

152, 153, 157, 178, 179, 183, 184, 185, 187, 190, 192, 193, 195, 196, 200, 201, 202, 203

Bâyazid Bastâmi (804-874; Persian Sufi): 32, 50, 65

Bly, Robert (1926-; American poet): 123, 129, 133, 151

Brown, John Porter (1814-1872; American diplomat and Sufi scholar): 131

Browne, Edward Granville (1862-1926; British scholar): 123, 132, 201

Buddha, Siddhartha Shakyamuni Gautama (5th-6th century BC): 15, 50, 57, 58, 59, 60, 61, 62, 63, 64, 66, 67, 68, 70, 71, 73, 75, 76, 77, 88, 197, 198

Burckhardt, Titus (Ibrahim Izz al-Din) (1908-1984; German Swiss scholar): 143

Burhânuddin Mohaggeg Termezi (d. 1241; Rumi's teacher): 31, 41, 42, 43, 53, 134, 161, 162, 196

Carrière, Jean Claude (1931-; French film critic): 145, 147

Chittick, William (1943-; American scholar): 126, 133, 155, 176, 177, 193, 196, 200, 202

Chopra, Deepak (1947-; Indian-American author): 122, 184

Conze, Edward (1904-1979; Anglo-German Buddhist scholar): 60, 197, 198

Dalai Lama, 14th: Tenzin Gyatso (1935-, Tibetan Buddhist leader): 73, 74, 198

Dashti, Ali (1894-1982; Iranian scholar): 96, 124, 138, 200, 202, 203

Davis, Frederick Hadland (Author of *The Persian Mystics: Jalal ud-Din Rumi*):

Dawkins, Richard (Author of *The Selfih Gene*): 20

Dōgen Zenji (1200-1253; Japanese Zen master): 21

Easwaran, Eknath (1910-1999; Indian-American author): 198

Eckhart, Mesiter (1260-1328; German Christian mystic): 19

Eiseley, Loren (1907-1977; American scientist and author): 17, 116, 117, 190, 201

Emerson, Ralph Waldo (1803-1882; American poet and writer): 131

Ergin, Nevit O. (1928-2015; Turkish translator): 11, 12, 127, 133, 151, 157, 179, 187, 192, 195, 196

Erguner Kudsi, Suleyman (1952-; Turkish Sufi musician): 147, 184

Ernst, Carl W. (1950-; American scholar): 126, 143

Esin Chelebi Bayru (1949-; 22nd great grand-daughter of Rumi): 143, 186

Este'lâmi, Mohammad (1936-; Iranian scholar): 183

Eyre, Ronald (BBC producer of *The Long Search*): 62, 197

Fakhruddin Râzi (1149-1209; Persian Islamic philosopher): 30

Farhadi, Rawan (1929-; Afghani scholar): 156, 158, 181

Faruk Hemdem Chelebi (1950-; 20th great-grandson of Rumi): 186

Fâtemeh Khâtun (Sultân Valad's first wife): 162, 163

Field, Reshad (Richard Timothy Field) (1934-2016; English Sufi writer): 184,

FitzGerald, Edward (1809-1883; English poet and translator): 157, 172

Foruzânfar, Badi uz-Zamân (1900-1970; Iranian scholar): 39, 120, 157, 164, 171, 181, 182, 183, 189, 191, 192, 193, 194, 196, 197, 199, 200, 201, 206

Frankl, Viktor (1905-1997; Austrian psychiatrist): 45, 194

Friedlander, Ira Shems (Turkish Sufi artist and journalist): 185

Fromm, Erich (1900-1980; German social psychologist): 99, 100, 125, 190, 200, 202

Gamard, Ibrahim (1947-; American translator): 133, 156, 158, 181, 187

Gandhi, Mahatma Mohandas (1869-1948; Indian political and spiritual leader): 138

Gauguin, Paul (1848-1903; French painter): 111

Gencosman, Mehmet Nuri (Turkish Rumi translator): 155

Genghis Khan (13th century Mongolian leader): 40

Ghazzâli, Abu Hâmed (1058-1111; Persian Islamic scholar): 51

Ghazzâli, Ahmad (1061-1126; Persian Islamic scholar; Abu Hâmed's brother): 51

Ghiyâsuddin Kay-Khosrow II (Seljuq king of Anatolia, ruled 1237-46): 161, 164

Gibran, Kahlil (1883-1931; Lebanese poet and painter): 128

Goethe (1749-1832; German poet): 131

Gölpinârli, Abdulbâki (1900-1982; Turkish scholar and translator): 39, 127, 149, 179, 187, 191, 192, 194, 196

Gorji Khâtun (daughter of Ghiyâsuddin Kay-khosrow II and wife of Prime Minister Mo'eenuddin Parvâneh): 164

Gowhar Khâtun (Rumi's first wife): 30, 42, 148, 160

Hâfez (Hâfiz), Khaja Shamsuddin Mohammad (1325-1389; Persian poet): 52, 123,

Hallâj, Mansur (c. 858-922 AD; Persian Sufi): 84

Hammer-Purgstall, Joseph von (1774-1856; Austrian Orientalist): 131

Harvey, Andrew (1952-; British author): 127, 133, 176, 184, 200

Hastie, William (1842-1903; British scholar): 131, 151

Hegel (1770-1831; German philosopher): 131

Helminski, Camille Adams (Mevlevi teacher and Sufi author): 127, 133, 154, 155, 156, 175, 178, 187, 191, 193, 195, 196

Helminski, Kabir (Edmund) (1940-; Mevlevi teacher and Sufi author): 124, 127, 133, 178, 187, 195, 202

Hewitt, Hugh (1956-; PBS producer of *Searching for God in America*): 74

Hossein ibn Ahmad Khatibi (Rumi's paternal grandfather): 58

Hudson, William Henry (1862-1918; American scholar): 12, 13

Hujwiri, Abul Hassan (1009-1072; Persian Sufi): 50, 215

Humâ'ie, Jalal (1900-1980; Iranian scholar): 190, 196

Husâmuddin Chelebi (d. 1284; Rumi's spiritual friend): 33, 43, 44, 46, 146, 162, 163, 164, 182

Husâmuddin Vâjed Chelebi Akbar (d. 1342; Sultân Valad's son): 164

Ibn Arabi, Shaykh-e Akbar Mohi ud-Din (1165-1240; Sufi master and author): 53, 68, 174

Ibn Sinâ (Avicenna, 980-1037; Persian scientist and Islamic philosopher): 50

Iqbâl, Afzal (1919-1994; Pakistani scholar): 39, 177, 191, 194

Iyer, Pico (1957-; British writer): 147

Jalâluddin Ulu Âref Chelebi (1272-1320; Rumi's first grandchild): 163

Jâmi, Nur ad-Din Abd ur-Rahman (1414-1492; Persian Sufi poet): 31, 51, 192, 197, 202, 203

Jelaleddin Bakir Chelebi (1926-1996; 21st great grandson of Rumi): 186

Jesus Christ (of Nazareth): 15, 37, 52, 68, 76, 80, 81, 82, 83, 84, 85, 86, 87, 88, 89, 92, 100, 136, 141, 166, 170, 199

Johnson, Samuel (1709-1784; English writer): 12

Jones, Sir William (1746-1794; British Orientalist): 131

Kerâ Khâtun (d. 1292; Rumi's second wife): 42, 46, 148, 149, 160, 161, 163

Keyvani, Majdeddin (Iranian translator): 164, 177, 194

Khâja Sharaf'uddin Lâlâ of Samargand (Rumi's father-in-law): 160

Khalili, Nader (1936-2008; Iranian architect and translator): 128, 133, 157, 184, 187, 195, 202

Kharagâni, Abul-Hasan (960-1033; Persian Sufi): 50

Kimiyâ (d. 1247; Rumi's adopted daughter): 42, 147, 148, 149, 150, 162

Kinney, Jay (1950-; American author and editor of *Gnosis*): 126

Khosh'nevis, Ahmad (Iranian scholar): 155

Kolin, Azima Melita (Bulgaria-born, London-based musician and translator): 127, 157, 180, 195

Kornfield, Jack (1945-; American meditation teacher): 126

Ladinsky, Daniel (1948-; American poet): 123

Lâhuti, Hassan (1945-2013; Iranian scholar): 196, 202

LeShan, Lawrence (1920-; Author of *How to Meditate*): 121,

Lewis, Franklin D. (1961-; American scholar): 39, 133, 149, 150, 152, 164, 177, 178, 191, 193, 194, 195, 196, 197, 203, 204

Lewisohn, Leonard (1953-; American scholar): 133, 164, 183, 186

Lings, Martin (Abu Bakr Siraj ad-Din) (1909-2005; British scholar and Sufi): 143

Lugmân (ancient sage mentioned in the *Quran*): 34, 35

Luke (*The Gsopel of Luke*): 84

Mafi, Maryam (London-based Iranian translator): 127, 133, 157, 180, 188, 195

Malakeh Khâtun (d. 1304; Rumi's daughter): 148, 163

Mary (Maryam) (Mother of Jesus Christ): 80, 81, 86, 88, 89,

Maslow, Abraham (1908-1970; American psychologist): 110

Matthew (*The Gospel of Matthew*): 76, 86

Mathieu, William Allaudin (1937-; Cold Mountains Music, CA): 184

Maufroy, Muriel (Author of *Rumi's Daughter*): 147, 148, 149

Meier, Fritz (1912-1998; Swiss scholar): 29, 192

Mill, John Stuart (1806-1873; English philosopher): 12

Mo'eeinuddin Parvâneh (Seljuq Prime Minister in Konya): 164

Mojadeddi, Jawid (US-based Afghani scholar): 180

Mo'meneh Khatun (Rumi's mother): 30, 159, 160

Mohammad Shah (Kerâ Khâtun's first husband): 161

Mosaffâ, Mohammad Jafar (Iranian author): 177

Moses (Prophet of Judaism): 37, 68, 81, 85, 141, 170

Movah'hed, Mohammad Ali (Iranian scholar): 155, 193, 196

Moyers, Bill (1943-; American journalist): 122, 201

Moyne, John (Javad Mo'in) (1921-2014: Iranian-American linguist): 127, 133, 151, 183, 192, 195, 196

Mozaffaruddin Amir Âlem Chelebi (d. 1277; Rumi's son): 163

Muhammad (570-632 AD; Prophet of Islam): 31, 32, 37, 62, 65, 68, 85, 103, 144, 159, 169, 170, 171, 172, 174

Muir, John (1838-1914; Scottish-American naturalist): 20, 190

Nâfezbek, Feridoon (Turkish scholar): 183

Nafisi, Sa'id (1895-1966; Iranian scholar): 190, 195

Naini, Majid (US-based Iranian Rumi scholar): 133, 188

Nan-in (Japanese Zen master in the late 19th century): 113

Nasr, Seyyed Hossein (1933-; US-based Iranian scholar): 62, 126, 133, 143, 144, 184, 197

Nassâj Tusi, Abu Bakr (d. 1094; Persian Sufi): 84

Nazeri, Hafiz (1937-; Iranian singer): 185

Nazeri, Shahram (1951-; Iranian singer): 185

Needleman, Jacob (1934-; American philosopher): 126

Nicholson, Reynold Alleyne (1868-1945; British scholar): 47, 65, 123, 126, 127, 132, 133, 143, 151, 179, 180, 182, 189, 191, 192, 193, 194, 195, 196, 198, 201, 202, 209

Nurbaksh, Javâd (1926-2008; Iranian Sufi master): 125

O'Kane, John (1940-; translator of *The Feats of the Knowers of God: Manâqeb al-ârefin*): 191, 193, 195

Oliver, Mary (1935-; American poet): 9, 132, 189

Omar Khayyâm (1048-1123; Persian poet and scientist): 50, 52, 128, 157, 172

Palmer, Edward Henry (1840-82; British scholar): 151

Parini, Jay (1948-; American author): 12, 13, 189

Petrova, Tina (Director of *Rumi: Turning Ecstatic*): 185

Poe, Edgar Allan (1809-1949; American writer): 12

Postneshin Jelaleddin Loras (Turkish Mevlevi teacher): 186

Râbi'a (8th century female Sufi): 84

Rahula, Walpola (1907-1997; Sri Lankan Buddhist monk): 75, 197, 198

Ram Das (Richard Alpert; 1931-; American meditation teacher): 126

Ramzi, Ahmad (Turkish scholar): 183

Rassouli, Freydoon (1943-; Iranian-American painter): 188

Redhouse, Sir James William (1811-1892; British scholar): 131, 150, 191, 195

Reiss, Hayden (Director of *Rumi: Poet of the Heart*): 185

Rilke, Rainer Maria (1875-1926; Austrian-German poet): 15, 16, 189

Roger Housden (1945-; British-American writer: *Chasing Rumi*, 2002): 147

Ruckert, Friederich (1788-1866; German scholar): 131

Ruskin, John (1819-1900; British art critic): 13

Saideh Ghods (Iranian author of *Kimya Khatun*, 2012): 149

Salâhuddin Zarkub (d. 1258; Rumi's spiritual friend): 33, 43, 46, 146, 162, 164

Sanâ'ie, Abul Majd (d. 1131; Persian Sufi poet): 31, 41, 50, 51, 134

Schimmel, Annemarie (1922-2003; German-American scholar): 39, 52, 130, 133, 135, 142, 143, 176, 177, 191, 194, 196, 197, 202, 203, 204

Sepah-sâlâr, Feridoon (14th century; Rumi's biographer): 39, 46, 50, 159, 190, 193, 195

Sepehri, Soh'râb (1928-1980; Iranian poet): 11

Shafi-ye Kadkani, Mohammad Reza (1937-; Iranian scholar): 182

Shah, Idries (1924-1996; Indian-Scottish Sufi writer): 132, 143, 191, 195

Shahâbuddin Gunawi (Rumi's son-in-law): 163

Shamsuddin (Shams-e) Tabrizi (d. 1248?; Rumi's mentor): 19, 24, 31, 32, 33, 42, 43, 46, 53, 54, 55, 58, 61, 73, 99, 102, 146, 147, 148, 149, 152, 154, 155, 156, 157, 161, 162, 164, 173, 181, 193, 195

Shamsuddin Amir Âbed Chelebi (d. 1338; Sultân Valad's son): 163

Shamsuddin Zâhed Chelebi Akbar (d. 1343; Sultân Valad's son): 164

Shahriari, Shahriar (1963-; US-based Iranian translator): 188

Shibayama, Zenkei (1894-1974; Japanese Zen master): 197, 198

Shido Bunan (1603-1676; Japanese Zen master): 67

Shiva, Shahram (Iranian-American translator): 127, 128, 133, 157, 180, 184, 187, 195

Singh, Simran (Editor of *11:11 Magazine*): 110

Smith, Huston (1919-; American scholar): 122, 126

Snyder, Gary (1930-; American poet): 132

Sob'hâni, Towfig Hashem (Iranian scholar): 183, 191

Socrates (469-399 BC; Greek philosopher): 45

Starr, Jonathan (Translator of *In the Arms of the Beloved*): 128, 133, 178, 195

Sulân Alâ'eddin Mohammad Khârazm-Shah (King of the Khârazmiân Dynasty in Iran, ruled 1200-1220 AD): 36, 40, 50

Suleiman Hayati Dede (1904-1985; Turkish Mevlevi teacher): 186, 187

Sultan Alâ'eddin Kaygubâd (Seljuq king in Anatolia, ruled 1220-1237 AD): 30, 41, 46, 53, 161, 164

Sultân Valad (1226-1312; Rumi's son): 39, 41, 42, 43, 51, 147, 148, 161, 162, 163, 164, 167, 190

Suzuki, Daisetz (1870-1966; Japanese Zen writer): 18, 69, 75, 190, 198

Tajadod, Nahal (1960-; Iranian-French scholar): 145, 146, 147

Thackston, Wheeler M. (1994-; American scholar): 181, 192

Thich Nhat Hanh (1926-; Vietnamese Zen master): 62, 72, 198

Thomas (*The Gospel of Thomas*): 87, 89, 199

Tillich, Paul (1886-1965; German American Lutheran theologian): 19, 112

Ulfat Isfahâni, Mohammad Bager (Iranian scholar of early 20th century): 120

Vitray-Meyerovitch Eva de (1909-1999; French scholar): 177

Washington, Peter (Compiler of *Rumi Poems*): 122, 178

Watts, Nigel (Author of *The Way of Love*): 147

Whinfield, Edward Henry (1836-1922; British scholar): 126, 131, 151, 180

Whitman, Walt (1819-1892: American poet): 132

Williams, Alan (Translator of *Spiritual Verses*): 179

Wilson, Charles Edward (1858-1938; British scholar): 131, 151

Wordsworth, William (1770-1850; English poet): 12

Yâzichi (Yazici), Tahsin (1922-2002; Turkish scholar): 191, 195, 199, 200, 204

Zamâni, Karim (1951-; Iranian scholar): 183

Zarrinkub, Abdul Hossein (1922-1999; Iranian scholar): 39, 160, 164, 177, 194

Zweigo, Connie (Author of *A Moth to the Flame*): 147

Acknowledgments

Since its inception in 2007, the Rumi Poetry Club has held monthly and annual meetings, all of which have been free and open to public. Our activities have been kindly publicized by several periodicals in Utah, including *The Salt Lake Tribune*, *Catalyst: Resources for Creative Living*, *Salt Lake City Weekly*, and *Slug Magazine*. The Salt Lake City Public Library, especially the Anderson Foothill Branch, has generously sponsored our meetings by providing space and facilities.

Many of the chapters in this books were previously published as articles in various magazines and journals (and some of these essays were actually based on the lectures I delivered at the annual Rumi Festivals in Salt Lake City, co-hosted by the Rumi Poetry Club and the Salt Lake City Public Library). Although I have largely revised, updated, reformatted, and partly rewritten the articles for this volume, I deeply appreciate the fellowship and support I received from the editors of the magazines and journals in which the earlier versions of these chapters were first published: Ali Reza Nourbaksh, Terry Graham, Shahrokh Ahkami, Allan Hartley, Nicholas Bawtree, Alan Godlas, Marina Montanaro, Robert Becker, Marie Arnold, John Einersen, Stewart Wachs, Ken Rodgers, Tim Miejan, Sydney Murray, Simran Singh, Alan Race, Cetta Kenney, Jim Kenney, Elizabeth Harris, Ron Miller, Richard Smoley, Sholeh Shams Shahbaz, Donna Baier Stein, Diane Bonavist, Melissa Studdard, and Steve Osmond.

Several dear friends from the Rumi Poetry Club read the entire typescript of this volume and gave valuable suggestions to improve the text. Here I express my heart-felt gratitude to Florin Nielsen, Teresa May Habibian, and Margo Andrews. Thank you! Any error is, however, mine.

Over the years, I have read books from a number of Rumi scholars who have deepened my knowledge of Rumi's life, work and poetic vision. I should especially mention Badi al-Zamân Foruzânfar, Jalâl Humâ'ie, Reynold Nicholson, Arthur John Arberry, Abdulbâki Gölpinârli, Abdul Hossein

Zarrinkub, Annemarie Schimmel, William Chittick, Towfig Sob'hâni, Hassan Lâhuti, and Franklin Lewis.

In the old days, it was customary for authors of Persian Sufi literature to begin their books with a sense of gratitude to God and creation, to ask for their blessings to accomplish their works free from egoistic desires (because, as the eleventh century Sufi author Hujwiri remarks, "no blessing arises from anything in which selfish interest has a part"), and to ask for forgiveness from the Lord and readers for any error and shortcoming in their books. This is a forgotten but beautiful etiquette. I would like that spirit to be the final words of this modest book.

ABOUT THIS BOOK

Rumi Essays: On the Life, Poetry, and Vision of the Greatest Persian Sufi Poet is a collection of essays about Mawlânâ Jalâluddin Balkhi Rumi (1207-1273). The serif font used for the text of this book is Garamond, originally designed by the French publisher Claude Garamond in the sixteenth century.

ABOUT THE AUTHOR

Rasoul Shams first learned of Rumi's poems in his Persian classes as a young boy growing up in Iran. The works of Rumi and other Persian poets have been his spiritual companions for over three decades. He has studied and lived in India, Japan and the US. He founded the Rumi Poetry Club in 2007, and is the translator of *Rumi: The Art of Loving* (2012).

ABOUT THE PUBLISHER

RUMI PUBLICATIONS are an imprint of the Rumi Poetry Club, founded in 2007 on the occasion of the eight hundredth anniversary of Rumi's birth in order to foster literature and art that nourish the human spiritual life and enrich our global culture. We celebrate inspirational words and perennial wisdom. For more information visit:

www.rumipoetryclub.com
www.facebook.com/rumipoetryclub

www.ingramcontent.com/pod-product-compliance
Lightning Source LLC
Chambersburg PA
CBHW020649300426
44112CB00007B/298